PAINTING, LANGUAGE, AND MODERNITY

PAINTING, LANGUAGE, AND MODERNITY

MICHAEL PHILLIPSON

Routledge & Kegan Paul
LONDON, BOSTON, MELBOURNE AND HENLEY

First published in 1985
by Routledge & Kegan Paul plc

14 Leicester Square, London WC2H 7PH, England

9 Park Street, Boston, Mass. 02108, USA

464 St Kilda Road, Melbourne,
Victoria 3004, Australia and

Broadway House, Newtown Road,
Henley on Thames, Oxon RG9 1EN, England

Set in 9 on 11 point Palatino Linotron 202
by Inforum Ltd, Portsmouth
and printed in Great Britain
by Billings and Sons Ltd,
Worcester

Library of Congress Cataloging in Publication Data

Phillipson, Michael.

Painting, language, and modernity.
Bibliography: p.
includes index.
1. Modernism (Art) 2. Painting—Philosophy.
I. Title.
ND196.M64P48 1985   759.06   85–1978

British CIP data also available

ISBN 0–7102–0480–9

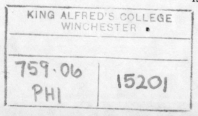

For Julia, only she knows

Contents

Acknowledgments

Conceived within modernity, against modernism, and nurtured through an emergent post-modernity, this text has a diversity of debts. Three are particularly significant in very different but complementary ways. The manuscript's transformations have been constantly provoked and informed in the course of a continuing dialogue with Jon Thompson; indeed it was he who originally convinced me of the worth of this writing project, of a writing that would be on behalf of painting. I still feel he was right. Similarly, the themes and concerns of the book are also, in part, responses to interests developed in the course of a long and close working relationship with Paul Filmer; although we interpret these interests differently our common concerns permeate the text. He has given his time unstintingly to reading drafts of the work and his sympathetically critical responses have been crucial for my writing. In rather a different way my understanding of and commitment to painting have benefited enormously from the many long discussions I have had with Hughie O'Donoghue; I learned much from him, both practical and theoretical, about the art of defending painting while our shared but war-torn studio was under siege by the St Mary Cray Neo-Dada-Post-Punk-Anti-Art-Happenings Mob.

I am also especially indebted to Basil Bernstein for his encouragement and support and for his constructive suggestions about and rigorous reading of my penultimate draft. Aaron Cicourel and Yehuda Safran made valuable comments too on early drafts of the text. Participation in the Goldsmiths' College MA in Fine Art has enabled me to work through some of the concerns of the book in an informal and always stimulating context; I am indebted to my colleagues and to the artists who have participated in the course whose intensity of commitment and quality of work exemplify the necessity of art. My thanks are also due to Sandra Koura, who with speed and equanimity transformed my execrable collage of a manuscript into an eminently legible and presentable, if still fractured and necessarily flawed, text. Finally, talking with Sam Fisher always helps me to remember that it is the painting which precedes the writing.

I am grateful to Oxford University Press for permission to quote from Arthur Rimbaud, *A Season in Hell, The Illuminations*, translated by Enid Rhodes Peschel, 1974.

1

A More or Less Contemporary Pluralogue
(Broken)

Scene: A ship at sea
Time: The present – twilight – running out

We are aboard the S.S. *MARie CELeste II* – a small, rather battered, occasionally leaky passenger ship which seems to be drifting somewhat aimlessly, destination apparently unknown; although it is rumoured amongst some of the passengers that the ship sailed originally from an obscure European port, it is no longer clear from the log whether she is returning from or is on the way to America (somebody appears to have tampered with the crucial entries). It is rumoured amongst the passengers (a rumour probably started by a member of the crew) that some of the lifeboats fall below current safety standards and there is concern that, in the event of a major disaster, not all could be saved. Many are thought to be poor swimmers (comfortable only in shallow waters); nevertheless the captain managed to reassure most people during an earlier conducted tour of the ship by pointing to the running repairs that the crew were continuously and assiduously carrying out.

Although the full passenger list has been mislaid it has become clear during the discussion (which we are still recording) that the expedition (for such it appears to be) comprises a heterogeneous collection of artists and writers (and not a few hangers-on). Many of these have contributed to the discussions, but, equally, many others seem constrained to silence, perhaps overawed by the company, or then again perhaps uninterested in the proceedings. The discussion re-presented here has been recorded (on admittedly inferior equipment – our Arts Council capital grant was withdrawn earlier this year) late one recent winter's afternoon after the cook's usual heavy lunch; the meal was accompanied and followed by the consumption of a large quantity of a rough (though nevertheless amusing) 'house' wine of clearly recent vintage from previously unestablished Italian and German vineyards.

No formal chair-person has emerged during the session, although someone representing him- or herself as an 'interpreter' appears to have acted as an informal link in the discussion. The microphone is

1

passed around amongst the participants and this accounts, in part, for the poor quality of reception at the beginning and end of some of the contributions; another factor affecting reception at these points is often the noisy response of the audience. As a result we have undertaken some editorial work and have reconstructed what we take to be the general tenor of the remarks that have been 'lost' in the recording; all these reconstructions are indicated in the text by being placed between stars, thus * . . . *. All text outside the stars is the text as recorded (or perhaps, we should say, as transcribed by our faithful transcribers who have generated as coherent a script as possible, given the interference and the notorious problems involved in transforming speech into writing).

We must add that the discussion was already under way by the time we had set our recording equipment up and established the best balance possible under difficult circumstances. Our transcript thus picks up a discussion that is already on the way. Unfortunately our sound engineer suddenly ran out of tape and the recording and the transcript break off rather abruptly. The discussion has continued and we were eventually able to acquire a further short length of tape to record a series of later exchanges. The two transcripts frame a collection of remaindered texts whose interosculation with the transcripts is not part of our editorial responsibility.

M.A.D.T.E.C.
(Modern Art Document Transcribers' Editorial Collective)

(tape runs)

PABLO PICASSO: . . . I just want to reproduce the objects for what they are and not for what they mean . . . I make a painting for the painting. I paint the objects for what they are . . .[1]

AN INTERPRETER: . . . for what they mean and are – meaning and Being – but can we separate these two, or is the painting of the 'being' of the objects, what they are, already bound to meaning? And is it the objects themselves that are painted or rather your and our relation with them through the languages of painting?

MAURICE MERLEAU-PONTY: . . . Ultimately the painting relates to nothing at all among experienced things unless it is first of all 'autofigurative'. . .

AN INTERPRETER: . . . you mean it is about itself, is a sign of itself, it re-presents itself?

MAURICE MERLEAU-PONTY: . . . It is a spectacle of something only by being a 'spectacle of nothing', by breaking the 'skin of things' to show how things became things, how the world became the

world . . . The effort of modern painting has been directed not
so much towards choosing between line and colour or even
between the figuration of things and the creation of signs, as it
has been towards multiplying the systems of equivalences . . .

AN INTERPRETER: . . . the languages of re-presentation . . .

MAURICE MERLEAU-PONTY: . . . towards severing their adherence
to the envelope of things . . . Vision alone makes us learn that
beings are different . . .

AN INTERPRETER: . . . I'm not sure that we can have vision 'alone',
but that's something else. By 'beings' you mean the 'objects' that
Pablo has just referred to?

MAURICE MERLEAU-PONTY: . . . 'exterior' foreign to one another,
are yet absolutely *together*, are 'simultaneity' . . .[2]

AN INTERPRETER: . . . are 'synchronic'; so one issue of the painter's
relation to the world is that vision seems to create our relation to
the world as one where the things, objects, others, events, are
separate, independent, while at the same time having this
independence only within what you call 'simultaneity', a
oneness, a whole, a system perhaps?

MAURICE MERLEAU-PONTY: . . . Vision encounters, as at a
crossroads, all the aspects of Being . . .[3]

AN INTERPRETER: . . . so we might say, as a beginning, that mute
'Being' speaks through the work of art; the work of art speaks or,
better, writes on behalf of the things, of their otherness. And the
work of art is the exploring and constant re-forming of the gap
between human being and nature that is always, as you have
shown, already full. Painting re-opens the gap and re-fills it
through its 'systems of equivalences' with something that may
potentially transform our relation to nature, to the other, to
Being; and at the same time it shows our solidity with nature,
our withinness. Perhaps it also proposes that that relation, that
solidity, is a possibility of Language. From what you say, Pablo's
desire to paint the objects for what 'they are', what we might call
the 'thingness' of the object, *that* they 'are', could only ever be
partially satisfied because painting works through a multiplicity
of systems of equivalence, or what might also be called codes,
signs, re-presentations, simulacra even, and firstly and lastly,
metaphors. Metaphor gives us both the thing and not the thing
and turns us towards Language; but does metaphor work at this
level of the 'Being' of things? Can you give us an example?

MAURICE MERLEAU-PONTY: . . . *well* . . . it is true and
uncontradictory that no grape was ever what it was in the most
figurative painting and that no painting, no matter how abstract,

3

can get away from Being, that even Caravaggio's grape is the
grape itself.[4]

AN INTERPRETER: . . . The painting gives us the grape itself, the
grapeness of grape, only, then, by giving us itself first, by being,
as you put it, a 'spectacle of nothing', because it is always finally
about itself, auto-figurative; it is about its own making of an
equivalence. It offers us the grape itself via the specificity of its
own language. The painting is caught between immanence and
transcendence, for while it needed this particular bunch of
grapes for its motif, all grapes need this particular painting to be
what they are for us. To desire, as Pablo desires, to paint the
'being' of objects is then to be committed to the being of *painting*,
for he takes painting as an opening on Being itself.

PABLO PICASSO: . . . *Take roosters* . . . we always have roosters,
but like everything else in life we must discover them. Just as
Corot discovered the morning . . . Everything must be
discovered – this box – a piece of paper . . .[5]

AN INTERPRETER: . . . must be discovered in its thingness as just
this thing. Revealing something as just *this* thing in its
concreteness paradoxically may allow it to stand for every such
thing. For a work to be a painting it must first of all be about, be
all in the service of, painting, for only then may it offer us a
glimpse of our relation-to-things. For painting is no longer
engaged in the impossible project of giving us things as they
'really are', as if they and reality lived a life absolutely
independent of us, but rather shows us the things as always a
matter of our relation to them and their relation to each other.
Painting is a practice of relating that relates us to things and in so
doing lets us see them as inseparably bound to us; this work of
relating draws our attention to the ways in which our being is
always a being-together, a being-as-relation.

GEORGES BRAQUE: . . . Let us forget things, and consider only the
relationship between them.[6]

IVON HITCHENS: . . . I am always fascinated by the space left
between the verticals of trees . . . These divide up the area into
separate movements which can be 'read', 'listened to' or 'looked
at'.[7]

STÉPHANE MALLARMÉ: . . . To paint not the thing, but the effect
that it produces . . .[8]

AN INTERPRETER: . . . where 'effect' may be read as a metaphor for
our relation to the thing . . . Perhaps we could call our glimpse,
this glimpse of relation-as-relation, the 'content' of the work of
art.

WILLEM DE KOONING: Content is a glimpse of something, an encounter, like a flash. It's tiny, very tiny, content . . .[9]

BOB LAW: . . . All around us we have unknown phenomena and mystery, we use art to bridge the gap of knowledge, to put something where there is nothing . . .[10]

DAVID JONES: In so far as form is brought into being there is reality.

AN INTERPRETER: So the painting helps to *make* reality; it is not against or apart from it?

DAVID JONES: 'Something' not 'nothing', moreover a new 'something' has come into existence. And if, as we aver, man's form-making has in itself the nature of a sign, then these formal realities, which the art of strategy creates, must in some sense or other be *signa*. But of what can they possibly be significant? What do they show forth, re-present, recall or, in any sense reflect?[11]

AN INTERPRETER: Ah! The painting as sign. This seems to open us onto a vast and open conceptual terrain! But from what has already been said, paintings must first of all be signs of themselves . . .

DAVID JONES: . . . the painter may say to himself: 'This is not a representation of a mountain, it *is* "mountain" under the form of paint.' Indeed unless he says this, unconsciously or consciously, he will not be a painter worth a candle.[12]

MAURICE MERLEAU-PONTY: It is the mountain itself which from out there makes itself seen by the painter; it is the mountain that he interrogates with his gaze. What exactly does he make of it? To unveil the means, visible and not otherwise, by which it makes itself a mountain before our eyes . . . The painter's gaze asks them what they do to suddenly cause something to be and to be this thing.[13]

AN INTERPRETER: Not, then, a description but the mountain's 'being'. This is to involve art with first questions – to say that art's realm is always ontological, always an address of what it is to seek to re-present the 'presence', the 'being', of something. Art puts the empirical (the unquestioned beliefs of the world of everyday life) into question through its insistent engagement of the practice of re-presenting, of relating to the 'presence' of phenomena; it does this through offering itself as an experience, Willem de Kooning's glimpse, of the re-presentation of that which is finally unre-presentable in itself – Being. But in a culture committed to and based upon the production, exchange and consumption of things, of information, this is a shocking question and a difficult one for any one to recognise, for we are prepared at very few points for confrontation with it. Neither

5

our conventional 'use' of Language as a neutral tool nor the critical practices of those who write about art may be able to face these questions without serious threats to themselves. Artistic practices which give primacy to Language's potential for constituting our experience continually marginalise themselves. There is a tension then between these two ways of relating to Language; and this tension also organises academic and critical inquiry.

MARTIN HEIDEGGER: Scientific and philosophical information about Language is one thing; an experience we undergo with Language is another.[14]

AN INTERPRETER: Yes, and in the former (and we might include much criticism here too) inquiry proceeds under the sway and control of Method, and Method prevents the possibility of either raising or following questions about 'presence' for it has already set up the limits, shape and form of the object of inquiry, what science knows as its object of knowledge; whereas art, however methodical the artist's practices, is always in the service of something other than Method.

MARTIN HEIDEGGER: *You have anticipated me; I was going to say that* Method, especially in today's modern scientific thought, is not a mere instrument serving the sciences; rather it has pressed the sciences into its own service . . . In the sciences not only is the theme drafted, called up by the Method, it is also set up within the Method, subordinated to it . . . Method holds all the coercive power of knowledge. The theme is part of the Method.[15]

AN INTERPRETER: Perhaps we can see in this the violence on which Method is founded and artists are frequent targets for this appropriative violence in the form of art-critical practices.

MARTIN HEIDEGGER: . . . Since modern thinking is ever more resolutely turned into calculation, it concentrates all available energy and interest in calculating how man may soon establish himself in worldless cosmic space. This type of thinking is about to abandon the earth as earth, . . . is already the explosion of a power that could blast everything to nothingness. All the rest that follows from such thinking, the technical processes in the functioning of the doomsday machinery, would merely be the final sinister dispatch of madness into senselessness.[16]

AN INTERPRETER: And, working out of this world of violent calculation, art may serve to remind us of what is other to the violence of technological-calculative thought; it re-presents other possibilities, other ways of relating to being (human and

6

natural). In such a culture human being is characterised by a self-assertive will that, for the most part, stands in the way of a listening relationship to things. And self-assertive practice seeks to control 'feelings' in the service of a violent instrumentalism.

MARTIN HEIDEGGER: Self-willing man everywhere reckons with things and men as with objects . . . He weighs and measures constantly *yet does not know the real weight of things*. Nor does he ever know what in himself is truly weighty and preponderant . . .[17]

AN INTERPRETER: . . . and we might also ask whether woman falls under the sway of measuring. However, you are suggesting that in spite of Method, of the power of calculative thought, we are no nearer to things?

MARTIN HEIDEGGER: Despite all conquest of distances the nearness of things remains absent.[18]

AN INTERPRETER: Scientific theories, methodic analyses, supposedly exhaustive factual descriptions, take us no nearer to things; they are particular kinds of metaphors for phenomena, for our relation to phenomena, rather than accounts of things 'as they are', of their 'presence'?

MARTIN HEIDEGGER: Is this reality (the statement of physics) the jug? No. Science always encounters only what *its* kind of representation has admitted beforehand as an object possible for science.[19]

AN INTERPRETER: It may be that the metaphors of art, then, offer a qualitatively different kind of relationship with things, with others, with world, precisely because their goal and ground is an experience that arises from something other than Method. The work of art exemplifies, it enacts and makes available another sense of relation to that of scientific theories or the rationalities of everyday life. The capacity of calculative thought to measure distance quantitatively is now extraordinary, and yet this thought cannot help us to begin to understand what nearness and farness, what distance itself, are and is. Perhaps part of art's work is to offer us the possibility of experiencing distance itself, as our relation to the 'being' of things. I think, for example, of Morandi's pots.

MAURICE MERLEAU-PONTY: *Depth is not a dimension,* . . . (it) is the experience of . . . a voluminosity we express in a word where we say that a thing is *there*.[20]

AN INTERPRETER: Depth as distance here, perhaps, is that differing and deferring through which, paradoxically, we experience our metaphoric identity with the world, and the work of art is a trace of this relation. The painter's faithfulness to his or her vision, that amalgam of what is seen with the eyes and what, in Klee's terms, comes 'from the depths' is one guarantee of what has already been called painting's autofigurative character, that it is a sign of itself first of all. And this faithfulness is always other to what we conventionally understand as accurate observation. Observation, after all, roots us firmly in a now disparaged empiricism.

AVIGDOR ARIKHA: Observation can be achieved at will, and is a search for facts, it is factual. But one cannot through that alone achieve a truly faithful portrait. More is needed to achieve that which is not about measure. (It is) a double-track trace: the sitter through the painter. Two lives marked on one surface . . . Since I regard art as an echo of being, in its most elemental sense, I see the role of observation submitted to a sort of igniting power . . . Painting from life in its submission to observation, a given space and limited time, by restricted means, is a sort of seismic trace. It is provisional but intensive . . . art is not science. It is about knowledge. It is the depository of what remains unsaid. It is insignificant in comparison with world events. It is about the little event of being.[21]

AN INTERPRETER: The tension seems to be, then, that paintings, as metaphors for relation itself, can only be experienced as traces of the thereness of things, through our experience of their absolute independence of those things. They are and are not of this world . . .

FRANCIS BACON: To be and not to be . . .[22]

MARK ROTHKO: . . . I express my not-self . . .[23]

AN INTERPRETER: . . . and precisely in their not being the things, they are as art. Here art's being seems to be nothing; or, better, it is art's being to be no-thing, where no-thing is not yet nothing: that which is not-a-thing is still some(thing). Art's question for no-thing is simultaneously a celebration of a being that cannot be confined in thingness but is other than nothing. As no-thing, the painting hovers between, constitutes the space between, is the hyphen between, the things as we know them mundanely and Nothing.

AD REINHARDT: . . . Make something out of nothing, that would stand alone
Not to have to lean on anything external to work . . .[24]

AN INTERPRETER: Yet, if I understand you, that something is always on behalf of nothing . . .

AD REINHARDT: An artist, a fine artist or free artist,
An artist-as-artist,
Has always nothing to say,
And he must say this over and over again.
Especially in his work
What else is there to say?
In work or words? . . .[25]

AN INTERPRETER: The work of art may write on behalf of Nothing, hence being itself always a something that is no-thing. Art is, in this sense, the other side of things. The absolute other that you say art speaks – nothing – has then to be differentiated from the no-thing that art itself *is*. This already begins to entangle us in the thicket where saying and being are inextricably intertwined, where art, in order to be, is always already a practice within Language. But can you say more about this realm of absolute otherness that is the reason for art?

AD REINHARDT: . . . 'Creation' as content of modern art . . .

AN INTERPRETER: . . . that sounds like Klee . . .

AD REINHARDT: Void, absolute liberation, not attributes, ineffable
Beyond name, form
Transcendency, transfer from everyday
experience, timeless,

trans-mundane
. . .

Numinous, 'wholly other', profound,
nothingness, remote
. . .

Object becomes something else, yet continues to
remain itself
Threshold, limit, boundary, frontier, entrance,
guardians

AN INTERPRETER: Your terse poetics have a certain relentless power . . . These metaphors for the absolute other that is art's Reason, point to the need for a specific kind of relation to the work of art. If the work of art, as the concretisation of art and as a 'saying', both is and is not a thing, the relation it needs cannot be that of the relation of an everyday observer to things.

AD REINHARDT: Not distinguish knower and known
Sanctuary is invisible
Not 'see' it but 'oned' with it[26]

AN INTERPRETER: . . . 'oned' with it . . . to be at one with . . . to lose oneself to . . .

MAURICE MERLEAU-PONTY: Modern painting, like modern thought

9

generally, obliges us to admit a truth which does not resemble things, which is without any external model and without any predestined instruments of expression, and which is nevertheless truth.[27]

AN INTERPRETER: This truth is not, then, something to be seen through as a matter of observation but is an experience of relation itself perhaps, of the limits of re-presenting . . .

MAURICE MERLEAU-PONTY: It is impossible to say that nature ends here and that man or expression starts here.[28]

JACKSON POLLOCK: I *am* nature . . .[29]

AN INTERPRETER: . . . and being Languaged, culture too! So, the relation that the work desires of us is a 'being with' rather than a neutral observation of it as a thing. In a culture where the calculative assessment of things is the rule, we have to tear ourselves out of this calculative mode to make the work possible, and for this to occur we need to place our trust in the artist from the beginning. We have to believe in the seriousness of the artist's commitment, and be prepared to suspend our mundane doubts by placing ourselves under the sway of the work. This trust requires a certain giving up of our-selves to the work.

GASTON BACHELARD: . . . a little impulse towards admiration is always necessary if we are to receive the phenomenological benefit of a poetic image. The slightest critical consideration arrests this impulse by putting the mind in second position, destroying the primitivity of the imagination. In this admiration which goes beyond the passivity of contemplative attitudes, the joy of reading appears to be the reflection of the joy of writing, as though the reader were the writer's ghost.[30]

AN INTERPRETER: And if we think of our reading of the work of art, it has the potential for pulling us under the sway of the work's difference; this comes from nothing intrinsic to the artist but rather from our own willingness to allow the work to play with us. The difference that the work requires us to make is from seeing nothing in it to seeing no-thing in it, from the inert seeing that merely notes the absence of information relevant to mundane needs, to the participatory sharing that may re-cognise the full emptiness of Nothing's absolute otherness; mystery of genesis: genesis of mystery. And this difference is accomplished partly by our being . . .

ROLAND PENROSE: . . . prepared to accept the artist's 'magic prestige' . . .[31]

ANTHONY TAPIES: . . . A picture is nothing. It is a door that leads to another door . . . And the truth we seek will never be found in a picture; it will only appear behind the last door that the viewer succeeds in opening by his own efforts . . . For art is like a game and only by becoming very innocent – and perhaps this is true of all human activities – shall we grasp the profound meaning that it possesses . . .[32]

AN INTERPRETER: . . . or *may* possess. But to achieve that innocence may require an immense act of willing that would seek to suspend itself as will.

BARNETT NEWMAN: The image we produce is the self-evident one of revelation, real and concrete, that can be understood by anyone who will look at it without the nostalgic glasses of history . . .

AN INTERPRETER: . . . well, I'm not sure about your 'self-evidence'; can something within Language *be* self-evid . . .

BARNETT NEWMAN: . . .*don't interrupt my evocation of art and the sublime! Anyway I was asserting that* . . . in his desire, in his will to set down an ordered truth, that is the expression of his attitude towards the mystery of life and death, it can be said that the artist like a true creator is delving into chaos . . . for the artist tries to wrest his truth from the void.[33]

MAX BECKMANN: If you wish to get hold of the invisible, you must penetrate as deeply as possible into the visible . . . Art resolves through form the many paradoxes of life, and sometimes permits us to glimpse behind the dark curtain which hides those spaces unknown and where one day we shall be unified . . .[34]

AN INTERPRETER: Yes, perhaps. But we must remember that these are always art's solutions and not life's. . .

AUGUST MACKE: To look at plants and animals is to feel their mystery.

To look at the thunder is to feel its mystery.

To understand the language of form is to come closer to the mystery, to be more alive.[35]

AN INTERPRETER: And your metaphor of art as the 'language of form' again raises the issue of painting's relation to Language. Perhaps we could ask where and how painting places itself in Language. What kind of 'saying' takes place in painting?

HERBERT MARCUSE: A subversive potential is in the very nature of art . . . Art can express its radical potential only *as art*, in its own language and image, which *invalidate* the ordinary language . . . and since the tension between idea and reality, between the universal and the particular, is likely to persist until the millenium which will never be, art must always remain *alienation* . . . Permanent aesthetic subversion – this is the way of

11

art . . . power of the negative . . .[36]

AN INTERPRETER: . . . art as the text of otherness – permanent alienation: sounds like a programme for modernity . . .

AD REINHARDT: Art-as-art is always a battle cry, polemic, picket sign, sit-in, sit-down, civil disobedience, passive resistance, crusade, fiery cross, and non-violent protest . . .[37]

AN INTERPRETER: . . . at least in theory, and perhaps in intention too, but we mustn't forget the social conte . . .

PAUL KLEE: . . . permanent wine . . .[38]

ARTHUR RIMBAUD: . . . I is an other . . . alchemy of the word . . .[39]

SAM FRANCIS: . . . Painting is a way out . . .[40]

AN INTERPRETER: . . . and way out, and out of the way, maybe . . .

AD REINHARDT: In reading and rereading and making art history we can see now that there was a negative progression. The still life, landscape, the pure still life and the pure landscape and the pure portrait were negations of all kinds of narrative, mythological, and historical painting. This has happened from period to period in the West. There was less of that in the East. For thousands of years artists in the Hindu and Buddhist traditions did the same empty images over and over again.[41]

AN INTERPRETER: A history of negations but still within Tradition – and these negations have accelerated partially to define the modern tradition itself . . .

OCTAVIO PAZ: . . . a form in search of itself . . .[42]

HAROLD ROSENBERG: . . . the tradition of the new . . .[43]

AN INTERPRETER: . . . which ironically may also encapsulate the 'post-modern' attempt to say 'no' to modernism . . . And curiously, in spite of art's radical otherness to science, the metaphor of 'No' in art finds an echo in the dialectics of contemporary science. For science changes through a series of rejections or criticisms of its preceding moments and organising principles. A new scientific paradigm says 'no' to what has preceded it by including what it denies. The development of scientific reason has necessitated breaks with the common sense reason that informed classical science because the latter's logic was unable to contain the apparent contradictions that scientific work was revealing. The surrationalism of the new scientific mind necessitated the negation of the logic of previous organising principles of knowledge and practice in order to hold together phenomena that were irreconcilable within existing scientific rationalities.

GASTON BACHELARD: Negation must remain in touch with previous training. It must permit a *dialectical generalisation*. Generalisation

by negation must include what it denies. Indeed the whole
impetus of scientific thought for a century now stems from
dialectical generalisations of this sort, which embrace what has
been denied. Thus non-Euclidean geometry embraces Euclidean
geometry; non-Newtonian mechanics embraces Newtonian
mechanics; wave mechanics embraces relativist mechanics . . .[44]

AN INTERPRETER: Are you saying that, unlike the realism of
classical science, the negations of contemporary science produce
generalisations that put our mundane conception of reason itself
into question, because they embrace contradictions which
mundane reason cannot reconcile?

GASTON BACHELARD: Conceived as a prolongation of common
sense or of common reason, classical science clarified opinions,
sharpened experiments and confirmed elementary knowledge.[45]

AN INTERPRETER: And as well as being a realist conception of
knowledge it also worked with an absolutist conception of mind
and Reason. . .

GASTON BACHELARD: If one allows classical science or classical
technology as a proof of the permanence of mental structure,
one finds oneself in a strangely embarrassing position upon
entering a new scientific domain in which such principles are
absent . . . In order that knowledge may have its full efficacy
mind must now be transformed. It must be transformed down to
its very roots in order to reproduce the like result in its buds . . .
In general the mind must adapt itself to the conditions of
knowing . . . the traditional doctrine of an absolute unchanging
reason is only one philosophy, it is an obsolete philosophy.[46]

AN INTERPRETER: So, you are proposing that the emergence of
contemporary science, through a sequence of no-sayings which
embrace what is negated, has resulted in a rupture with common
sense. Common sense can no longer hold together the negations
that science must find ways of embracing. And for this reason
science's reason is sur-rational, its worlds are sur-real.
Contemporary science requires that we suspend the realist
aesthetic of its predecessors in favour of a metaphoric sense of
the relation between knowledge, the language of science and the
world. Now, if the modern tradition in art, the tradition of the
new, is a tradition of no-sayings which both embrace what they
deny (Tradition itself) and also call for a suspension of common
sense norms of seeing, this would seem to require a re-
structuring of our sense of the relation between imagination,
mind, and practice. Where science requires an opening up of
Reason to its own continuous potential transformation, art

requires an emancipation of the receptivity of the imagination to the power of metaphor, to unreason; and in art, as a matter of practice, the work must be given the imaginative space within which to effect its work. Contemporary art is the continuous transformation of ways of exploring the consequence for the imaginative experience of 'being' of contemporary physics' discovery of . . .

MICHAEL CRICHTON: . . . the limitations imposed by the idea of the objective observer. Einstein struck the first blow with his Special Theory of Relativity in 1905 . . .

AN INTERPRETER: . . . and Cézanne died in 1906 . . .

MICHAEL CRICHTON: Relativity destroyed . . .

AN INTERPRETER: . . . said 'no' to . . .

MICHAEL CRICHTON: . . . the concept of the stable, objective observer . . . Einstein showed us that in many situations two observers would see things very differently, and their instruments would record differently.

AN INTERPRETER: And subsequently Heisenberg, in the uncertainty principle, showed that . . .

MICHAEL CRICHTON: . . . if you measured mass you altered direction, and if you measured direction you changed mass . . .

AN INTERPRETER: . . . and the theory had to embrace these contradictions, it had to say 'no' to commonsense and to classical science's reason. At the same time this seemed to point to some kind of limit of scientific practice . . .

MICHAEL CRICHTON: . . . because in order to observe, the observer had to change the outcome. Observation could not be made in a neutral uninvolved way.[48]

AN INTERPRETER: So it appears to be the character of the observer's *relation* to the observed that determines the observations and therefore the theoretical understanding of the phenomena. This relativising of the observer is grounded not in any reality or absolute, then, but in metaphor, in the very practice of relating itself.

COUNT KORZYBSKI: The map is not the territory.[49]

JEAN BAUDRILLARD: *And I'd go further than that,* the territory no longer precedes the map, nor survives it. Henceforth it is the map that precedes the territory . . .[50]

AN INTERPRETER: . . . you mean in the post-culture of the spectacular information society? Well, at the least, contemporary art is a continuing recognition that the relation beween the map (the work of art) and the territory (the work's other, its referents) is always indirect. There is no territory that can be grasped 'in-itself'; there are 'only' metaphors for it, re-presentations, simulacra, that are relative to the vision, the discourse, of each artist. Unity is, in any case, always absent, occluded by the self-fragmentation of the post-modern culture. The specificity of each work of art, its concreteness and absolute otherness to every other work, is precisely what draws us towards it, and yet in its concreteness it is still metaphor, in and as itself it writes on behalf of something other than itself. But for us to grasp this other of the work of art, of the poetic image, we have . . .

GASTON BACHELARD: . . . to seize its specific reality.[51]

AN INTERPRETER: But if it is so specific how can we, the respondents, grasp it? Perhaps this brings us, following the preceding references to the word in the remarks on science, back again to Language.

GASTON BACHELARD: As a general thesis I believe that everything specifically human in man is *logos* . . .

AN INTERPRETER: . . . and woman too?

GASTON BACHELARD: . . . *mais c'est bien sûr* . . . One would not be able to meditate in a zone that preceded language.[52]

AN INTERPRETER: Perhaps, but isn't there a difference between language and Language? Hasn't logos identified itself with speech and the erasure of writing? Let's say, then, that it is the work's or image's relation to Language that, for you, provides for its transsubjectivity?

GASTON BACHELARD: The image . . . is youthful language . . .

AN INTERPRETER: . . . Language . . .

GASTON BACHELARD: . . . it places us at the origin of speaking-being.[53]

AN INTERPRETER: And if we think of the painting as text amongst texts placing us at the origin of writing-being, this resonates with modern painting's relation to Language.

ROBERT MOTHERWELL: The interest in language so dominant in modern art is not an interest in semantics *per se*: it is a continued interest in making language (whatever the medium) to fit our real feelings better, and even to be able to express true feelings that have never been capable of expression before.[54]

AN INTERPRETER: And yet, while this acknowledges that the work of art lives in a language it seems to recommend a rather assertive relation to Language where the latter is 'made to fit' some anterior 'feeling' that must be 'expressed'. Language here seems to be something that the painter can more or less control. If only André Breton were here I'm sure he would have had something to say against that! The rhetoric of expressionism can no longer support a self-critical painting practice that treats its own language seri . . .

BARNETT NEWMAN: (cutting in) . . . For a work of art to be a work of art it must rise above grammar or syntax, *pro gloria dei* . . .[55]

AN INTERPRETER: . . . Now who's interrupting! O.K., but it can't rise above Language! Well, this seems to move us away from the means of 'expression', the supposed fitting of the mark to feeling, hinted at by Robert, to a different plane . . .

PABLO PICASSO: . . . I want to say the nude, I don't want to do a nude as a nude. I want only to *say* breast, *say* foot, *say* hand or belly. *To find the way to say it*, – that's enough. I don't want to paint the nude from head to foot, but succeed in *saying* . . . I've won when that which I'm doing begins to talk without me.[56]

MARTIN HEIDEGGER: . . . thing and word . . . being and saying . . . this relation . . . announces itself in . . . 'logos' . . . (logos) speaks simultaneously as the name for Being and for Saying.[57]

AN INTERPRETER: . . . always remember that logos represents writing. So Pablo's search for the way to say implicates his search with the inter-twinedness of Language and Being, and Language is here not a specific language, such as French or English, but the very possibility of our being-together, of being-as-saying . . .

MARTIN HEIDEGGER: . . . To be involved in saying is the mark of a saying that follows something to be said, solely in order to say it. What is to be said would then be what by nature belongs to the province of Language . . . beings as a whole.[58]

AN INTERPRETER: And Pablo wins when the saying is said through him, when saying has freed itself of will. For painting, this is a saying before speaking, before words: a sign of itself as saying, as in-scribing.

AD REINHARDT: Sign which refuses to signify.[59]

AN INTERPRETER: Now that's an interesting way of putting it, Ad, because it preserves both Language and refusal! If we seize painting's specific reality we are relating to its saying. And here its saying is a possibility and a condition of Language. Does the modern tradition, through the multiplicity of ways of saying that constitute it, enable us to recognise this mute saying-without-words as a trace, a sediment of that writing-in-general which is Language before languages?

LUIGI LAMBERTINI: It is similar to the discovery of a trace left for us centuries ago by a hand moved with the desire to communicate, to write in a language which is still without an alphabet . . .[60]

AN INTERPRETER: So, every painting is a re-memoration of the first marks and gestures that inaugurated it within Language and as the very possibility of being-in-the world. Painting's marks, hovering between reference and abstraction, between something and no-thing, offer us a glimpse of the re-presentation of significance itself. And painting as a marking is immediately implicated with writing. It is the metaphor of painting as writing that underwrites the modern tradition's relation to Language. Luigi has just spoken of painting as a writing without an alphabet, a proto-writing before the phonetic linear script, a re-memoration, a reminder of what we name in the word 'origin': that already fragmented 'moment' of marking – the opening of relation itself. Painting's mark is a trace of that hyphen which opened up a space and a relation between nature and culture. And at the 'same time' it is the invention of a new sign that expands however slightly the possibilities of Language itself. It re-presents the Desire for another world through its dissatisfaction, not with Language, but with existing languages of this world. In painting we 'see' the double movement of deconstruction and construction already in play, under way . . .

FRANK AUERBACH: . . . reinvention of the physical world. . .[61]

AN INTERPRETER: . . . within Language . . .

MARCEL BROODTHAERS: the hope of another alphabet . . .[62]

(tape runs out)

Our transcription could not capture the groundswell of muttering and choking that rose steadily during the interpreter's last piece of polemic, gradually drowning the participants' contributions. Various participants, mostly critics together with a handful of artists (mostly English) left, indicating their disapproval by knocking over chairs, coughing loudly and falsely, belching, farting and jeering on the way out. A few insults were thrown across the lounge although it is not clear at whom they were directed (handfuls of human hair and ground glass were subsequently found under some of the tables by the bar staff). Some who had been sleeping woke up rather noisily, while others who had been listening attentively fell asleep and began to snore. Yet more remained completely silent, although it was not clear whether their silence represented tacit agreement with the interpreter, sullen hostility, or total indifference. Eventually the tumult subsided and there was a period of comparative silence for what seemed like several minutes (although in reality it must have been somewhat less than this) and just as it seemed as if the interpreter's remarks might have brought the discussion to a premature end, it began to take off again. Our engineer, however, had still not returned with fresh tape. To re-present this break we fill the gap between the two parts of the recorded discussion with a collection of textual fragments found, apparently abandoned, in a battered leather briefcase outside a bank in Brixton High Street. They appeared to us to bear directly and indirectly on the matters under discussion and we include them here without editorial comment.

The Editorial Collective.

2

In Advance of the Broken Ar. . .

Why paint now? Why look at, respond to, paintings now? Why write about painting now? Why criticise paintings now? And why just painting (here)? Why not sculpture, land art, video, film? And why not poetry, fiction even? Why separate painting from the other arts, from art? We are no longer, apparently, shocked by 'the new' (well, only some of us and then only a little) so surely painting is no longer 'timely'? How could it be in a culture organised around the instant exchange of visual representations, images and information?

What purchase could painting possibly have on us in the face of the spectacular power (?) of the mass image media? Are not even photography and film (let alone painting) being squeezed of their remaining drops of cultural and experiential relevance by the over-arching interpenetrating system of electronic media? And is not what little painting there is so contained by the market and museum systems that exchange value and art-historical judgment have elim-inated the possibility of any excess, any surplus, that we might seek in engaging painting for ourselves?

And surely, in any case, modern painting has run itself out, exhausted itself, on the rack of reduction? Did we not recognise through the work of the minimalist and conceptual artists that a reduction to apparent essentials of form and idea had finally elimin-ated, put a stop to, finished off, the need for painting? Didn't the over-developed avant-garde, exclusive to the visual arts, with its manic trajectory and its obsessive attacks on both itself and the structures which enclosed it, result in a final kamikaze flight of unspectacular self-destruction? And who noticed anyway apart from those paid to notice? Isn't painting, then, as something to do, to engage now, finally unrecuperable? Aren't we at last left with nothing but death, the Tradition, the past, the museum, old masters (and a few old mistresses)? Surely no one could still want, Desire, to paint once they were familiar with this history? And even if they did, what could their work possibly do other than repeat what's already been done? After all, didn't painting in its vanguard course explore, exhaust and move beyond every possibility of its own life? Surely in these circumstances to paint now could only be to mimic the past, to parody in a practice of endless repetition? Surely the only recourse for contemporary visual artists is to abandon painting (and perhaps even art) and turn to other media, other practices?

And yet. . . . And yet. . . .

Are there not at least in Western societies more artists practically committed to exploring the question 'what is painting?' than at any previous time? Is not painting reaching larger audiences than ever? Has so much ever been written and read about contemporary painting? And hasn't painting, as a 'specific signifying practice' (enter the concepts!) made a highly specific contribution to the life of modernity in the arts, a contribution whose very particularity calls for an equivalently specific response? Might not such a response in any case open on to more general questions of practice and theory across the arts?

And could it not be that, in a culture dominated by the mass reproduction of images and the simulations of the electronic media, painting, precisely because of its untimeliness, might valuably preserve and exemplify the necessity of otherness? Isn't it precisely the 'virtue', the 'Good', of the works of art which we come to know and value partially to transcend the constricting conditions of the context in which they were made? Doesn't the ability of images and texts across the arts to take us over, to keep open the possibility of our own self-transformation, certify to art's continuing relevance? And does not the attempt by totalitarian regimes to eliminate modern art practice testify to the continuing power of this possibility?

Could it be that modern painting's reflexive address, far from terminating the practice, has widened the scope of painting's possibilities? Hasn't one of the roles of avant-garde practice in the visual arts been to highlight the restrictive practices of both formalism and politically grounded criticism? And are we not witnessing now not the death of modern painting but the death of modern criticism? Do we not need to re-view the emergence and life of modern painting practice and search for an alternative reading of its significance? Might not such an alternative require us to re-think contemporary diagnoses of the death of the modern commitment and to see the 'post-modern' as a move within modernity?

Could it still be possible to write for, to show, a sense of painting's possibilities that preserved the 'Good', indeed the absolute necessity, of the commitment to an absolutely modern vision of painting practice? And might not such a recuperation of the modern commitment, far from disvaluing Tradition, recover a strong version of the value of the pre-modern tradition of painting practice? Would we then be able to participate in the generation of and response to a painting practice that valued both its identity with and its differences from its own roots?

3

Recuperating Modernity

In a culture where criticism appropriates its objects according to its own violent interests there is a need to write on behalf of the objects. A writing on behalf of painting, from within its folds, might seek to show what painting brings, has already brought to writing, to being. And more concretely, within the visual arts and perhaps across the arts generally, it is on the site of painting that the question of modernity has been most explicitly fought over and worked through. From the emergence of the modern commitment through to the post-modern era it has been painting which has been at the very centre of the critical debates both within art (among artists) and within the realm of critical/analytical practice. Indeed a turn towards other media practices and object-making in the 1960s and 1970s (performance, film, photography, video, land art, installations, mixed media objects) was precisely in response to questions that had been raised about and on the terrain of painting, about painting's very possibility.

Modern painting too has focused in its recent life, uniquely amongst the arts, the political, economic and moral issues concerning the relation between art and its social context. And this is clearly in part because of all forms of art practice, its artefacts – paintings – have characteristics that make them peculiarly vulnerable to economic appropriation: the public and private life of paintings is partially (some would say wholly) determined by their possible and actual market status. The uniqueness of the painting as an object, with its associated 'aura', however much this latter may have been transformed by the mass photographic reproduction of paintings, provides for its status and potential as a commodity. Sculpture is obviously open to similar processes, but its very material properties (dimensionality, scale, partial reproducibility) restricts its commodity potential. The commodity status of the painting thus makes explicit the political and economic context of artisitc practice and for this reason it is in painting rather than the other arts that the

22

question of the possibility and potential of an avant-garde has been most consistently articulated, tested and practised.

Similarly, in the context of developing a theoretical understanding, there is every reason to treat painting, at least to begin with, on its own as a 'specific signifying practice'. Clearly each kind of artistic practice (writing fiction/poetry/drama/music, painting/sculpting/ filming/videoing, and so on) works in a medium or media and in a relation to a tradition of practices that have distinctive properties; concomitantly each of them structures its relation to its audience, its respondents, distinctively. So while a commitment to modernity may generate dilemmas, paradoxes and tensions common to all areas of artistic practice, each one has to work these out according to the specific possibilities of its own context and medium. If we want to look at art as a 'system' of practices, it is structured precisely through the differences between each realm of practice. As long as this specificity is carefully preserved as an initial strategy we can move back and forth between the specific and the general in the confidence that we are not glossing or losing the differences, the necessary peculiarities that in the last analysis resist generalisation. This also is to separate the practice, the making, from the product of the practice, the work of art; that which differentiates painting from other art practices cannot necessarily ensure that the work of art preserves such differences. The work of art finally stands over against the practices from which it emerges. It is their other.

Painting on or into a (relatively) flat surface requires a specific address, has had a specific life, precisely because of what differentiates it from other art practices, however closely related these may be. It is these differences which place it in a specific relation both to us and to its past – Tradition. Nevertheless we can find in painting practice not only echoes of the life of other artistic practices, but also, precisely because it has concentrated its energies on central questions of modernity, crystallisations of the dilemmas and tensions of art practice generally.

And nowhere within the arts has the question of what it means, what it is, to be 'absolutely modern' been so explicitly, restlessly and violently explored as in painting. This question refers us immediately to the possibility of a distinctively modern practice in painting and also opens directly on to the issue of the so-called death of modernity and its other – post-modern – practice. The latter carries us over into wider issues of cultural and socio-political analysis with its connotations of radical changes in the very structures and processes of 'industrial society' itself. Some of these will be touched upon in the subsequent discussion of post-modernity.

Having argued for the need for an address of painting's specificity I want to qualify this immediately. If we turn from the practice to its outcome, the work of art, it may be increasingly difficult to preserve the specificity of the painting precisely because of the role of the other – the audience as respondent – in the painting's subsequent life. For paintings are already implicated in wider cultural practices of re-presentation: they seep out of art into not-art. If we include painting within the overarching metaphors of re-presentation, textuality and text which gather all processes and products of signification, the constitution of meaning itself, it may be impossible to show where painting stops and other texts begin. The painting, the work of art as text, stands in relation to all other textual phenomena both within and beyond the conventional 'boundaries' of painting and art.

This general inter-textuality, the play of relations between this apparently absolutely heterogeneous, expanding-contracting, self-transforming non-system of texts, is characterised by an inter-penetration of texts. Inter-textuality is intra-textuality – one within another(s). Because every text is already however tacitly and implicitly, a reading of, a response to, a comment on, a critique of, a Desire for at least one other text (and typically of many more than one), so there is a general seepage, a flow, of texts into each other. The 'empirical' boundaries of texts, their inside-outside, frames, edges, covers, first and last words, and so on, merely serve to channel this inter-penetration, in certain directions. Indeed an understanding of 'framing' in general is central to any exploration of textuality for it draws us directly into the issue of the relation between one text and another (see Derrida, 1978a). Painting is approached here within this context of inter- and intra-textuality. And it may be that this very sense of the unlimited, unboundaried, unfinishable character of texts has emerged in part out of the very course of modern artistic practice and exploration; art work has confronted criticism, thought, analysis, everyday practice, with this as a critical issue for their own self-consciousness. Artistic practice itself has in a variety of ways continuously moved back and forth across this issue. Works of art directly confront their respondents with it. For example, and most concretely, the practice of collage, a dominant feature of modern painting across a wide range of genres, works precisely through juxtaposing textual fragments from heterogeneous sources; although in the service of the specific work, such 'internal' juxtapositions already deconstruct the boundary between the inside and the outside. And this limitless dispersion, dissemination and displacement of texts, this folding back of texts on to and

24

into each other, means that art and life are, in principle, inseparable, although in practice we continually make concrete judgments about the limits of art.

Now this points to an important tension within modern practice between work (practice and products) which identifies itself as avant-garde and work which has a more open sense of modernity. And in the present post-modern condition this critical division is very much to the fore. The two senses of practice join over the criticality of the boundary 'between' art and life with the politicised avant-garde exploring the 'boundary' with the aim of negating and transcending it; art's radicality here would be certified by its ability to ally itself with other forms of critical practice aiming at specific sites of cultural and social change. Political avant-garde practice in art seeks to transcend itself on behalf of some other, non-art 'good'. The alternative sense of modernity, committed to a radical art-for-art's-sake practice, confronts the 'same' division between art and life but reads it differently; the telos of the practice here is constantly to affirm art's otherness to life through a critical questioning of those taken-for-granted conventions of re-presentation and signification that provide for the 'natural' or for the commonsense of the realities of everyday life. Both senses of practice run risks: the avant-garde sense of practice risks losing its difference by submerging itself completely in an instrumentally oriented cultural criticism. The alternative sense of practice constantly risks losing its difference, its otherness, through falling under the sway of, being trapped by the everyday conventions it seeks to put into question. Both also run the related risk of subordinating themselves to theories of practice generated within the sphere of art criticism. The threat here is of a criticism treated as the authority for the work rather than as a response to it. These risks are acknowledged here in the movement between treating painting both in its specificity and in its dispersal into the general text. No matter what the desires and intentions of artistic practice the latter is finally absolutely unable to prevent its art work being recuperated by the surrounding culture on its own terms – this is the risk, the hazard of practice.

But none of this yet seems to engage modernity 'itself'; we are still dealing with consequences of its differential interpretation. Is there a 'modernity-in-itself', a centre, a site, from which we can trace divergences and declines? The example of the avant-garde can be instructive for it already opens us to the possibility that modernity is not and never has been 'one', a common ground assuring the fundamental identity of those subscribing to a unitary code of practice. And yet in a culture whose self-understanding includes a

CONSEQUENCES OF MODERNITY –

grasp of and a belief in itself as committed to modernity, the question of what 'it is' is vital. We need only think of the implications of the term 'modernisation' for a contemporary society or some sub-system within it. Modernity crystallises the violence of a moral political force. Perhaps even at this most general level the arts, and painting specifically, through the intensity of their involvement with the question of modernity, re-present significant moments in the culture's grasp and experience of itself. What, for painting then, does modernity name (for the effects of a commitment to it clearly go beyond a merely descriptive sense of the painter's own contemporaneity)?

In 1863, at the suggestion of the Emperor Louis Napoleon, a separate Salon, the 'Salon des Refusés', was held for the first time for those who were rejected by the official Salon in Paris; the latter represented the only public opportunity in France for artists to show their work and was dominated by the Academicians in the Institut de France under whose auspices it was held. The Academicians' Salon preserved the values of a classicism that rigorously excluded work which departed from its ideals of re-presentation: unquestioning adherence to rigidly interpreted codes of realism and naturalism, composition, chiaroscuro, and so on, put to work on a narrow range of subject matter (historical/symbolic narrative, society portraiture, etc.). The Salon des Refusés was a crucial institutional and symbolic break for it opened up and consecrated an absolute split, the terms of whose legacy we are still living within. After 1863 there were two types of painting, that of the Academy and that of the rejected; this act inaugurated for painting what might now be called, paradoxically, the modern tradition. It can also remind us that the critical question we still need to put continually to 'modern' painting is whether the art of refusal (initially, lest we forget, the refused) is becoming academicised.

The first Salon des Refusés included works by Whistler, Pissarro and Manet, painters whose work explicitly engaged in different ways the conditions of modern life and in this already displayed its otherness to the worn out classicism of the Academy (Picon, 1978). The practical effect of making this work visible was immediate, for, from that moment on, artists who sought to place their work before the public, at a time when the system of private dealers was in its infancy, had to make a choice. Were they to ally themselves with the Academy or with the rejected?

Some ten years later, also in France, the young poet Arthur Rimbaud asserted in *A Season in Hell*: 'It is necessary to be absolutely modern' (Rimbaud, 1974, p.104, my translation). If we read his own

26

writing as an enactment of this necessity, it is clear that in the context of poetry too it entailed a refusal. If Rimbaud's bald injunction throws down the challenge to the artist who would be 'absolutely modern', and if the subsequent life of the modern tradition represents an attempt to confront, explore and map his instruction, we find crucial issues raised already in his brief writing practice. 'A Season in Hell' itself abandons traditional constraints of rhyme and meter and opens up a new space in poetry. Certainly Rimbaud regarded himself as a revolutionary, but a revolutionary of a very particular kind and not one that fits easily within stereotypes of the political revolutionary. Two years earlier in 1871, when only 16, he had written his 'Lettre du Voyant' in which he dismissed all preceding poetry and set out the terms of his search for new ideas and new forms. For Rimbaud the 'new' was to be achieved through a conversion of the self into a 'voyant', a poet-prophet, a visionary searching through self-knowledge for a state called the 'unknown', a transcendence which was to be attained by what he called a 'reasoned deranging of all his senses' (ibid., p.7). The products of this state might have little to do with the conventional aesthetics of the beautiful and a lot more to do with the search for the sublime which modernity itself inaugurates (see Lyotard, 1982 for a discussion of this distinction).

Rimbaud completed 'A Season in Hell' when he was 18, and he followed this with his 'Illuminations'. By the time he was 20 he had ceased writing poetry altogether, and subsequently became a wanderer and occasional gun runner across Europe and Africa. His search for visionary transcendence through his poetry ended therefore long before we could begin to locate the arrival of what contemporary criticism might call his poetic 'maturity' or the emergence of a style.

In the conjunction of his poetry and his life we can find key pointers to those questions that were to become crucial, although interpreted in different ways, for the subsequent life of the 'modern tradition': a rejection of the past as the dominant source for the conventions of artistic practice; a search for the 'new' through that paradoxical 'reasoned deranging' of the senses; an absolute commitment to be true to whatever resulted from this deranging; and, crucially, a recognition of the limits of his own ability continually to find the 'new'. The poetic 'place' which Rimbaud delineated as the space in which the modern commitment had to work is anything but easy to enter or sustain a life within. The implications for artistic practice are radical and uncomfortable. And not least because we can now consider them from within both our knowledge of what has

27

happened to modernity in art subsequent to Rimbaud, and also the relative comfort of the Academy or its contemporary equivalent (the College, the gallery system, the systems of public and private patronage). To inaugurate a practice of refusal is very different to maintaining it as a way of life in a culture where specific features of it may already be valued and institutionalised. Being absolutely modern would seem to necessitate the continual critical re-assessment of the history of modernity itself as an intrinsic feature of practice. The crucial question for contemporary artistic practice, then, must be whether it is still necessary to be 'absolutely modern', and, if so, whether the experience of the modern tradition itself has changed our understanding of this absolute modernity. Is the quality of Rimbaud's radicality still definitive of what it is to be 'absolutely modern' or have the terms, have the possibilities of modernity changed through its own very history? What after all could be more radical, as a gesture of negation, than Rimbaud's choice of poetic silence, of artistic death, at the age of 20?

Part of Rimbaud's search was for a new language, for, as he said, 'I no longer know how to speak'; past or existing languages of both poetry and everyday life were irrelevant because 'I do not find myself again in any time other than the present' (Rimbaud, 1974, pp.47 and 101), and his rhetorical rejection of past poetry has already been noted. The paradox is clear (at least to formulate if not to face): we face the present as something alien because we no longer know how to speak/write. The modern experience for Rimbaud is thus doubly alienated: it cannot be comprehended in the languages of the past, of Tradition, and yet we do not find ourselves except in this present – hence the need for a new language, a language of the present, a language that owes nothing to the past, a language without history, without memory, a language for beginning again, a language against repetition.

This begins to show us the central paradox as well as the inaugural Desire of what we now recognise as the modern tradition: for does not the very fact of this tradition *as* tradition testify to the impossibility of its attainment? We know too, from our very 'withinness' in Language, that the radicality of Rimbaud's rejection of the past and his search for a new language, a language that has no past or memory, a language that is beyond Language, cannot be achieved. For we know that Rimbaud's work is read not as ending poetry, or from poetry's outside, not as an absolute rupture or a new beginning, but rather as an exploration into the very heart of the poetic region. His writing is a de-centring that re-opens the question of centring itself. If we only attended to his rhetorical rejection of past poetry we would be turned aside from his practice which was a radical revivifying of poetry's potential, an 'expansion' of the Tradition's possibilities. And his writing can be read from no other site than that of poetry without both transformation and radical loss. We can only politicise its radicality through turning it away from poetry, poetry as its end, to another end. This is the avant-garde's dilemma: if it sees its end as beyond art (life) it immediately risks losing itself to, turning itself into an instrument for, a tool for, another practice. If, then, this absolutely new language, which is the apparent guarantee of modernity, of commitment to the 'present', is unrealisable *from the beginning*, what does this do to Rimbaud's project? Has modernity always been impossible?

The question of modernity confronts us unavoidably with the relation between Language, our languages, and the 'present', our 'presence', the 'presence' of things and others for us; we are faced with how to re-present 'the times' in which we live and with what 'it is' to be 'timely' in such re-presentation. It confronts us, as Rimbaud has shown us, with the problem of the relevance of what we bring, carry over and forward, from the past of the language we learn from others, the language of the past, the artistic tradition, to our relation to the 'present'. The experience, the diagnosis, the dilemma of modernity seem to begin with this refusal of what the Tradition delivers to us as the expected, indeed the required, conventions for making art. It is these rather than Tradition itself which are no longer experienced, lived, as 'timely', because they prevent the artist from re-presenting the quality of his or her relation to the 'present' in its specificity. This is a diagnosis not only of the legacy of the languages of art but also of the world in which art is practised too, for it asserts that the reason for the untimely quality of existing languages is that the world itself has changed, is changing, in a way which calls continually for new languages to grasp the changing conditions of the artist's experience and practice. But in what ways might our very experience of a tradition of refusal and innovation have acted back upon and transformed these first assertions of modernity's difference?

Clearly the terms 'modern' and 'tradition' are in tension with each other, and equally clearly artists now practise in a culture which itself is organised around the principle of innovation, at least on the plane of production and consumption. The centrality of innovation to the life of the culture extends as far as artistic practice in so far as the demand for the new has been partially institutionalised within that practice, and this is fostered within certain limits, by the art support systems. Modern practice and its art works may live a precarious and marginal life but this marginality is secured through public and private systems of connoisseurship (museums, galleries, arts councils, collectors, educational institutions, mass media) which have given limited approval to a version of innovation. Indeed they have depended upon and sought to control and re-work the dynamic of innovation to further the interests of their own security. The patterns of change in modern art practice cannot be divorced from this institutional context. Modern art may still be marginal to the central concerns of the culture and contemporary consciousness, to instrumental reason, but perhaps its marginality has changed in quality through the forms of its institutionalisation. There is still an 'academic' tradition supporting the traditional aesthetics of realism and naturalism which are loosely used to underwrite the practices of re-presentation that dominate the mass media, while the alternative tradition, modernity, has a marginality secured by those institutions which use it according to their own interests and needs. We have thus to distinguish between the sense of innovation which may be operating in any artist's work and the sense which is used in the wider art world and culture to provide for the stability and long-term survival of organisational interests.

But if refusal and innovation partially define the modern commitment they do not exhaust it; as Rimbaud found, the artist does not escape from the Tradition even though his or her work may re-define the significance and potential of Tradition. The work always returns to, places itself in a relation to Tradition. It is not Tradition itself which is refused but only specific languages, specific conventions of re-presentation within it. How could it be otherwise, for to refuse Tradition itself, to say 'no' to practice itself, could only lead to the abandonment of art. On the contrary it is only from within the deepest commitment to Tradition, to the very possibility of art, that any artist could generate the need to refuse its specific languages. The modern refusal arises precisely from the Desire to celebrate the continuing possibilities of the Tradition, the conviction that it has a future, in the face of the signs of its decline in its currently dominant languages. It is this affirmation of the absolute necessity of continuing to paint, of finding ways to sustain Tradition in the face of worn out, lifeless, untimely languages, which places the artists in tensions only partially resolvable in the course of practice itself. To practise *art*, rather than something else (criticism or theory for example) is already to begin to display the Good of art, and here of painting specifically.

Every practice or work that seeks to context itself as painting, that begins with and from within painting, first of all displays its commitment to, its Desire for, the continuance of painting. It is a celebration of painting in the face of every other kind of re-presentation. Criticism and theory find it very hard to comprehend this commitment and its consequences. If the experience of and commitment to modernity require the artist, the painter, to make painting, its very possibility, the question, this question can only come from within; it comes from itself and returns to itself. It remains always a question of and for painting. This self-directed questioning, this reflexive turn, can thus never be an absolutely negative questioning because the very practice is a celebration of the value of carrying out painting as questioning. Even those works which seem to be at the 'limits' of painting (think of Malevich's 'White on White' paintings, Rodchenko's 'Red, Yellow and Blue', Klein's 'Blue', Reinhardt's 'Black', Rauschenberg's and Ryman's 'White' paintings and so on) are still paintings of their relation to 'limit'. Only if painting could be reduced absolutely to a negative self-questioning, a self-obliteration, could it seek to be the final painting; but then what would it be to want to paint such a painting – an unpainting? How can one paint in order to end painting? One makes such a gesture only by not painting. Every gesture of painting exceeds and denies the Desire to end painting. To begin painting is to re-member and to celebrate the liveliness of the Tradition.

The radical alternative is obviously to stop painting; and this has happened both in individual cases (think of Jackson Pollock) and also in the late modern and post-modern turn to other media and other practices. But at the same time and also partially defining post-modern practice there has been a resurgence of painting, a renewal that insists upon the necessity of re-opening the question of the necessity of painting in the face of both the vanguardist critique of it as an anachronism and the materialist reduction, performed within late formalist and minimalist practice.

The displacement of modernist abstraction from the centre of the critical stage has been manifest across every institutional area of the art world – markets, galleries, academies and art press – and has entailed a de-centring of art practice itself. Art-historically it serves to remind us that an extraordinarily wide range of non-abstract painting continued alongside, indeed surrounded, the dominant modernist abstraction; post-modern painting gives this work that had been marginalised by avant-garde critical practice equal if not greater significance in its attempt to comprehend the meaning of modernity (we need only think of the renewed interest in Picasso's late paintings which exemplifies the post-modern turn). More specifically, geographically the art world itself is de-centred as the abstraction grounded in American painting and critical practice gives way to the emergent European painters, especially in Germany and Italy, whose work is taken to exemplify the shift in painting's values. Indeed it is a very feature of post-modernity to deny a centre and to disperse and fragment practice on behalf of an alternative vision of modern painting which brackets the materialist assumption of a progressive linear trajectory for painting. The regionalism that post-modernity displays (witnessed in the very different kinds of painting produced by the German and Italian painters associated with post-modernity) itself reasserts the primacy of the personal and cultural context within which the painting is produced, and distances the work from the unifying internationalism of American modernism.

As a practice that is highly knowledgeable about and responsive to the history of modern painting, post-modernity has called forth a variety of categories amongst critics, and these tend to focus on the ways that it relates to modern painting (the range of genres, schools, styles and gestures) as a resource in its pursuit of the question 'what is painting?' Allegory, appropriation, parody and citation are to the fore in this critical canon, for criticism seeks to grasp post-modernity as an ironic practice that puts yesterday's gestures to work in contexts to which they are no longer appropriate. Critical distrust of what is seen as a nostalgic return to outworn modes of practice, is sharpest where the critic writes for either the maintenance of 'given' formalist values or a politicised sense of avant-garde practice: post-modernity is condemned as the subversion of the avant-garde. Indeed Oliva's term for gathering the post-modern Italian artists – The Trans-avantgarde (Oliva, 1980) – proposes post-modernity as a going beyond of the avant-garde.

It is not however part of my concern here to review the play of both painterly and critical differences that assemble the region of the post-modern, but rather to offer a re-reading of modernity itself, a reading necessitated by the post-modern diagnosis of modernism's death. The following texts provide an introduction to the debate about post-modernity in art and the range of critical differences which structure the field of discourse: Ashton (1976), (on Guston); Brock (1981); Buchloh (1981, 1982a, 1982b, 1982c); Buchloh, Krauss, and Michelson (1980); Crimp (1981); de Duve (1983); Faust (1981); Fineman (1980); Foster (1982, 1983, 1984); Gohr (1982); Kramer (1983); Krauss (1981a, 1981b); Kuspit (1981, 1983); Lischka (1984); Lyotard (1981, 1982); Melville (1981); Oliva (1980); Owens (1980a, 1980b, 1984); Parmesani (1984); Pohlen (1984); Ricard (1981); Wildermuth (1984).

In the course of this re-reading the issue of post-modernity will be raised frequently for, by definition, this text itself is written from within post-modernity, that is from a site of painting and writing which seeks to re-cover an alternative version of the Good of modern painting and which sees post-modernity as inevitably caught within modernity. Written on behalf of painting this text is partly a response to and seeks to distance itself from much of the writing within whose interests varieties of post-modernity have been both adumbrated and dissected. My argument is that before we can grasp the significance of the kind of break which post-modernity seems to mark with its immediate past we have to reconsider dimensions of the relation between painting and modernity which modernism and vanguardism may have occluded and repressed. And this means trying to approach painting on its own ground, on its own terms, and not through critical categories which have already fitted it to a unifying vision of painting and criticism that grounds itself on a site of Method and writing beyond painting (philosophy, psycho-analysis, semiotics, sociology, politics, or whatever). The brute 'fact' which systems of contemporary criticism have to face and which they cannot accommodate is the ever-present Desire amongst artists to preserve and constantly renew painting in the face of both critical disbelief in its possibility and absolute cultural marginalisation.

In the face then of both theoretical and practical attempts to find and diagnose the death of modern painting and to surpass painting's limit many artists find it absolutely necessary to carry on, to start, to return to painting on a site other than of modernist abstraction. Are they uniformly deluded about painting's present and future? Are they sacrificing their commitment to modernity or could it be that the theoretical conventions that have surrounded and supported modern painting practice have missed or actively repressed alternative possibilities for it? But, before the significance of the transformation of the modern into the post-modern can be explored, the text of modernity in painting must be re-traversed and alternative readings broached.

If painting, even in self-questioning, always celebrates painting, is always a re-memoration of Tradition, then even that painting which sought to re-invent painting in the service of the commitment to the absolutely modern, *starts in the middle of painting*. It finds itself always already in the middle of painting but begins from the assumption that this middle is, like the dark continent's interior, still an unexplored, unknown and finally unknowable territory. Middle here is an ever-expanding and retreating region: not a point, not a mid-point, but absolutely non-punctual. When modern painting practice is offered as a search for its origins the latter names the still to be explored middle region. There can thus be no absolute beginning again, no absolute innovation, free of all repetition, for modernity cannot, nor does it Desire to, perform an ontological break with Tradition itself but only with the legacy of its inert languages. Modernity names that liminal practice that incessantly re-maps painting's terrain; it is, borrowing from Deleuze and Guattari, both a deterritorialising and a reterritorialising of painting (Deleuze and Guattari, 1983). To say that modern painting, as a search for its own beginings, is an archeaology is not to show it as a search for some absolute origin, a moment of past presence when it 'really began', but is rather to metaphorise it as the constant attempt to recover a territory which, because it is the artist's own territory, has always provided for the need for its recovery 'from the beginning'. The middle names a region without a 'dead' centre, for each attempt at mapping so re-structures our sense of the terrain that the centre is perennially deferred. And will always be deferred, for in spite of our apparent technical conquest of the means of re-presentation (the 'instantaneity' of the satellited televisual image) *we still do not know what re-presentation 'is'*, what it is 'to re-present'.

The modern tradition is not *only*, then, in Paz's term a 'tradition against itself' (Paz, 1974), or solely a 'tradition of the new' (Rosenberg, 1962). Precisely as tradition, and as painting, modern painting entwines itself with the Tradition through its sharing of the celebratory character of painting-in-general, and indeed of art-in-general, of art as that array of practices which respond to the Desire to engage the imaginative possibilities of relationality in and for themselves. The modern tradition is also a tradition-for-itself as well as against itself: it is against itself in its recognition of itself as already part of the past in the very 'moment' of its becoming, for it knows that its effort to re-present the present is impossible; but it is for itself in its very attempt to place itself as art, for it celebrates the 'thereness', the absolute necessity, the being, the 'taking place' of art.

And in being for art, painting declares its unutterable, absolute weakness, its total powerlessness. Painting, as Arikha says, is 'very small' (Arikha, 1978). But this very weakness, this absolute rejection of the very bases on which power and authority are sought and claimed in our culture, already makes it a potential threat. The irony of its display of absolute otherness to the violent conventions of instrumental reason, of calculative thought and practice, lies exactly in this continual exemplification of the alternative commitment – the commitment to weakness, to non-violence; to be on behalf of, to display, to exemplify, to perform this otherness in a culture founded upon violence and the will-to-power is to invite distortion, repression and incorporation. And the culture's answer is typically to find ways of absorbing and neutralising the display, and of turning it to its own instrumental ends (for example through the inter-related market and museum system), of transforming it into what vanguard theory and criticism would call 'ideology'. But such criticism all too frequently works from within the same violent framing practice as the culture it so violently criticises: it has to assert itself as the voice of authority and in doing so needs to subdue its topics, in this case painting. In this, its overwhelming need to place, to have, painting on its terms, it preserves its absolute otherness to painting. And painting's problem is precisely that its helplessness, its vulnerability, is almost aggressive; its very up-front character confronts us, is unavoidable. This aggressive humility itself seems to invite attack by making a virtue of weakness, and what could be more threatening to those practices committed to the ruthless project of overcoming and containing their topics? 'Art is an embodiment of the anti-war. The body doesn't want to die, so the voice of the body is anti-war, so I think it is urgent to listen to the body's voice' (Francesco Clemente, 1981, p.27). But in order to hear 'this voice of the body', to read painting's writing, already requires that we suspend just those thought forms that criticism has to bring to bear on the work of art to be what is – critical.

Nothing points more clearly to the need for an alternative reading than the emergence and dominance of 'formalism' as the essential ground from which to comprehend modern painting. Formalism as a critical response produced 'modernism', a term avoided here precisely because of its alliance with formalism. It is that approach which begins with a separation between 'form' and 'content', subsequently privileges form over content, and finally subsumes content within form. Reductive in intent it seeks to establish the 'essence' of painting in its formal features (the application of colour to a flat two-dimensional supported surface); painters' exploration and handling of these 'essential' forms are then seen as defining the possible quality of aesthetic response to be gained from the work. The term 'modernism' has been most consistently applied to that painting which appeared to follow the formalist programme of painterly questioning and has dominated critical (and much painting) practice, especially American, until the emergence of the postmodern; it also defined that sense of avant-garde practice which saw itself as the search for the material and conceptual essence of painting. Coming in upon the coat tails of abstract expressionist painting and providing criteria for 'colour-field' painting and 'post-painterly' abstraction, it offered a retrospective reading of modernity in painting which re-presented the latter as a historically linear progressive questioning practice. Modern painting was reconstituted as a trajectory of self-inquiry the telos of which was to establish the absolutely and minimally necessary terms for painting, to show what formally differentiated painting from every other art practice, and then to work rigorously within these differentiating terms. Through this questioning painting would come to know itself, its own identity, its material essence and limits, it would truly come to itself and into its own. Or so the theory had it. . . .

In arguing for painting's difference, formalism, epitomised in the writings of Greenberg (1961) and Fried (1967), used a covert empiricist philosophy which sought to separate 'sight' off from the other senses. Painting was to be for the eyes alone, and thus its essence and therefore its effects would be found in their pure form only along an isolated dimension of sight, eyes cut off from consciousness, from signification, and most importantly from Language. Empiricism in the last analysis has to assert and enforce an absolute separation between physical sensation (for painting, that of sight) and meaning or significance, and it has to give sensation priority over significance. Living within a classical dualism of Western metaphysics, the body-mind dichotomy, it asserts that our experience of painting is first of all a matter of pure sensation: of sensation before significance. There may be a variety of subsidiary metaphors for these 'sensations' which are conventionally associated with aspects of 'emotion' or, more vaguely, 'feelings'. Any significance we attach to a painting must always be, for empiricism, a secondary and derivative process, an epiphenomenon, that has to effect some kind of absolute transformation of one 'thing' into something else, of 'sensation' into 'significance'.

The conversion of modern painting into 'modernism' through this conjunction of formalism and empiricism was considerably aided by the much earlier emergence of abstraction established in different ways by Kandinsky, the Delaunays and Malevich. The rejection of conventional versions of figuration, the re-presentation of others and objects drawn from either everyday or imaginary experience, provided the grounds for the formalist interest, for, in eliminating conventional signification painting already seemed to be involved in a painterly reduction. Modernism thus comes to be identified centrally with abstraction, with the apparently essential elimination of the signified as conventionally understood, the 'real world referent'. To be absolutely modern according to the requirements of modernism involves a reading of modern painting via its trajectory through a linear series of necessary stages of development. And the concept of development ties it to a version of progress; to follow the trajectory is to go beyond, to be ahead of what is left behind. Tradition is rendered diachronically as a series of surpassed moments each of which was necessary to its progress but none of which could now be relevant to present practice. To engage such past work as either artist or respondent could only be seen from within modernism as an act of pure nostalgia.

But to impose this unitary and one-dimensional reading on to modern painting is to relegate to the margins, to make a historical footnote of, most of the painting that has been practised in the name of modernity. Even at the level of 'movements' (symbolism, the Viennese secession, dada, metaphysical painting, most surrealism, new objectivity, much constructivism, vorticism, neo-dada, pop art, super realism, new image painting and so on), let alone of individual artists, the list of exclusions, of footnotes becomes absurd. Alternative readings of modernity have thus to comprehend this multiplicity, these differences, in a non-reductive way; another reading practice is needed to relativise the formalist and vanguardist strategies and to recuperate and re-new acquaintance with a lost, critically repressed, modernity.

One site from which this can be done is that offered here – the site where painting is gained, is won, is achieved, within Language. To offer painting (and indeed all the arts) as an engagement of and within Language is already to distance the reading from any kind of formalism or empiricism for it already puts out of play both the form-content dichotomy and the primacy of sensation (as some supposedly separable realm of being) over significance. 'Beginning' from its own being-in-Language it treats the questions of painting's relation to itself, to the world, to respondents, as always questions that can only be posed from the 'withinness' of, from within the thickness of, Language. The relevance of the turn towards Language in twentieth century thought, although running off in many different directions, can be acknowledged for all the arts precisely because this was already *their very own problem*: they are all and always have been concerned with 'presencing' or better 're-presencing' 'something' within a language. The specific languages of the arts put themselves into relations with Language, with the very possibility of each of their languages. It is not merely that, as Lévi Strauss would argue, language is what makes culture the other of nature, but rather that the very possibility of our having a 'nature' as the other of Language is already a gift of Language. If we can treat

Heidegger's metaphor of Language as the House of Being (Heidegger, 1967) with the utmost seriousness then we are already beginning to face the questions that art has always faced for itself. For art is both the very exemplar, the explorer, and the first celebrator, of that nagging doubt about the impossibility of a 'transcendental signified': that the referent, the signified, of every signifier, of every act of meaning (be it speech, writing, painting, gesturing or whatever) is always itself as Derrida proposes (Derrida, 1981, p.28) another signifier. We cannot get outside Language or a language to the 'things themselves'; there can be no absolute 'presence' of some 'thing' outside the skin of language through which we constitute that thing and give it the only life it has for us. The 'nothing' that we posit beyond Language as the absolute other of something is first of all, as a word, the grant of Language; we can only conceive of the abyss, the without of Language, from our withinness – to name the unnameable as dread is to show the depth of our withinness.

It is in this context that the earlier metaphors of text and textuality take on some pertinence. Painting offers us an array of languages of re-presentation, of coded practices readable in specific texts (paintings) which are already highly reflexive; that is, they refer first of all to *themselves* as precisely languages of and for painting, as explorations and celebrations of what it is to re-present in paint. To metaphorise painting as language is thus to inter-relate it with other creative cultural practices (literature, the arts generally, criticism even) in a way which on the one hand preserves its difference through attention to the specifics of its own practices of re-presentation, and on the other shows its unavoidability for those practices precisely because of these specifics. Gathering painting within Language, showing painting's question to itself about itself as a question about its own specific ways in Language, draws it into the play and circle of those practices whose 'being' it is to make Language and their modes of re-presenting within it, the very point of their project. From such a site the empiricist sensation becomes yet another 'transcendental signified' for as Derrida puts it: 'Empiricism is thinking by metaphor without thinking the metaphor as such' (Derrida, 1978, p.139). And the form-content dichotomy is displaced in the very term metaphor and the associated range of tropes and figurations which could be brought into play in such a poetically grounded response. Instead of the authoritarian destruction of much current critical practice, art, painting and writing would move into relation in the region of a deconstructive practice in which art and painting are already fully engaged.

To put painting into this relation to Language, to re-insert it into the folds of Language, also allows us to bring to the fore and assert the importance of a defining feature of modern painting practice – the role of the work of theorising as an active critical 'moment' intrinsic to that practice. Painters have often written and spoken about their work, we need only think of Leonardo and Delacroix, but only with modernity did practice clearly require an explicit address by painters of the very grounds of their commitment and their ways of working. It is because modernity understood itself as a self-questioning of the relevance and possibilities of the Tradition's legacy to each painter that painters have treated their own theorising as intrinsic to their work: not as replacing, or standing for their work but as a necessary complement. And it is no accident that both the movements of modern painting and artists working independently of such movements have written and published extensively about their own work; such group and individual 'manifestos' display artists' need to extend their practice from the visual into the verbal text. More recently, with the emergence and relative stability of art world journals and papers, both the opportunity and demand to extend this secondary area of practice have increased greatly. Interviews with artists in which the artist publicly rehearses and formalises his or her theoretic interests are staple features of such organs. And in this context artists may be asked to confront and to theorise issues which had not necessarily entered into their practice or concerns in any explicit way; in a wider sense too the art press acts constantly to re-invent the critical-theoretical context of making art, not only by the theoretical argument employed by their contributors, but also by their patterns of selection and juxtaposition. Modern painting practice is now absolutely intertwined with the theoretical work of both its practitioners and those who mediate art practice to the art world and to the wider culture (see Rosenberg, 1972, p.55).

A re-reading of the modern tradition needs to attend to this multi-dimensional textuality of painting practice for it displays the ways that words cannot be kept out of painting. We cannot come to any painting (we never could) with our mind as a 'tabula rasa'; we only relate to every work through the conventions that enable us to read it as a painting in the first place (rather than, for example, an advertisement or a photograph). And our engagement of the work will only continue if we can establish a common 'ground' through our reading for both what we bring to and desire from it and for painting's own language. In this context the artist's own related or accompanying texts are typically treated as major allies; we need only think of the role of titling as a resource for the respondent and the near universal practice of titling in the public display of paintings. Of course titling performs part of the art-historical task of authentication too but this is of less importance in the public gallery setting where its role as information is to the fore. The inter-twining of words and paintings is even more explicit in those works which contain texts or fragments of texts (from Picasso through to Twombly and Kiefer). However much we may seek to eliminate the linguistic character of such texts and transform them into 'painterly' marks their resistance is always and inevitably absolute. We cannot escape from theory *in* the painted text either.

But there is another side to this interplay between theorising and painting, for it seems increasingly as if there can be no final distinction between practice and theory. Each breaks up, fragments, the other. Theory does not stop at the frame. We need it and already have it in play in moving within the frame, but then our theorising will be confronted by the work of the painting itself, will be forced back on itself, will be split into oppositions, tensions, confusions, elisions and so on. And theory is even more explicitly fragmented when words, bits of words, scraps, are part of the painting itself; the painting performs the fragmentation, the dispersal of theory and in this, perhaps, makes explicit the condition of modern painting for us. For, from the divisionist brush mark of the impressionists onwards, painting has in a multitude of ways both experienced and explored fragmentation and taken it as a metaphor for its own life and, more generally, for the experience of the subject in the wider culture in which painting is practised.

Fragmentation is necessarily tied in part to the questioning dimension of modern practice for, in so far as questioning always threatens repetition, always asks repetition to justify itself, it proposes concomitantly the difference of each work or body of work. Practice and its artefacts are always likely to appear fragmented precisely because what sufficed for one work or collection of works is no longer felt to suffice. Finding what suffices, where what suffices is the other of repetition, of sameness, is always likely to produce ruptures, breaks, cuts, jumps, in practice: fragmentation becomes the very condition of practice because there is no comfort to be had from the lapse into repetition. And fragmentation leads us towards multiplicity, towards the possibility that painting, and perhaps art generally, re-presents: that, as subjects, we are always already several, not one ('Je est un autre' – Rimbaud); that art's truth is that there are many truths; that critiques, methods, theories, which unify and gather everything within unifying metaphors cannot face the otherness of art's multiplicity; that the system, the boundaried structure, the closed exit, the closed text, *exist only in and for theory*, and that art *practice* and its works always exceed such theoretical closures, however uncomfortable it may be for theory to admit that in the last analysis (and in some cases the first too) art escapes and exceeds it.

If the inter-relation of theory, of words, with painting explicitly displays fragmentation and is a recurrent theme of modern painting practice, and if it opens us on to painting's life in Language, it may be that what de Duve calls the 'discourses of justification' (de Duve, 1983) can provide vital resources in re-viewing modernity. In the context of a critical analysis of the post-modern question of whether painting has a future following the 'death of modernism' he proposes that 'the future of painting . . . addresses its demands for legitimisation to the modernist past . . . to a modernism that is still waiting to be interpreted' (op.cit., p.34). This need for a return to the past of modernity is required because the 'discursive history', the history of interpretations written by critics and art historians based on their aesthetic judgments has predominated over (and and even dominated) the 'operative history', the history of the relations between the works themselves produced through the aesthetic judgments *practised* by the artists. Each art work is a concretion of artists' aesthetic judgments which are themselves interpretations, readings, of the works of Tradition; thus each painting is always a judgment on at least one other painting. The judgments which each work embeds both relate the work to Tradition and display the artist's interpretation of his or her relation to Tradition. This reiterates my earlier point that painting is through and through a practical theorising, an engagement of and within Language.

The written texts which may accompany or be affiliated to an artist's work thus take on an important function in any re-reading of modern practice for they draw us into a reconstruction of this alternative operative history as always partially independent of critical and all historical interpretations and judgments. They have the function both of authorisation and of 'fecundity' for the aesthetic judgments that constitute practice, and they thus belong to the order of practice not that of critical discourse. By showing art practice as unavoidably theoretical and asserting the necessity of including such theorising in any response to the work de Duve shows the possibility of avoiding 'launching into ideological criticism while at the same time avoiding the hypostasis of a purely visual, pre-linguistic practice often seen as the only alternative to a philosophy of art as language or ideology' (op.cit., p.37). By treating art works seriously *on their own terms as theoretical acts*, both the

negative distancing of ideological criticism and the lapse into empiricism (the 'purely visual' school of criticism) can be avoided. For de
Duve a re-reading according to the different but inter-related planes
of theorising is essential if the legacy of abstraction within which the
modern tradition confronts the post-modern is to be faced respons-
ibly. Sharing this interest in offering a strong version of painting as a
practical theorising, as thought-full rather than thought-less practice, but from within the wider concern with the Language-painting
relation, I also treat artists' 'discourses of justification' as fundamental to their practice. Such a treatment is an essential part of
any recuperation of the modern tradition in the face of the post-
modern question about the death of modernity. If, as I have suggested, we always find modern painters in the midst of Tradition
and celebrating painting itself as the display of that withinness, then
de Duve's question to criticism is highly pertinent: 'What pushes us
to repeat the tradition of a break just when we are beginning to
understand that modernist ideology erred in its image of a break
with tradition?' (op.cit., p.32).

If we do not yet know what 'modernity' in painting 'is', and if we
are prepared to consider that it might be something other than
'modernism', any judgment about its death is entirely premature
for, 'we don't even know what it is we have to mourn' (ibid.). The
only way of conquering the fear that 'makes us so anxious not to be
modern any longer' (ibid.) is by confronting it on the terrain established by the moderns themselves, but through a reading that seeks
a qualitatively different relation to Tradition (and within it, the
modern tradition) to that of modernism.

4

Modernity Underwrites Itself

If I put time and care into my writing it's because I feel that words have a certain strength, and their power shouldn't be monopolised by so-called specialists, but should be shared. If, as someone once suggested, the art of warfare is too serious a matter to be left in the hands of soldiers, writing about the visual arts is a much too serious occupation to be left in the hands of critics alone (Daniel Buren, 1981).

If the act of painting is always a celebration of painting, each work paints itself into a relation with every other work, with Tradition itself; and yet the modern commitment, questioning the very terms through which painting can re-present, can be true to the specificity of its 'moment' (its context), and is clearly committed to difference, to putting some 'distance' between itself and what has gone before (and what is going on synchronically with it). Robert Motherwell points to this identity-in-difference in the following terms: 'Every intelligent painter carries the whole culture of modern painting in his head. It is his real subject, of which everything he paints is both an homage and a critique, and everything he . . . says is a gloss' (Motherwell, 1978, p.7). And we might add to Motherwell's 'modern painting' the totality of painting itself – Tradition. Every work takes on the fact or being of Tradition but only within a specific historical context where the Tradition has taken on a very particular meaning; each work displays the artist's relation to this particularity. The 'fact' of Tradition can thus be contrasted with specific concrete traditions, such as the modern 'tradition of the new' where painting inaugurated a de-construction of the prevalent languages in which it found itself. This re-territorialising of painting by modernity was itself an attempt to re-constitute the very terms of the relation between painter, painting, painting's 'subject matter', and painting's respondents. The difference modernity sought to make was a difference in relationality itself; and of course this

43

difference would re-constitute not just our relation to modern painting but to painting as such, to Tradition. From within modernity we would have to view Tradition as a part of modernity, to judge it according to the criteria which modernity fought to establish for itself: the value of the past for modernity can only lie in its absolute unrepeatability at the very moment it is in-forming our contemporary relation to painting.

To re-cast art's (painting's) relation to the world is necessarily to reveal its engagement of Language, for this re-structuring of relation was necessarily a practical theorising; not only, as we have seen, did the paintings themselves re-constitute the terms of their possible relations through their concretion of aesthetic judgments on other works, but the very practice of their making was highly theorised. There is continuity between modern painting's 'operative history', its embedded aesthetic judgments that provide for our relation to it, and the 'discursive justifications' (de Duve, 1983) that painters themselves developed in the course of their practice. It is the latter upon which I focus here.

My concern is not to show how the individual moments and movements of the modern tradition ground themselves, but rather to re-open the theoretical region within which an inexhaustible variety of concretely different ways of practising painting could co-exist, and to consider some of the general concerns that define the modern commitment. Foundational to the tradition is precisely the thesis of difference itself: modernity is the tradition of multus, of dispersal and dissemination. The contemporaneity of a wide range of 'movements' is an index of this scattering. Some movements such as futurism and surrealism have extensive 'discourses of justification', while others, such as cubism, are less explicitly supported, and many artists practising either in isolation from or with only passing relation to self-grounding movements have nevertheless written extensively about their work. My interest is in exploring, through the writing of painters whose work, although associated with movements or groups, is generally distanced from any narrowly defined commitment, some of the justifications and self-analyses that seem to have taken on a more general significance within the modern tradition. If the space opened by these and other painters has a coherence it is to be found in the ways that 'relation' itself, the painter's and our relation to the work of art as well as the relations that constitute the work itself, is radicalised. Every innovation and everything specific to the modern tradition bears upon the issue of art as relation, where relation already places us in the thrall of Language.

Even the most passing acquaintance with the work and life of modern painters, and most obviously those whose work provides keys to the trajectories of the modern tradition, dispels absolutely the myth of popular fiction of the artist as an inarticulate practitioner. For what must immediately confront anyone who inquires into the roots and ground of contemporary painting is the complexity of such painting's engagement with and necessary commitment to theory (the word); painting is always a practical theorising and this is an absolutely explicit and usually self-acknowledged feature of all contemporary practice. The clearest index of this, and also one of our most valuable resources in the modern tradition as a set of practices, is the writing of painters themselves, for the practice of painting has continually involved a complementary activity of writing. Every work of art can only be such in the ways that it is related to a tradition and thus to art itself, and we can only relate to it in and through some 'knowledge' of this tradition, however tacit or taken-for-granted this knowledge is. And as it has been a defining feature of modernity to put its own past into question, theorising has been intrinsic to it, for such questioning necessitates a conceptualising of the relation between past and present. It is not merely that modern painting has been performed within a critical context, has been enveloped by some kind of external criticism, but rather that it is critical in its constitution, in its own practices, in so far as it questions its relation to the other of Tradition. The questioning always entails a theorising of the practice that painting is, and it is always also both a communal and an individual practice; that is, both the community or 'sub-culture' of art practice, which would include the structure of relationships between artists, educational and art-supportive institutions, artists' audiences, and also each individual artist, are, in part, sustained through the continual construction and reconstruction of theories which make sense of art practice. In other words art practice is not a process that occurs independently of versions of theorising and critique, for such theorising permeates the works of art themselves. It does not exhaust them but is a major contributor to the ways in which works place themselves in relation to the Tradition.

Drawing selectively from these materials I try to show here how they can be read as underwriting a distinctively modern sense of painting practice in which it is relation itself which is radicalised and transformed, before and apart from the intervention of any 'external' criticism of theory. My concern is to show how the context of artistic practice is always an explicitly theorised context, where the theoretical 'work' does more than just document 'intention'. For such texts can be read as constituting the very possibility of art itself in the ways they open up a conceptual space within which art practice can live. This is above all an articulation of the space in which Desire is transformed into necessity in the construction of specific works of art, and the conventional notion of 'intention' barely begins to recognise let alone engage this transformation and its consequences.

Now this is to turn us towards art's celebratory dimension, for if theorising seems to be bound up with art's commitment to questioning, we must still ask 'questioning on behalf of what?' The answer, I suggest, is that it is a questioning of Desire itself, of the erotics of our relation to Being and to the other in all its senses (a putting of the question 'Why paint here, now?'). Questioning celebrates relation itself. So the texts which provide senses of the space within which artists practise are not merely descriptions of how and why they work in the way they do, which stop at some concrete sense of intention, but are rather themselves, like the works they relate to, metaphors for that other realm which makes concrete intentions possible. As metaphors, they write for and refer us to the erotic origins of specific intentions in a generalised polymorphous Desire for the other, and to the relation between Desire and Language or writing-in-general.

Thus if we approach and are open to painters' written texts as metaphors, they can guide us in complementary ways towards the textuality, their relation to Language, through and for which their art is instituted. And it is worth emphasising that this metaphoric reading of their texts is facilitated by the very senses of Language and writing manifested in these texts, for in each case the writers display similar kinds of sensitivity to the life of Language that is available in their painting. Their writing, then, is not just to be read as autobiography, description, or information, for it does much more than just inform us concretely about their life and the place of painting within it. What it immediately displays and offers are specific relationships to Language itself, and particularly to its granting and withholding character, the work of metaphor itself.

The modern tradition in its historically brief life appears to have undergone enormous internal transformations which are typically represented retrospectively by criticism as more or less discrete movements or moments. However I want to argue that this plur-alectics of constant change and multiplication of difference is a surface manifestation of the modern tradition's theoretical under-pinnings, the basic themes of which are displayed but not exhausted in the painting and writings of a few artists. This work creates and articulates a region as the very working space of modernity; it offers possibilities and provides justifications, or what we might call 'deep motives', that both provide for modernity's partial breaks with the past while at the same time ensuring an essential cotinuity of art itself. This is accomplished by the modern tradition's gradual re-velation of an ontology of art that provides both for the past and the present, that, in other words, enables us to re-read the past, the pre-modern, as always secreting the modern within itself as a future potential moment.

My present concern is not to attempt to provide for the surface of concrete differences of modern practice, but to point to the adum-bration and display of certain deep commitments in the work of a few artists who were and are influential as individuals in the securing (always relative and in question) of the modern tradition. I am suggesting that these commitments are intrinsic to and are defining features of modernity. These artists are drawn together through the common sense of Language, painting, writing, and relation which all share metaphorically, even though their works assemble and display considerable concrete differences. What they can be shown to share is as important as their most obvious and exciting differences; and in some ways these very differences, arising from the inter-play of biography, aesthetic judgment and Desire, index the life of modernity itself as the constitution of concrete difference. And if, as I am proposing, modern painting, in the course of its journeys, has shown us that it needs, it Desires, to be 'read', this is also to show itself as a writing. This gathering of itself on the site of writing-reading necessarily disrupts the conven-tions of writing-reading which we inhabit in everyday life. To metaphorise painting as writing is to seek to preserve the perennial openness of the work of art to an erotics of interpretation. The present reading of artists' 'discursive justifications' hopefully en-hances this openness and at the same time shows how modernity finds itself in the midst of Tradition.

In some ways Cézanne's oeuvre stands as the watershed of the modern tradition, already incisively opening many of its possibili-ties and defining fundamental features of the modern artist's rela-tion to the world. Yet while he exemplifies some of the basic features of the modern 'soul' in painting, he is at the same time thoroughly entangled with and committed to his reading of the pre-modern tradition. And I might suggest that in this very characteristic Cézanne's work already points us to a defining feature of the modern tradition: that it *is* tradition, that its links with the past are paradoxically as strong as its breaks, that in a sense the modern tradition is never truly or never just modern. Indeed we can see in the history of modernism after Cézanne that every one of those thoroughly modern 'radical' attempts to end art, through anti-art or through merging art with life, was simultaneously absorbed into the tradition. Anti-art in the very moment of its production is at the same time art (or it is nothing, dispatched to the absolute margins of the cultural memory); such gestures could only be made sense of in the context of art, from within the life of art, and this preserves them within Tradition.

If impressionism is that interlude between the classical past and the modern future, neither one nor the other, the movement of Cézanne's painting from outside of impressionism, through it, to its transformation, inaugurates the modern while preserving the past in a way that impressionism did not and could not do. Cézanne transforms the relation of artist to nature from the impressionist observer who is external to nature, to that of the dialectician who is already *within* the very phenomenon he is trying to represent, and for whom that same nature is already within him. And perhaps precisely the same can be said about Cézanne's relation to Tradition; his work displays and celebrates a dialectical relation to Tradition which knows that Tradition can only be changed from within and that each act, each work of art, is a contribution to the re-definition of Tradition itself:

> To my mind one does not put oneself in place of the past one only adds a new link (to Roger Marx, 23.1.1905, Rewald, 1976, p.313).

> The Louvre is a good book to consult but it must be only an intermediary (to Emile Bernard, 12.5.1904, op.cit., p.302).

> You see that an era of a new art is opening, you feel it coming (to Charles Camoin, 21.1.1902, op.cit., p.280).

We know well enough about the long hours that Cézanne himself spent in the Louvre studying and working from the works of his predecessors, and so the museum itself becomes a metaphor for the Tradition which he inherits and adds a 'new link' to. It is moreover a metaphor which displays the centrality of Language to Cézanne's conception of art by showing past art as something *to be read*. And we can note in passing that the metaphor of reading itself occurs frequently, as Gowing has shown (Rubin, 1977, p.62), in the opinions transcribed by Bernard from his conversations with Cézanne, where Cézanne frequently speaks of 'reading nature'. Tradition and nature, then, are metaphorised as texts to be read, the interpretation of which modifies Tradition itself through what it adds to it; and in addition Cézanne already anticipated the radicality of the changes about to occur in painting, and which his own work inaugurates, for it is a 'new era'.

The radicality of this new era is anticipated in Cézanne's two letters to Bernard in 1905 where the conventions of the past are both preserved as the ground of his own work but also presented as what must be transcended in the name of the self. Thus he passes from the inferiority of the official salons which only 'encourage more or less widely accepted methods', to the classical tradition itself where similarly, 'we must not . . . be satisfied with retaining the beautiful formulas of our illustrious predecessors. Let us go forth to study beautiful nature, *let us try to free our minds from them*' (to E.B., 1905, op.cit., p.315). And again, 'we must render the image of what we see, *forgetting everything that existed before us*' (to E.B., 23.10.1905, op.cit., p.316). The suspension of the past, this calculated amnesia, is proposed on behalf of 'personal emotion' and self-expression 'according to our personal temperament.' Forgetting in the service of a rendering of the image of the seen 'must permit the artist to give his entire personality, whether great or small' (ibid.). This freeing of the mind from past conventions, the attempt to forget the ways in which nature has been previously rendered, is to be performed on the behalf and in favour of the specificity of the personal emotional response to nature, and it is this latter which the work of painting strives to re-present. Perhaps we can also note that this suspension of previously taken-for-granted conventions on behalf of a particular kind of inquiry (Cézanne's study of nature through painting) is a skeletal practical formulation of the 'reduction' of the classical phenomenological method of inquiry; Cézanne presents himself, the artist, as a practical phenomenologist

The conventions of Tradition thus provide the starting point for work and the work itself requires a bracketing of these conventions and a concomitant search for that which is distinctively personal, the unique personal emotion which is the relation of the artist to nature; this personal emotion, Cézanne's 'sensation', is what is transformed into the work of art in the course of artistic practice. And of course, at the level of practice, Cézanne's own work displays the impossibility of the stated aim, the impossibility that is, of the absolute reduction, the complete suspension of the past, for Cézanne's work is a continuous display and affirmation of certain classical ideals, some of which he himself acknowledges when he writes of doing Poussin again but 'from nature'. In other words only some of the conventions are suspended in practice, namely those which tended to hold the artist apart from nature on behalf perhaps of some literary ideal; this is alluded to elsewhere where Cézanne says that the artist 'must beware of the literary spirit which so often causes the painter to deviate from his true path – the concrete study of nature' (to E.B., 12.5.1094, op.cit., p.250). Thus when Cézanne says that, 'Art is a harmony which runs parallel to nature' (to Joachim Gasquet, 26.9.1897, op.cit., p.250) he preserves through the metaphor of art as music, a strong continuity between his own sense of painting and the classical, the difference being for him that the harmony he seeks must be rendered from the sensations which constitute the artist's personal response to a close and continuous relation with nature. The specific sense of harmony which Cézanne arrived at in his later work, the *re*-presentation of the motif and its objects through the precise and highly organised (partially theorised) colour modulations, is itself a display of both Cézanne's conformity with classical conceptions of composition (harmony) and the difference that personalising the artist's relation to nature makes to the work of art.

In the same moment that he maintains the classical tradition Cézanne subverts it by moving it on to another site, a site which is at the same time a radical display of modernity, for it absolutely relativises the artist's relation to nature, to the other. There is no longer 'one' given nature 'over there' lying independently of all of us, but rather a nature 'for me', that is, the way nature *is itself within me*, and similarly a tradition within and 'for me' rather than a tradition external to me. This transformation of the artist's relation to nature and Tradition, which Cézanne's work inaugurates, is a defining feature of modernity itself, and finds its parallel in modern science in the transformation of the observer's relation to the observed in post-Einsteinian physics. A necessary feature of this relativising of the relation is the way it begins to require and display an alternative sense of Language, for if 'reality' is not some absolute pre-given external to human being, is not a 'transcendental signified', but rather obtains its sense from the ways in which human beings methodically make sense of it from within specific contexts and languages, then the relation of Language to its other (nature) can no longer be that of correspondence but rather of constitution. The implicit sense of Language here, then, is that founded in metaphor; world is grasped and constituted in the creative confusing work of metaphor itself.

Cézanne thus underwrites this defining feature of the modern tradition in his articulation of a dialectical relation of the painter, for whom nature is both inside and outside, and the world. An interesting comment on this very feature of Cézanne's being-in-Language is provided by the American artist, Mary Cassatt, who noted with some astonishment after visiting Cézanne in 1894, that,

> Cézanne is one of the most liberal artists I have ever seen. He prefaces every remark with: 'Pour moi it is so and so', but he grants that everyone may be just as honest and as faithful to nature from their own convictions; he doesn't believe that everyone should see alike (op.cit., p.237).

This 'pour moi' speaks precisely to the radical relativising of the language of art that Cézanne's work provides for. The artist no longer writes on behalf of an assumed absolute vision of everyman, the positivist-empiricist conception of a given independent reality, but rather invites us to collaborate in a creative re-construction of his own 'method' and, if we begin this collaboration the work then seems to exhort *us* to do likewise, to put our own relation to the world to the test; in other words the work takes on an exemplary character in the service of that Desire to disclose, however fleetingly, the trace of a contact with relationality itself. Art is thus always interpretation for Cézanne, and hence the issue of the relation to the viewer is crucial; Cézanne writes of this as 'make see': 'make the reader see what you see' (to Octave Mirbeau, December 1894, op.cit., p.238); and writing of method he says, 'technical questions are for us only the simple means of making the public feel what we feel ourselves and of making ourselves understood' (to E.B., 21.9.1906, op.cit., p.329). The re-siting of the artist's relation to the world and Tradition is thus what Cézanne's work begins, through its emerging transformation of art's languages, and it is this which opens the 'new era' which he himself feels is approaching.

If art is a questioning celebration then Cézanne affirms both dimensions in the strongest terms with his passion for nature (and the other) as their ground and mediation. His questioning of nature is not a dry search for and representation of empirical information, but is a passionate affair, an interpretation, every moment of which indexes and affirms its erotic character. And, inversely, his work is never pure celebration, that moment of absolute excess which falls entirely under the sway of the erotic. Rather his practice and his paintings exemplify and live through a tension where questioning restrains the erotic in the service of the disclosure of our relation to other. That Cézanne defined his work as questioning is everywhere

51

evident in his writing, and indeed one of the most frequent metaphors he uses for painting practice, for work, is that of 'study', and we can already note its common root with that of every artist's place of work – the studio; for example in writing to Vollard he says, 'I do not think that I shall in any way harm the course of my studies by exhibiting' (To A.V., 17.3.1902, op.cit., p.287). And to Vollard again,

> I am not giving up work or my study which, I like to believe, has obliged me to make efforts that will not be sterile. . . . I am going on with my search and shall inform you of the results achieved as soon as I have achieved some satisfaction from my efforts (To E.B., 12.4.1904, op.cit., p.302).

The concern with study and search are ever-present in Cézanne's writings and tend to confirm the label applied earlier of 'practical phenomenologist', where the object of study or questioning is 'the manifold picture of nature' (To E.B. 12.4.1904, op.cit., p.302). And of course the driving force of this continual felt need to study nature is his erotic attachment to it. Nature stands perhaps as metaphor for the other, with whom Cézanne seeks the passionate relation, for 'beautiful nature' includes 'man, woman, and still life' (To L. Lydet, 17.1.1905, op.cit., p.312); this is what the questioning that his studies speak of celebrates, and we find continual references to this relation in his letters. Thus, 'pleasure must be found in the work' where the work, the act of painting itself, is precisely the making of a relation with a loved one for '. . . I am deeply in love with the landscape of my country' (To J.G., 30.4.1896, op.cit., p.245). Passion is assigned to temperament, unique to every individual, and this is a 'primary force', a name in other words for that founding Desire which pushes the artist continually forward through pleasure and pain towards the 'end he should attain' (To C.C. 22.2.1903, op.cit., p.294). And all the time Cézanne knows that the primary force of Desire can never be satisfied because art itself is endless, it moves ever ahead of us whenever we try to grasp it, for as he writes to Monet, art is 'the chimerical pursuit' (6.7.1895, op.cit., p.242).

The kind of hold Desire has over him is frequently indicated in both his actions and words for, although racked by diabetes, he insists on working at his motif outdoors in all weathers to the very end of his life; to the end he remains, 'in the grip of sense-perceptions, and in spite of my age, riveted to painting' (To E.B. 27.6.1904; op.cit., p.304). These extremely graphic images show the way Cézanne embodies painting as Desire; and it is in this sense that he epitomises and preserves the 'wild' character of painting, its continual excess. His work is a highly sophisticated response that nevertheless keeps intact the absolutely primitive character of Desire itself, surfacing and being concretised in the sense of art, that sense that 'is without doubt the horror of the bourgeois' (to E.B. 25.7.1904, op.cit., p.306). It is this sense, which art re-presents and writes for, that is the anathema of bourgeois culture – for it always stands as its other. Whether or not every work of art can be seen as a threat to bourgeois culture, art's questioning celebration, projecting from the subversive site of Desire, stands for and enacts its always potential transformation. To be a 'painter by inclination', as Cézanne signs himself in a letter to Geffroy (4.4.1895, op.cit., p.240), is always an act of de-centring in a bourgeois culture, for it is in the 'nature' of inclination to deviate from the centre: following one's own inclinations necessitates the suspension of conventions.

The surfacing of the dialectic of questioning and celebration in Cézanne's work, as the erotic conjunction of studying and passionate sensation, is the grounding of theory in practice. Thus Language is ever-present in painting practice for the latter is for Cézanne a continual testing of theory. And Cézanne's sensitivity to Language and writing-in-general can be traced back quite clearly to his youth for he was, for example, a prolific poet, and much of his early correspondence, especially with Zola, circles around poetry and a fascination with Language. Zola and Cézanne used to exchange rebuses, charades and language puzzles of various kinds that often relied on puns and hidden meanings, odd rhyming schemes and so on; it is also clear from his letters that Cézanne spoke Latin well enough to use it informally in correspondence. Powerful and direct images abound in his letters displaying at the most general level Cézanne's strong feeling for and interest in Language, which is transferred to his painting practice as a proto-writing. His interest in developing the theory of his painting practice then needs to be placed in this wider context of his involvement with Language. And when we turn to his concern with theory it is not a casual or occasional concern but rather a constitutive feature of his work, and in this way we can see, again perhaps for the first time in the way that it enters the work, what comes to be a defining feature of the modern tradition, the permeation of all subsequent work by theory.

The increasingly explicit concern with theory emerges strongly late in the 1880s and becomes a familiar theme of his later correspondence. Apart from the related repeated reference to his studies already noted, the idea of theory informing practice is constantly present; thus he writes to Camoin, 'one says more and perhaps better things about painting when facing the motif than when discussing purely speculative theories in which as often as not one loses oneself' (28.1.1902, op.cit., p.280), and in a further letter to the same person, 'Everything, especially in art, is theory developed and applied in contact with nature' (22.2.1903, op.cit., p.294). Theory is always to be rigorously opposed to the literariness of speculation – for it has its life in the interminable dialectic with practice; as, perhaps, a gentle admonition to Bernard for this kind of thinking, Cézanne says of the painter, 'He must beware of the literary spirit which so often causes the painter to deviate from his true path, the concrete study of nature – to lose himself too long in intangible speculation' (12.5.1904, op.cit., p.302). And a month before his death he writes to Bernard:

> a vague state of uneasiness persists which will not disappear until I have reached port, that is until I have realised something which develops better than in the past, and thereby prove the theories – which in themselves are always easy; it is only giving proof of what one thinks that raises serious obstacles. So I continue to study (21.9.1906, op.cit., p.329).

Theory is only good when its proof can be located in the paintings themselves, so it must be developed on the site of painting practice itself, in and through the relation with the motif. Whilst we do not have an explicit reference to the experimental model of the natural sciences, the analogy with science is fairly obvious through, for example, Cézanne's reference to proof. Yet, as we have seen, the upshot of the practical theorising will not be like the object or theory of science, it will not be a determinate statement in a rational theoretical system, but will rather be a representation of the Desire to found and offer an absolutely personal sense of the *relation* to other. Cézanne is perhaps the first to show explicitly that he does not paint objects themselves but rather the relationships between them (and in this of course his practice is also akin to modern science). His theorising then leads up to the moment of painting practice in which the act of marking the surface marks on behalf, not of the things-in-themselves independent of the artist, but of the relationships between phenomena that give them their space (what Stokes calls the 'affinities' betwen objects (Stokes, 1978b, p.259)), and of the relationship between these relations and himself: 'it is all a question of putting in as much inter-relation as possible' (To his son, 14.8.1906, Rewald, 1976, p.323). A brief look at Cézanne's practice, and more specifically at the kinds of mark he made in his painting, can show some of the ways in which his particular theoretical practice began to provide for the future flowering of the nascent modern tradition.

In his division and differentiation of every part of a 'plane' of an 'object' through often minute brush strokes of modulated colours Cézanne confronts us with a radical question of interpretation, for this is art as the absolutely concrete practice of deconstruction and reconstruction. We are faced with the need for our own active collaboration, our re-construction of the work of art, and are drawn into a re-enactment of this deconstructing; to join the work on its terms we have to try to re-construct for ourselves the decisions which led to the specific marks. Each painting becomes an occasion for at least this, as well as many other types of constructive reverie, for the marks invite us to ask about the kind of work they are doing in the painting. And perhaps we can begin to see, at this level of the marks themselves, their relation both to each other and to the whole (what Stokes (loc.cit.) calls 'the sum of affinities'); we are invited to participate in the work of re-presentation they enact. For the quality of our interpretive relation to the painting, the differences it makes to us, will be constituted in our recovery of the work of these marks. The phenomena painted by Cézanne, portraits, still-lifes, land-scapes, landscapes with figures, live through these differences. A painting writes these phenomena into being for us in and as the inter-relationship of each brush stroke; every phenomenon re-presented is constituted as such through these differences, and the 'sum' of these differences, the whole picture, Cézanne's rendered motif, is only significant in their terms. Nature itself, and we have seen that nature always includes man, woman and still-life for Cézanne, is re-presented and thus forever deferred in these tiny movements of difference, re-presentation as fragmentation. And by confronting the mark itself we are then required to re-read Tradition through the dialectic of marking; we can only re-view every past work of art through a knowledge that has been radicalised by Cézanne's own practice, his reopening of the question of the limits of marking.

In separating art from nature and showing it as a practice whose very being is a seeking to be other to nature, to world, to 'reality', the differentiating work of Cèzanne's brushstrokes confronts us with both art's otherness to and its relatedness to nature. As a mark in relation to a set of marks that constitute the painting as a whole, each mark has its specific significance in and is bound up with the reality of the whole painting, Stokes's 'sum of affinities'. But at the same time, in so far as the mark is contributing to the re-presentation of natural phenomena, it puts the possibility before us that nature itself is constituted in and through differences, through in fact a structure of relations which we ourselves constitute in the act of reading either art or nature. In this way we can perhaps read each mark as a metaphor for nature, for life, as relation through difference and deferral. The radicality or revolutionary quality of Cézanne's paintings would then lie in this kind of reading, the reading that turns eventually to its own method of construction, of making or marking sense and 'sensation'. And this quality would have to be located in the very explicitness with which these questions of art's relation to nature, of the character of our relation to nature and other (and thus of relationality itself), and of the demands on representation, are broached.

The phenomena 'in' Cézanne's paintings (fruit, his wife, the Monte Sainte-Victoire, and so on), what would traditionally be called 'content', and each painting as a whole, are re-presentations of or metaphors for relationality itself, that is, for the possibility that there are no 'things-in-themselves' but only phenomena constituted in, through and as specific relations. And this is to say that, at the level of specific marks themselves, the site or surface where significance emerges, the 'place' at which our gaze is directed, the conjunction of eyes and surface, is the space that *is no space* between two or more adjacent marks. This absent space, the space that we experience as gap while knowing it to be always a space both created and repressed by the very adjacence of the brushstrokes themselves, is the space through which we are pulled down towards the differing-deferring work of the 'trace' itself – 'differance' (see Derrida, 1973, p.129).

Here is one possible 'place', this full gap, that the possibility of Language itself, of writing-in-general, may be disclosed. And as we can see, the writing that painting is, as a writing in advance of writing, begins by metaphorising the gap, the differance, that allows significance to emerge. For in painting the gap *is not there*; that is precisely why it is a writing before writing or speech, an absolutely mute saying, which in spite of and because of itself inscribes the possibility of writing. If painting was for Cézanne, in part, a process of 'forgetting everything that existed before us' in the name of an exploration of relation, this exploration must be seeking to re-present the always absent 'origin' of relation itself; each painting seeks to constitute itself as a metaphor for original relating, the coming-to-be of relation, of writing and of significance, knowing that 'origin' itself has always been metaphor and not full 'presence'. This re-membering is a further display of modern painting's commitment to wild being, to will a primitivity without will.

If Cézanne's painting and writings begin to open on to a region for painting which is specifically 'modern' in the way it reconstitutes a relation to Tradition, then Kandinsky, especially in his early works, both confirms the general shape of this space and opens and develops possibilities latent within it that provide the ground for much twentieth century painting. For Kandinsky opened and theorised the possibility of abstraction which came later to define 'modernism' and its associated formalist criticism. The affirmation and development of Cézanne's openings come particularly in the ways that Kandinsky provides for the difference that the self makes to the genesis and construction of the work of art, for at the very centre of his thesis is what he calls 'inner necessity'. In *Concerning the Spiritual in Art* (Kandinsky, 1964), first published in 1912, some six years after Cézanne's death and following the first phase of cubism, Kandinsky articulates an utterly modern conception of painting that nevertheless, as with Cézanne, preserves strong links with Tradition. In other words modern painting is not, for Kandinsky, a negation of the past but a radical expansion of the possibilities of Tradition itself through a re-definition of the artist's and the spectator's relation to the process of creation itself; and this need for a new art is contexted quite precisely by him as a move (called forth by the quality of contemporary social relationships) away from certain dominant themes in nineteenth century painting. For Kandinsky, changes internal to art are very much tied to the character of historical experience itself, so that the specific character of art's 'harmonies' will refract the context in which the harmonies are produced:

> from the fact that we live in a time of questioning, experiment and contradiction, we may draw the conclusion that for a harmonisation on the basis of individual colors our age is specially unsuitable. The strife of colours, the sense of the balance we have lost, tottering principles, unexpected assaults, great questions, apparently useless striving, storm and tempest, broken chains, antithesis and contradictions – these make up our harmony (op.cit., pp.65-6).

And, elsewhere, locating the feature of the nineteenth century which defines the inner content of contemporary work, he speaks of the 'disintegration of the soulless, materialistic life of the nineteenth century, i.e. the collapse of the material supports that were considered the only solid ones and the decay and dissolution of the various parts' (Kandinsky and Marc, 1977, p.186). Clearly there is no sense here of any simple causal relation between external social processes and the content of specific works of art but rather a showing of the contexted character of all artistic practice, and the suggestion that a feature of the inner necessity to produce works of art will always be a tendency for the process of creation itself to make reference at a variety of levels to those external processes. We might suggest that it is the distinction between internal and external that is itself in question, for if the supposedly external processes are indeed partially constitutive of the processes of artistic creation itself, the sense in which we can hold external and internal apart becomes problematic. Kandinsky, however, stratifies the origins of inner necessity into three elements:

1) Every artist as a creator has something in him which demands expression (this is the element of personality),
2) Every artist . . . is impelled to express the spirit of his age (this is the element of style). . .
3) Every artist as a servant of art, has to help the cause of art (this is the quintessence of art) which is constant in all ages and among all nationalities (Kandinsky, 1964, p.52).

Personality, style and Tradition structure the inner necessity and it is a defining feature of modernity that the self, or what is specific to the individual artist, must be allowed ultimately to define the character of the practice. 'Inner need' is thus what the artist must attend to and is the arbiter of artistic practice itself:

The artist must watch his own inner life and hearken to the demands of inner necessity. Then he may safely employ means sanctioned or forbidden by his contemporaries. This is the only way to express the mystical necessity (op.cit., p.53).

And Kandinsky proposes that it is a moral obligation of the artist to follow the impulse, thus defining the specific kind of relation between the artist and the society in which he practises: 'The artist is not only justified in using but is under a moral obligation to use, only those forms which fill his own need' (op.cit., p.74). And the need for this obligation is again socially contexted, for, while it may seem to produce a version of 'art for art's sake', this is precisely the kind of art which is required in an age dominated by materialism. In such a time art becomes a voice on behalf of that which is other to the dominant social forms, and for Kandinsky it is precisely art's responsibility to enact this role of otherness:

58

The phrase 'art for art's sake' is really the best ideal such an age can attain. It is an unconscious protest against materialism and against the demand that everything should have a use and a practical value. It is proof of the indubitability of art and the human soul, which can never be killed but only temporarily dazed (op.cit., pp.75–6).

If subversion is intrinsic to modernity, subversion as criticism of what has been and what is, of instrumental values and relations, then it is a subversion grounded in a sense of the need for preserving a space for that which is other to the dominant forms. It is, in other words, a positive subversion, for art's responsibility is continually to remind us of this other, and the guarantee, for Kandinsky, that it will do this is the artist's honest response to inner necessity for this will continually produce work which transcends contemporary stylistic conventions; it is in the nature of the creative process itself to enact that which is other to convention.

If 'inner necessity' metaphorises Desire, names that which moves the artist, then we can see Kandinsky as offering us a strong sense of Desire as the Reason for art. Art writes for, or on behalf of, it is the saying of Desire; and this is to affirm in the strongest way art's celebratory dimension. The artist's searches and studies, particularly (in Kandinsky's case) the questioning and exploration of colour and spatial relationships, can be read as a questioning in the service of celebration, for what is celebrated is the 'inner necessity' itself. Modernity is located in the ways that this celebration is performed, in an essential part, through a questioning practice. For Kandinsky shows art as a questioning practice that is a search for the new, for what is unconventional because it breaks through style and tradition, but always in the 'cause of art' itself. This is concretised in the presentation of 'art for art's sake' in a technicist culture.

If we consider briefly the way Kandinsky understands inner necessity then we are faced with a paradox because, in spite of the primacy which he appears to give to the 'spiritual' or the 'soul', his constitution of inner necessity is open to what I have earlier described as an empiricist reading: Kandinsky proposes that the inner is 'the emotion in the soul of the artist' and that

the soul is affected through the medium of the senses – the felt. Emotions are aroused and stilled by what is sensed. Thus the sensed is the bridge, i.e. the physical relation, between the immaterial (which is the artist's emotion) and the material,

which results in the production of the work of art. And again
what is sensed is the bridge from the material (the artist and his
work) to the immaterial (the emotion and the soul of the
observer) (op.cit., p.23).

A literal reading of this would locate the sense as the original
pre-meaningful source of emotion and therefore of the artistic
impulse; however, a metaphoric reading recovers an alternative
sense. Although 'what is sensed' is said to arouse the emotions, the
'sensed' is immediately constituted through the powerful metaphor
of 'the bridge', as the relation between the material and the immaterial. Now it is precisely a defining feature of relation that it is not a
'thing' in the way, for example, that (in empiricism) the senses are
treated as things. A bridge only 'is' when it joins up two sides; it has
its being precisely in and as relation. So in naming the sensed as the
prime mover of artistic impulse, as pure relationality through the
metaphor of the bridge, Kandinsky can be read as preserving the
origin as no-thing, which is in keeping with his description of it
elsewhere as 'mystery' (op.cit., p.75).

Kandinsky points directly to this absolute otherness, this non-
presence of the origin, in his discussion of the 'language of forms
and colour' (op.cit., pp.45 et seq.); in contrasting 'purely abstract
form' with 'purely material form' he argues that the impossibility of
any absolute reproduction of a material object by the artist provided
for what was conventionally called 'stylisation' (the following of
'purely pictorial aims') where the 'resulting harmony had an entirely personal character but with a prevailing external expression.' In
contrast to this, the new art that he writes for and which his own
painting partially inaugurates, would aim directly towards 'inner
harmony':

> The coming treatment and change of the organic form aims at
> baring or uncovering inner harmony. The organic form here no
> longer serves as direct object but is only an element of the divine
> language, which needs human expression because it is directed
> from man to man (op.cit., p.48).

The uncovering of this inner harmony, which comes through the
artist's attention to the demands of inner necessity, produces organic forms in the work of art which are themselves only elements in a
language that is absolutely other – the divine language. Such a
language could only be made reference to, pointed towards,
through the metaphors that concretely constitute expression be-

tween human beings. The truly modern artistic practice, then, for Kandinsky, is one that faithfully follows and explores the demands of inner necessity on behalf of the absolutely other; its work is realised as metaphors that write for and point to this other. This reference to the 'divine language' in the context of a discussion of the 'language of form' and colour can be read as Kandinsky's display of art's implication with ontology for it stands as a metaphor for Being. Elsewhere, contrasting the arts, Kandinsky says that each art has its own language and equates this concrete sense of language with methods, but even these are only externally different between the arts and are identical in their innermost core (Kandinsky and Marc, 1977, p.190).

Thus, at the centre of the new art, in its very telos, is the metaphorisation of Being as Language which allows Kandinsky to develop the Language metaphor quite concretely in his analysis of the inter-relation between pictorial space, form and colour, and the work of art's relation to an audience. And it is in this part of his discussion that he directly confronts the question of abstraction. The connections are clear for Kandinsky: commitment to inner necessity is essential in developing an art that is other to materialism and this art will therefore be, as a moral necessity, an 'art for art's sake'; and, as a turning away from materialism, the response to inner necessity is likely to constitute the work of art through forms which make no reference to 'direct objects', for in an art which is 'above nature' the representation of nature is subordinated to inner necessity. Likewise, because they detract from the spectator's experience of the purely pictorial, of the 'vibrations' set up in the spectator by the harmony between the artist's rendering of inner necessity and his or her own inner responses, the literary, anecdotal and narrative elements, the 'fairy tale effect', 'must be abandoned'. This bracketing of 'conventional beauty' (Kandinsky, 1964, p.71) and the literary element does not produce however a loss of reality, for both contemporary abstraction and contemporary 'great realism' (epitomised for Kandinsky by Henri Rousseau) are concerned with the 'inner sound of the thing' (Kandinsky and Marc, 1977, p.162). Outer beauty, the conventions of artistic form, are abandoned in great realism in the service of revealing the 'soul of the object'. And this reduction of the 'artistic' in realism which aims beyond the outer shell of things is regarded by Kandinsky as the 'most intensely effective abstraction' (ibid.). Complementing this, 'great abstraction' performs a similar liberation for here 'it must be possible to hear the whole world as it is without representative limitation' (op.cit., p.164). So, it is not the abstracting forms, lines, planes and so on, which are important but only their 'inner sound', their life: 'The "representational" reduced to a minimum must in abstraction be regarded as the most intensely effective reality' (op.cit., p.165). Realism and abstraction, although externally radically different, thus live through their revelation of the inner, in internal equality. Kandinsky also anticipates the problem of formalism in his proposal that there is 'in principle' no question of form because form is dependent on inner necessity and this may lead to either 'real' or 'abstract' forms; form is an indifferent matter in principle because it is always only the vehicle for and product of inner necessity, and is therefore to be subordinated in the spectator's experience of the work of art to the exploration of the inner necessity. And the royal road to this inner necessity is that of colour.

Although there is a residue of empiricism in Kandinsky's assertion that the experience of colour is initially a 'purely physical effect' (Kandinsky, 1964, p.43), this is immediately qualified by the description of this effect as the enchantment of the eye by the 'beauty and other qualities of colour' (ibid.). The apparently purely physical at the same time is always a matter of meaning in the way that the eye is taken over by beauty which, as Kandinsky shows elsewhere, is itself always conventional. The experience of colour is always within meaning and it is precisely this which Kandinsky explores at some length, for the starting point of the artist's exercise of his spirit is the study of colour and its effects on men' (op.cit., p.54). Colour is theorised in terms of two sets of poles, warm and cool, and light and dark, and each of the primary colours is explored in terms of the quality of its associations and potential for movement; these are constituted through a wide range of metaphors relating to music, mood, social relations and so on which Kandinsky admits are both provisional and general. He notes that each colour will find some expression in words but that there will always be something 'left over', what is referred to here as surplus or excess, so that words will remain 'hints, mere suggestions of colour'; the meaning of colour is, in other words, absolutely metaphoric. Thus yellow 'might be said to represent the manic aspect of madness' (op.cit., p.58). The feeling ultimately created by blue 'is one of rest' (ibid.), while green represents the passive principle and 'the social middle class self-satisfied, immovable and narrow' (op.cit., p.59). Red is a 'sound of trumpets, strong, harsh and ringing.' (op.cit., p.61). White and black have particular significance as exemplars of two poles of association: 'White acts upon our psyche as a great, absolute silence, like the pauses in music that temporarily break the melody' (op.cit., p.60). And here we are immediately reminded of Mallarmé's 'whites of writing', the gaps between the words. However Kandinsky suggests that white's 'silence' is not a dead silence but 'one pregnant with possibilities. White has the appeal of the nothingness that is before birth, of the world in the ice age' (ibid.). Here the metaphor of pregnancy points us back to the coming forth of meaning in this silence that is not dead, of the nothingness that already contains the something within itself. Perhaps, then, if we follow Kandinsky, the life of white in painting can refer us to what might be called painting's archaeological character in that it can be read as a metaphor for origins and beginnings themselves – beginning as differance. White's life points to relationality itself, the gap between human being and nature that we 'are', and its continued renewal as writing-in-general. The hermetic sealing of being in and as absolutely undifferentiated nature is broken in 'differance', through which being comes into itself as *ex-istence*.

On the other side Kandinsky proposes black as 'a silence with no possibilities' for 'The silence of black is the silence of death' (ibid.). As with the constitution of white, these and other associated metaphors for black can take us directly back to writing and Language. In a culture saturated with print, black is the conventional colour of printing and of writing. And Kandinsky's metaphors for black, turning on death and absolute silence, resonate with the phonocentric view of writing in which the written word is treated as the death of speech, where the voice that speaks is presented as first, as the source of life. In this view of writing, which implicitly defines the history of Language in the western philosophical tradition, the written word is a positive sign that, as the other of speech is itself dead. It is this position that provides the space for the structuralist analysis of the sign, where the signifier (in this instance, the printed shapes of a word in phonetic writing) is *nothing in itself* and can only point beyond itself to the signified. Each signifier is a convention for ideas beyond it. Kandinsky's contrast of black and white can be heard as a strong echo of this conception of Language in the context of what he himself has metaphorised as the *language* of colour and form in painting.

We can also note that Kandinsky anticipated subsequent debates concerning two-dimensionality and flatness in painting in his brief comments on space. For in discussing the exclusion of the third dimension, he argues that the step forward in which the concrete object was made more abstract through the abandonment of modelling, has also limited the possibilities of painting to the actual surface. Painting thus 'acquired another material limit'. And we can note that this is one of the material limits addressed in the reductions of minimalist painting. But he writes for the freeing of painting from this limitation through the destruction of 'the theory of the single surface' (op.cit., p.66).

Finally we can see that the inter-twining of Language and painting is intrinsic to Kandinsky's conception of art for not only does Language stand as a powerful metaphor for painting in his writing, he is also a committed theorist about and for art. Theory is clearly indispensable to artistic practice for understanding both the past and the character of one's own inner necessities, but Kandinsky also is committed to a specific relationship between theory and practice. Thus, on the one hand, 'Theory is the lamp which sheds light on the crystallised ideas of the past' (op.cit., p.31), and is therefore an essential tool for the artist in exploring how internal necessity may require a break with these crystallised ideas. But on the other hand,

> In real art, theory does not precede practice but follows it. Everything is at first a matter of feeling. Even though the general structure may be formulated theoretically, there is still an additional something which constitutes the soul of creation. Any theoretical scheme will be lacking in the essential of creation – the internal desire for expression – which cannot be formulated (op.cit., p.53).

All artistic practice then is surrounded by theory, but in the work of creation itself theory is bracketed in favour of a dialogue with inner necessity of which the painting itself is the writing up. There is an ontological break between theorising and practice for Kandinsky. And this sense of the relation between art and Language provides too for his version of criticism:

> *The ideal art critic* would not want to discover 'mistakes', 'errors', 'ignorance', 'plagiarism', etc., etc. Rather, he would try *to feel* how this or that form works internally, and then he would convey his total experience vividly to the public (Kandinsky and Marc, 1977, p.172).

Such a critic would need the 'soul of a poet'. Kandinsky offers the lay-person or critic two questions the force of which are still pertinent today: he or she should ask, 'what did the artist do?' or 'which of his inner wishes did the artist express here?' (op.cit., p.180). And emphasising his rejection of the 'negative' criticism, he suggests that

The attitude toward a work of art should be different from the attitude toward a horse one wants to buy. With a horse one important negative quality outweighs all the positive ones and makes it worthless; with a work of art this relationship is reversed: one important positive quality outweighs all the negative ones and makes it valuable (op.cit., p.182).

Kandinsky's own theorising, then, complements and adds to that of Cézanne in clarifying the space of the modern tradition. He provides a way of understanding contemporary practice that gives absolute primacy to the inner necessity of the artist's impulse to create while preserving a strong sense of the Tradition. Art and Language are shown as reciprocal metaphors so that theorising is integral to artistic practice and, further, this relationship of Language and art is always explicitly explored through metaphors themselves. Moreover his very stance towards painting and Language provides us with a way of reading his work and of working out its relationship to his own and others' paintings. If we read his own analyses as an attempt to exemplify his own sense of the 'ideal art critic' then it would be missing the point of this writing to treat his work as a set of prescriptive rules for practice or interpretation; for, as an exemplification, we should rather treat his writing as an attempt to display what he regards as 'the Good' of being a respondent. His essays lay out the grounds for the respondent's stance towards the work of art which would be in harmony with that of the artist. We might, then, read his interpretation of, for example, the life of colours, as a display of how we, as respondents, might relate to the work of art, rather than as attempts to define the absolute properties and associations of specific colours. We would be true to the inner necessity of his text if we treated his metaphors as displays of the kind of attitude that contemporary painting requires of the respondent, rather than as rules which limit our response. The invitation would be to substitute our own metaphors for his in exploring our relationship with the work of art.

This concern, partially developed by Kandinsky, with the necessarily active role that the spectator plays in the life of the work of art is at the very centre of Marcel Duchamp's contribution to the modern tradition. And it is Duchamp above all who provides for the absolute inter-twining of art with Language not only as a relationship of practice and theory, but also as the very substance of artistic practice itself. His own oeuvre and life continue to provide apparently inexhaustible and endlessly controversial resources for artists and writers, and especially for those avant-garde subtraditions which explore, often in the name of anti-art, the limits of art. My concern here is not with the intricacies of the diverse ways in which Duchamp's influence concretely works itself out, nor is it to undertake a detailed analysis of his own work, but is rather to try to show that the exemplary character of his work is a crucial contribution to the self-transformation of the modern tradition; defining this exemplary character and intrinsic to its contribution is Duchamp's display of a relation to Language.

One of the most significant features about Duchamp's oeuvre, his works and writings, is that whilst he is intensely theoretical he never writes a developed 'theory of art practice' in the way that Kandinsky, Mondrian, Klee and other twentieth century artists have done. Apart from the dialogues with Cabanne (Cabanne, 1971) in which he retrospectively reviews his 'career', there are only occasional and brief pieces in which any conventional theorising occurs (as in 'The Creative Act' of 1957, in Sanouillet and Peterson, 1975) and even here his writing has a cryptic epigrammatic quality. And yet, as his collected writings show (ibid.) he wrote continuously. Indeed writing was intrinsic to his work, so that what emerges is a distinctive sense of the relation between theory and practice, between Language and art, where theory is not some moment independent of practice, but where artistic practice is itself the display of theory. For Duchamp art has to be theoretical in its very doing, its being done, so that the work of art is a display of theory that requires a self-conscious act of theorising by the respondent to re-constitute it.

The fragmentary character of Duchamp's writing displays the way it is bound to the process and context of art's creative constitution itself; theorising in the context of art for Duchamp is always absolutely contextual as it is bound up with the creation of particular works. In other words the theory of the work of art can never be external to the work of its creation and re-creation, for it is a defining feature of art that it lives in and as the 'personal art coefficient' (op.cit., p.139) displayed in every work of art. This coefficient is the difference or 'gap' between what the artist intended to realise and did realise, and it in turn requires 'refining' from its raw state ('à l'état brut') by the respondent in a process which transmutes the work: 'the creative act is not performed by the artist alone; the spectator brings the work in contact with the external world by deciphering and interpreting its inner qualifications and thus adds his contributions to the creative act' (op.cit., p.140). Duchamp reminds us that the work of art is a text to be deciphered and that this process of deciphering transmutes the work from its wild state, inert matter, into a quality. The respondent's interpretation is already this side of the gap between the artist's intention and its realisation; that is to say the intention is not available in the work, for the work stands as the residue of the artist's 'personal art coefficient' which has already escaped intention, and it is this residue which the respondent deciphers. The 'personal art coefficient', as reconstructed by the respondent, is the theory of the work; it is theorising as a practical accomplishment which is fulfilled in every interpretive act of a respondent and *is tied to the occasion of practice itself*, for it is the other of theory as generalisation. The sense of theory which Duchamp's work exemplifies is thus one which stands for the absolute concreteness of the work of art in the way that it ties interpretation to each work in its specificity; it shows us that the work of art cannot be 'had' or possessed by a generalising theory that seeks to subsume it under some rule of interpretation external to the relation between the work and a respondent. Theory for Duchamp must begin and end with the concreteness of the work of art no matter where it goes to in between. Art in its very concreteness already fragments all systematising theory.

In his remarks on the 'personal art coefficient' Duchamp pointed to the gap or difference between intention and realisation and proposed that 'in the chain of reactions accompanying the creative act, a link is missing' (op.cit., p.139). Now I want to suggest that this lacuna or absence is implicitly tied to Desire in the creative process, for it 'represents the inability of the artist to fully express his intention' (ibid.). An intention here can be heard as the concrete rendering of the Desire that can never be satisfied or exhausted because it defines 'being' itself. This seems to parallel Kandinsky's inner necessity, except that Duchamp renders this as the gap between intention and realisation which, like all gaps, requires a leap. If the work of art stands for the unsatisfiable Desire for complete expression of intention, then Duchamp's gap, which constitutes the work, in its specificity as just *this* work, is another name for that space which the movement of differance itself releases, for the movements of differing and deferring in which the origin of significance is itself re-presented. The work is both gap and the leap which fills the gap; it is a missing link in a chain which is paradoxically complete because the work of art itself completes it, or rather is the penultimate link which provides for its completion by the respondent. This full absence, the space between intention and realisation writes into being a work whose significance lies precisely in its constitution of, its bringing forth of significance, for, as a new 'beginning', each work recalls for us this originating movement of significance itself. In a sense the work of art *is* that gap, for the 'personal art coefficient' is the artist's own 'handwriting' and this is art in its raw state ('à l'état brut') – the encounter with the absolute primitive beginnings of wild meaning.

There is an inchoate poetic recognition of that which Derrida points to as the movement of differance or trace at the beginning of Duchamp's genesis of the *Large Glass* (*The Bride Stripped Bare by her Bachelors, Even*). The collection of texts which accompanied the production of the *Large Glass* between 1912 and its non-completion in 1923 was published in 1934 as *The Green Box*, and the second note in this collection, dating from 1912, writes of a 'Kind of Subtitle' for the *Large Glass* as a 'Delay in Glass'. Duchamp later spoke of the poetic aspects of the choice of the word 'delay':

> I wanted to give 'delay' a poetic sense that I couldn't even explain. It was to avoid saying 'a glass painting', 'a glass drawing', 'a thing drawn on glass', you understand? The word 'delay' pleased me at that point, like a phrase one discovers (Cabanne, 1971, p.40).

If 'delay' appears to be a substitute for the word 'painting', we must be careful, for the note in *The Green Box* says,

> delay in glass does not mean picture in glass. It's merely a way of succeeding in no longer thinking that the thing in question is a picture – to make a delay of it in the most general way possible, not so much in the different meanings in which delay can be taken, but rather in their indecisive reunion 'delay' – a delay in glass as you would say a poem in prose or a spittoon in silver (Sanouillet and Peterson, 1975, p.26).

Certainly the *Large Glass* is unlike any other 'picture' in the western tradition of painting and this helps us to stop thinking of it as a picture, but the choice of 'delay' is crucial, for what it immediately points us towards is deferral. If the work is not to be thought of as a picture, this is partly because the *Large Glass* marks an epistemological break in Duchamp's own oeuvre, for with it he effectively abandons painting pictures as they are conventionally understood within the Tradition. In one sense it is *painting itself* which is delayed in the *Large Glass*; for Duchamp, painting is permanently deferred, and if we treat the *Large Glass* as a reference to twentieth century painting generally, it represents his sense of the need to re-literarise art practice. Painting is delayed on behalf of Language for Duchamp's concern was to re-inject art with ideas: 'I wanted to get away from the physical aspect of painting. I was much more interested in recreating ideas in painting . . . I wanted to put painting once again at the service of the mind' (op.cit., p.125). These retrospective remarks of his, made in a 1946 interview, are confirmed in his later interviews with Cabanne when he speaks of his 'anti-retinal' attitude (Cabanne, 1971, pp.43, 93). Against the sensuous in painting for its own sake, a painting's supposed immediate appeal to the eye as its apparent end, Duchamp's practice pointed in another direction, towards Language. Thus the 'delay in glass' is Duchamp's way of deferring what he saw as the domination of the sensuous in painting, the responsibility for which he attributes to impressionism and post-impressionism. But if the picture is deferred on behalf of Language, and if Language has its life through the movement of differance, then we might suggest that painting is delayed on behalf of delay itself. The work of art which defers the sensuous on behalf of the word also provides for a radical openness of interpretation by deferring any sense of a final or absolute interpretation. There is indeed a picture trapped between the glass in the *Large Glass* but it is a picture whose meaning is forever delayed by the very ways in which it is implicated with and equivocated by the word (and most concretely with the texts of *The Green Box*). The work as text, together with its accompanying texts, ensures that it will forever deny an absolute reading.

Language is a continuing concern of the texts in *The Green Box* both as a topic and as a problem for the reader, for the writing's fragmentary character encourages and provides for a metaphoric reading where each fragment can be more easily treated on its own than as part of an unbroken text. Any sense which the reader produces on the metonymic dimension, through the combination, association and relation of texts, is explicitly a product of the reader's own constitutive work, for continuous sense can only be provided through an active filling of the gaps between the fragments themselves and between them and the *Large Glass*. And these searches are clearly guided by the reader's interests rather than something intrinsic to the texts; yet the latter are required reading for the construction of a sense for the *Large Glass*, they are part of the work. Thus what the reader does make of the *Large Glass* will be very much a matter of the specific associations through which a sense of these texts is generated, thus confirming the context-bound character of theorising in Duchamp's work. This encourages the reader to be reflexive towards his or her own interpretive work, for the reader is required to confront the fact that interpretation is a product of *his or her* methods of theorising. Duchamp's interest in the disruption of metonymy, of the ability to reconstruct sense through the combination and association of semantically related linguistic elements, is pointed to directly in some of the early fragments in *The Green Box*. Thus Duchamp writes,

> to *lose* the *possibility of recognising* 2 *similar* objects – 2 colours, 2 laces, 2 hats, 2 forms whatsoever to reach the Impossibility of sufficient *visual* memory, to transfer from one like object to another the *memory* imprint. – Same possibility with sounds; with brain facts (op.cit., p.31).

And again, in the text immediately following, where he outlines the 'Conditions of a Language' (consisting of signs for all the abstract words without concrete reference taken from a Larousse dictionary) that would have an alphabet which would be suitable only for the description of the *Large Glass*, he notes the need for an 'ideal continuity' of meaning. In the first case Duchamp envisages the possibility of the absolute loss of that metonymic connection which allows the constitution of similarity and thus difference, while in the second he recognises the need for continuity as intrinsic to the possibility of a language. Perhaps both these texts can also be read as metaphors for Duchamp's sense of the work of art and artistic practice, for the first envisages the possibility of indifference, of seeing without any memory trace, and this would be a seeing for the first time outside any convention or tradition. In the second, if we treat Language and art as reciprocal metaphors then the work of art is the search for prime words that are indivisible and exemplify unity; and the alphabet of signs for these prime words provides for groupings of signs which would make up the work.

There is a fine irony in Duchamp's paradoxical recognition that this alphabet would probably only be suitable for the *Large Glass*, for Duchamp knows both that every work of art is unique, constitutes itself in and as its specific language, but also that it is a condition of Language that it be infinitely translatable. The *Large Glass* can be seen as standing, then, for art as a paradox in the ways that it lives through a variety of tensions and it centres these tensions in Language. In particular while it resists and always absolutely escapes from any symbolic reading, it nevertheless requires an active interpretative search and re-constitution by the respondent which always ironically leaves the respondent realising that his or her own interpretation is only a product of his or her own methodic work, for at the unfinal end of the search the *Large Glass* still confronts the respondent mutely with its infinite deferral of significance. If we treat the *Large Glass* as a metaphor for every work of art, it displays the absolute otherness of the work and shows us that its life is always a dialectical tension between the work of interpretation and a meaning whose completion is forever deferred. It is both a language in itself, and, at the same time, untranslatable, for it is a sign that, having no references other than that of deferral itself, cannot be seen through. We are left finally to confront the metaphoricity of our relation to the world and its other.

Art and Language are thus inseparable for Duchamp, and his work is a display of this inseparability from the epistemological, and perhaps also ontological, break of 1912 onwards; the work of art is transformed into an occasion for theorising about the occasion itself in its concreteness. Not only are there further texts related to the *Large Glass* which explicitly treat the question of Language (for example, see op.cit., pp.38 and 77–8), but the variety of works subsequently produced are bound to questions of Language. If, for example, we consider Duchamp's fascination with the pun and his continual play with the alternative possibilities that arise from the disjunction between reading (seeing) and hearing, these works exemplify a relation to Language of celebratory questioning.

They are involved with questioning in the way the respondent is required, through a confrontation with alternative readings, to question the sense of Language through which a work of art is approached; each object or text faces us with the 'fact' that it is neither one thing (interpretation) nor the other, for it hovers between the two and only the respondent's interest can institute a preferred sense. At the same time because the activity is performed for itself in the service of a specific sense of art as the play of ideas, it is a celebration of what Language makes possible. Puns and word play turn, very frequently, on the difference between an interpretation constituted through the process of reading or seeing a text, and the possible phonological transformations that can occur when the text is spoken aloud. Language is experienced in the pun as ever open to this play of differences and, referring us forward to the issue of phonocentrism taken up shortly in relation to Derrida's work, the pun is precisely an opening up of the difference between writing and speaking. It shows us how phonetic writing's apparent superiority as a representation of sense, its economy in relation to its referent, is confounded by the very voice for which it is the signified. For what occurs in the pun is that the voice as signifier confounds its own signified (the writing that 'represents' the voice) in the ways that it can offer other sense possibilities to those of the phonetically written text. Speaking what is written leads to another meaning which requires that we confront the difference between speaking and writing: 'Objet Dard', 'Belle Haleine', 'Lits et ratures', and so on. And again this difference takes us back to differance, because it is in just this full absence between speaking and writing that the origin of significance itself is here disclosed and deferred in and as a matter of play. We are shown this ultimate instability and fragility of the most 'advanced' sign system in the gap between reading for sense and hearing sense – alternative moments of the 'same' which constitute difference. How might this stand to writing-in-general? If we take this playful disclosure in conjunction with Duchamp's anti-retinalism and his other comments on Language, it begins to show the ways that the sign is utterly dependent upon the work of the reader/hearer, and it is another element in Duchamp's displacement of artistic intention in the way that it shows how it is the reading which creates the possibilities. The work is wild ('à l'état brut') until led somewhere by a respondent.

The difference between seeeing-as-reading and hearing is a central theme of Duchamp's works and is seen most obviously in the relation between a work's title and its object-referent, for with Duchamp it is precisely this relation which provides for the work's life. And at this point we can begin to see how Duchamp's involvement with Language has nothing to do with the technical and everything to do with Desire. If the personal art coefficient pointed us towards Desire through its disclosure of the gap between intention and realisation, then the practice of art, as the playful celebration of Language, brings us there even more explicitly, for Duchamp's relation to Language is nothing if not a display of Language's implication with the erotic.

In his 1946 interview Duchamp acknowledged the influence of Brisset and Roussel, the former being an extraordinary philologist who developed an analysis of Language based on the pun, while the latter was a novelist whose writing obtained its imaginative release by following certain linguistic rules based often on the difference between the written and the spoken. Richter confirms Brisset's influence on the Dada painters and poets more generally (Richter, 1965, pp.168–9) and the relation between Roussel and Duchamp is discussed in Sanouillet's analysis of Duchamp's relation to the French intellectual tradition (d'Harnoncourt and McShine, 1974, p.47). One rule Roussel used for some of his work was that the last phrase of a poem or novel was to be an almost identical repetition of the first, except that one minor change such as the loss of a letter, would provide for a transformation of its meaning, the transformation arising in part from the difference in pronunciation required from the slight change. A detailed critical appraisal of these rules can be found in Heppenstall's study of Roussel's principal writings (Heppenstall, 1966). The homophone, basic to punning, was a constant feature of Roussel's 'technical' devices; an example from Heppenstall's study, drawn from Roussel's astonishing novel *Locus Solus* (1970) is the transformation of 'deluge' into 'de l'eus-je?' (Heppenstall, 1966, p.53). Roussel's novel *Impressions of Africa* was performed on the stage in Paris in 1912 and was seen by Duchamp in the company of the poet and art critic Apollinaire; Sanouillet argues that it is most unlikely that Duchamp was familiar with the complexity of Roussel's word-games and was probably more taken with the spectacle and the 'delirious language' (d'Harnoncourt and McShine, 1974, p.52). Nevertheless Duchamp himself attributes the genesis of the *Large Glass* directly to Roussel:

It was fundamentally Roussel who was responsible for my glass, 'The Bride Stripped Bare by her Bachelors, Even.' From his 'Impressions d'Afrique' I got the general approach . . . I felt that as a painter it was much better to be influenced by a writer than by another painter. And Roussel showed me the way (Sanouillet and Peterson, 1975, p.126).

The literary influence can be seen in the homophones, slight displacements, reversals of phrase positions and puns which are a continuing feature of Duchamp's writing. Most of these are of course lost in translation, as is the case with the work of Brisset and Roussel, but the well known example to be found in the French title of the *Large Glass* already shows Roussel's influence at work and exemplifies the way this playful relation to Language defined Duchamp's work from the very beginning of his break with 'painting pictures'. And it is an example which also points us towards the erotic underpinning of Duchamp's work, for what we begin to see is a sense of Language that is the other to the technical manipulation or mere subversion of its surface rules. It plays with Language and allows Language to have its way in the name of a work whose very being is a radical displacement of technicism and instrumentalism.

All systems, all instrumental practices, are confounded by the 'Large Glass'. The French title, 'La MARiée mise a nu par ses CELibataires, même', already contains the two syllables of Duchamp's first name and identifies the first syllable (MAR) with the top half of the *Large Glass* (that relating to the bride) and the second syllable (CEL) with the bottom half (that relating to the bachelors): the artist seems to stand for oneness, for the union of male and female. But this is complicated by the title's last word, 'même', which homophonically can also be heard as 'm'aime', and this alternative immediately provides for a multiplicity of possible senses which are partially dependent upon who is taken to be speaking the title. We are at liberty to see the 'm'aime' referring (perhaps ironically) either to the relationship between the bride and the spectator, or we can read the title as a speech by Duchamp in which case it becomes perhaps a statement (ironic?) of self-love (MAR-CEL m'aime), or of the bride's love for Duchamp. But then again we could preserve the 'même' . . . we are tantalised with different erotic possibilities, through the play of Language; and if we begin to further complicate the matter by asking, for example, what the bride and the bachelors could be metaphors for, then the affair gets completely out of hand, which is just what we may suspect Duchamp desired. Quite apart from the *Large Glass* and his last work *Etant Donnés* the erotic is an ever-present theme in his oeuvre, even though frequently ironised as in some of his objects (such as *Please Touch* of 1947, *Female Fig Leaf* of 1950 and the *Wedge of Chastity* of 1954); but the unavoidable centrality of the erotic to Duchamp's sense of art is at its most explicit in his self-transformation into Rrose Selavy, the alter ego photographed by Man Ray in 1920, while Duchamp was still working on the *Large Glass*. Rrose Selavy is, among other possibilities, a homophone for 'eros, c'est la vie', which we may take as a metaphor for art's relation to life as well as Duchamp's own motto as an artist.

Indeed *The Green Box* is itself a continuous testament to the erotic, both ironically and otherwise for the texts move continuously into the languages of mechanics and physics only to subvert them immediately into their other. Duchamp himself refers to his own work at one point as a 'playful physics' (op.cit., p.49), putting, as it were, the external 'form' of physics (its writing) in the service of Desire through his erotic subversion of the conventions of its language; his alternative physics transforms physics into a meta-physics, but a meta-physics whose object is not to generalise a philosophical system but to exemplify what art might be doing as the other of calculation, of the system. Nor is this the wilful play of some absolute anarchy for it is a practice that knows its own limits and treats them seriously; Duchamp himself acknowledges at one point that one of the consequences of the illogic of his alternative physics is 'much too far-fetched' (op.cit., p.61). Indeed the texts are continually walking the fine line between the conventional sense of geometry, physics and mechanics (non-Euclidean geometry, the relationship between the third and fourth dimension, gravity and so on) and the Non-sense or wildness of art that is this side of nonsense. And all this is done with no other end than that of the constitution of one particular object – the *Large Glass* – which itself neither explains anything nor is explicable. In spite of its internal complexities nothing could ultimately be a clearer exemplification of the in-itself-for-itself which elides art with the erotic on the terrain of Desire.

In Duchamp's case the line between art and life seems peculiarly hard to draw because he eschewed the role of professional artist and avoided the kinds of institutional ties which might have pushed his work towards a particular kind of output. This stance against art as an institution in part contributes to his iconic value to avant-garde movements in art, although the avant-garde necessarily lacks Duchamp's ironic detachment. Duchamp's detachment then is neither a simple negation nor a neutrality for, in ironising his detachment, Duchamp resites himself in the Tradition. What Duchamp detaches himself from is not art or the Tradition but is, rather, repetition; he needed to preserve himself from art as institution to avoid repetition and to keep alive the possibility of invention, and in this sense he is truly 'indifferent' to the art of his contemporaries (see e.g. Cabanne, 1971, p.98). The relation to Tradition which this attitude provides for is that articulated by T.S. Eliot in 'Tradition and the Individual Talent', an essay well known to Duchamp for he quotes it in his text 'The Creative Act' (Sanouillet and Peterson, 1975, p.138). In this view the Tradition makes available a set of creative possibilities to the artist; each work of art is then a creative response to, a reading of, these possibilities, which, as something new, redefines the Tradition's possibilities however slightly at the same time as it locates itself within it. For Duchamp it was necessary to preserve his detachment from contemporary art institutions to maximise the possibility of true invention and, hence, a re-definition of the Tradition's boundaries. At the same time it was ironic in recognising both his own limitations and those of art.

What Duchamp exemplifies, then, through his continuous exploration and celebration of art's languages, is a specific relation to the Tradition through an ethic of invention, and his works can lead us to a radical confrontation with art's possibilities in the way they require us to address the very assumptions we bring into play in relating to it. Whether each work achieves the radical inventiveness that Duchamp worked for is a decision that Duchamp well knew would be taken by history and it is this knowledge which ultimately ironises every artistic practice whatever the depth of its own commitment, integrity or sense of achievement. If the modern tradition is partially about the value of 'the new' then Duchamp exemplifies it, but not at the expense of either the Tradition or the respondent as the ultimate donor of the work's life and space. If Duchamp perhaps overplayed the distinction between retinal and anti-retinal (it is after all the present thesis that such a distinction is ultimately untenable) it was a distinction made in the service of clarifying and strengthening the relation between a work of art, the tradition within which it gains its identity, and the context in which it comes to have its concrete life.

The three artists so far considered underwrite the modern tradition by providing the terms and the grounds for a sense of practice that stands in a different relation to past art than preceding innovations within the Tradition; the modern tradition differs itself from other changes within Tradition in the ways that it re-defines the artist's relation to the world. As I suggested, this is epitomised in the dialectical sense of relation which informs Cézanne's work and which has subsequently defined the understanding and practice of relation in the modern tradition generally. If the basic terms of this relation and the directions of its possible development are broadly articulated in the work of Cézanne, Kandinsky and Duchamp, two other artists, Matisse and Klee, make contributions which expand modernity's region and elaborate the emerging possibilities of the transformation of 'relation'.

Matisse's work, his art practice and his writing, offers a synthesis of the meaning of modernity on the terrain of figuration and it does this through a strong version of painting as Language. What Matisse thus presents us with can be taken, if not as an answer to Duchamp's requirement that Language be reinstated in art at the expense of the 'retinal', then at least as a complement to this position. For Matisse preserves painting and painting as figuration, not with an empiricist insistence on the primacy of sensation over Language but rather through metaphorising art as Language and mediating the relations between art, nature, and Language, with the 'sign'.

One of the defining features of the modern vision has been its recognition and release of the possibilities of colour in painting and Matisse is often seen as one of the main architects and apostles of this release. If Kandinsky was, perhaps, the first painter to theorise the relation between colour and idea in painting in a way which provided for the exploration of colour in itself, Matisse was arguably the first to exemplify a similar sense and to develop and synthesise it in the context of figurative painting. And while in his own work his relation to colour is integrated into a thoroughly modern vision

Matisse himself recognises that this renewal of colour's possibilities has already been awakened in nineteenth century painting in the work of Delacroix and Van Gogh, the impressionists, and, above all, Cézanne, 'who gives a definitive impulse' (Flam, 1978, p.99). Thus, while the modern relation to colour may appear to be radically different to that of its predecessors, it nevertheless develops through direct continuities with the past, but at the same time, through its drawing on the sense of colour in non-western traditions, exemplified by Matisse himself, relativises the conventions of colour use that had framed traditional practice.

Now if colour is released, explored and celebrated by Matisse from his Fauvist period onwards, this occurs only in the context of a wider vision of artistic practice which his work and writing exemplify, and the significance of colour can only be approached in this wider vision. Crucial to this vision is the relation between modern artistic practice and its past, for, drawing from Cézanne, Matisse insists on the way that the past defines and informs the present possibilities, even though it is a defining dimension of the modern vision to create the new, that which is other to the Tradition. He acknowledges his debt to Cézanne – 'in modern art it is indubitably to Cézanne that I owe the most' (op.cit., p.123) – and echoes Cézanne's belief about the way the artist's relation to his subject was to be articulated with past work:

> Courage is essential to the artist, who has to look at everything as though he saw it for the first time; he has to look at life as he did when he was a child and, if he loses that faculty, he cannot express himself in an original, that is, a personal way. The first step towards creation is to see everything as it really is (op.cit., p.148).

And again. 'The painter should come to his model with no premeditated idea' (op.cit., p.152).

As noted in relation to Cézanne, this requirement to suspend the conventions of vision and marking in painting practice offers painting as a practical phenomenology for the exploration of visibility and relation themselves, especially as the goal is to 'see everything as it really is' (where what 'really is' is precisely relation 'itself'). But this bracketing or epoché is never performed in a void, as Matisse himself recognises; that is to say, he knows that there can never be an absolute suspension of, a clean break with, Tradition, for it is Tradition itself which provides the space for this very suspension. There is no void for Matisse because the artist is always *in between* the

Tradition and the object that he paints:

> If he is sensitive no painter can lose the contribution of the
> preceding generation because it is part of him despite himself.
> Yet it is necessary for him to disengage himself in order to
> produce in his own turn something new and freshly inspired
> (op.cit., p.102).

The problem of the relation to the past and to the present is a
problem of Language, and Matisse brings into play one of his
favourite metaphors in articulating the context of the modern painter's practice:

> it is perilous to fall under the influence of the masters of my own
> epoch, because the language is too close to ours, and risks taking
> the letter for the spirit. The masters of ancient civilisations had a
> language which was very full for them, but so different from
> ours that it prevents us from making too literal an imitation.
> Influenced by them we are obliged to create a new language, for
> theirs refuses us a full development of ideas and very quickly
> closes its doors on us (op.cit., p.126).

It seems that, within the metaphor of Language, the problem is
one of translation; Matisse offers us a view of the relation between
languages, those of the past and the present, which precludes any
kind of perfect (literal) translation. The ideas and experiences generated within each language cannot be translated into the terms of
another without loss, the loss of the possibility of development; thus
to try to move out of the contemporary language in order to re-live or
re-constitute past languages could only be performed through sacrificing the very phenomena which make the language a living
language for its contemporaries – the loss of the modern experience
itself. Past, present and future art, then, are related for Matisse
through languages which may overlap but which cannot be substi-
tuted for one another; the 'full' significance of a language is tied to
the specific context in which it is constituted, and any attempt by us
to grasp a language that is historically other to our own can only
result in an imperfect translation of its ideas and the experiences
which it makes available. Tradition, then, constituted by languages,
provides for continuity while ensuring difference at the same time.

If Tradition defines and imposes certain possibilities on the artist
this is always in relation to an object and for Matisse this object is
nature. The artist engages the possibilities, constitutes a relation to

Tradition in practice, only in response to the object, and Matisse, again echoing Cézanne, offers us an absolutely modern sense of the object and the artist's relation to it. The artist is not in a void precisely because he starts with an object, an object that produces a 'sensation' in the artist. However this sensation is not the sense-data of empiricism, nor is it a sensation which calls forth a version of naturalism or imitation, for the parameters of the modern relation to the world stand against both these. Art aims not at capturing a literal imitation of some assumedly independent object realm, but rather at exploring its own relation to a world which is both external and internal to the artist at the same time. The artist's rendering will be not of a world-in-itself separate from the artist – over there – but rather will be a rendering of the artist's relation to the world, a relation that is recognised as relative to where the artist practises from, relative to the languages of his or her own experiences:

> What possible interest could there be in copying an object which nature provides in unlimited quantities and which one can always conceive more beautiful? What is significant is the relation of the object to the artist, to his personality, and his power to arrange his sensations and emotions (op.cit., p.73).

The object, nature, is already within the artist as sensation, as emotion, so that what is painted is the response to this sensation, and in this way the painting comes concretely to stand in the space between the artist and the object as metaphor for his relation to it, for sensation here is nothing other than an experience of relation; what the painter paints is a metaphor for relation itself. Indeed in order to be true to the sensation, as an inchoate knowledge of relation, the painter needs to explore (and here Matisse points to the questioning dimension of painting) his knowledge and memory of his relation to the object with the aim of an identification with it. 'Adequate' painterly 'work', a practice, that is, that satisfies as nearly as possible the painter's compulsion to paint (Desire), is a work that involves an attempt to eliminate the space between, the relation of, self and other: 'A study in depth permits my mind to take possession of the subject of my contemplation and to identify myself with it in the ultimate execution of the canvas' (op.cit. p.92), and, 'I shan't get free of my emotion by copying the tree faithfully, or by drawing its leaves one by one in the common language, but only after identifying myself with it' (op.cit., p.94). Identification here points to the way the artist experiences the world within him- or herself and the work of art constitutes the meaning of this experience. The sensation whose significance is rendered in the work of art cannot then be divorced from Language for it only comes to be in the activity of creatively rendering it; it is constituted as this particular sensation in the creative act, and is, from the beginning, a sign. But it is a sign in a rather special sense, a sense that is not amenable in the first instance, that is at the level of origin, to a structuralist or semiotic conception of the sign, for it does not point away from itself to a referent or signified. It seems to be a sign first of all of itself.

If the work of art is defined as such a reflexive sign, a sign that displays itself in and as its own specificity, we can read this as another rendering in the context of Language of what Duchamp called the personal art coefficient, for this coefficient, what distinguishes the work both from other works and from the artist's intention, is its work as a sign that signifies only its own absolute difference within a tradition of continuity, of sameness. The sense of the work of art as sign is fundamental to Matisse and because he metaphorises art as Language we can find in his writing a coherent and developed sense of the relation between Language, art and sign. In writing about one of the founding motives for Fauvism as the 'courage to return to the purity of the means', he shows how this demands of the artist a remembering of the origins of Language itself; this journey back to the beginning of writing-in-general, of the possibility of the inscription of human being, is the practice of art for Matisse, so that art as the practice of this reconstitution of beginning, is absolutely inter-twined with Language: 'it is necessary to return to the essential principles which made human language. They are, after all, the principles which "go back to the source", which re-live, which give us life' (op.cit., p.74). This inter-twining of art with Language necessitates a view of the work of art as directed not towards some pre-meaningful realm of the respondent's sensations but rather to a dialogue with the respondent's being-in-the-world, and this relation with the respondent is accomplished through 'description' and 'speech'; thus he says that

> I have never considered drawing as an exercise of particular
> dexterity, rather as a means of expressing intimate feelings and
> describing states of mind, but as a means deliberately simplified
> so as to give simplicity and spontaneity to the expression which
> should speak without clumsiness directly to the mind of the
> spectator (op.cit., p.81).

The work is to speak to the mind and not to 'bodily' senses or emotions.

This description that the work of art performs is elaborated through the concept of the sign in a way that preserves the paradox in which art is Language constituted through a diversity of languages but the signs of each language are finally specific to each picture. Although art's signs are absolutely concrete, untranslatable, it remains paradoxically Language. The way that we can hold these two elements of the paradox together is by recognising that Matisse is offering us a sense of that return to the first principles of our being-in-Language, to the time of a Language before languages, or of writing-in-general, of differance. This return is referred to in one of Matisse's discussions of the work of signs in painting. He is discussing the relation between the object in nature and his representation of the object in his painting, and he articulates in this context his specific sense of sign: 'One must study an object a long time, to know what its sign is. Yet in a composition the object becomes a new sign which helps to maintain the force of the whole' (op.cit., p.137). The sign for the object in other words takes its meanings from its contribution to the whole that is that specific picture, thus, 'each work of art is a collection of signs invented during the picture's execution to suit the needs of their position. Taken out of the composition for which they were created, *these signs have no further use*' (op.cit., p.137, my emphasis). Each picture is a description which is assembled through signs whose significance is specific to that particular picture; what they signify first of all is that picture's uniqueness, its particularity.

> Thus the sign for which I forge an image has no value if it doesn't harmonise with other signs which I must determine in the course of my invention *and which are completely peculiar to it*. The sign is determined at the moment I use it and for the object of which it must form a part. For this reason I cannot determine in advance signs which never change and which would be like writing; that would freeze the freedom of my invention (op.cit., p.137, my emphasis).

The sign signifies the uniqueness of that picture first, and only derivatively an object external to the picture; the sign here is no longer about resemblance. Matisse insists that his signs must avoid being like the signs of writing (and we can assume that he is referring to the linear phonetic script) precisely because the latter are fixed, and working with fixed signs would deny the freedom of invention that produces the difference that each work makes to the Tradition. The signs in a painting signify, exemplify, and re-present the origin of writing itself and writing-in-general by showing their own absolute concreteness; they are for and of Language while remaining untranslatable. This proto-writing communicates itself as a writing that is a display of the Desire for other, for relation with other. It Desires to possess nature but knows that every attempt at possession results in a sign that, constituting a relation with nature, always falls short of possession. And each work of art, as itself a sign and an inter-penetrating of signs, signifies itself as a unique re-presentation of this relation. Of course, at a secondary level, the sign does have a referent, but this referent's transformed 'presence' in the painting as a sign has nothing to do in the first instance with its life outside the painting; it does not appear then as a copy or as information because it is in the painting in the form of a sign whose raison d'être is to signify the differences of that specific painting. Thus Matisse, in one of his conversations with the poet Aragon, points to modernity's subversion of the sign's resemblance to the referent:

> I have to create an object which resembles the tree. The sign for the tree, and the sign that other artists may have found for the tree . . . The importance of an artist is to be measured by the number of new signs he has introduced into the language of art . . . but the quest for signs – I felt absolutely obliged to go on searching for signs in preparation for a new development in my life as a painter (op.cit., pp.94–5).

The quest is for that paradox, a personal language, the peculiarities of which are that it may be understood by another, the respondent, but it cannot be used by another to produce art for to copy it would be to transform it into the equivalent of the hieroglyph. The specificity of the artist's signs, its disruption of conventions of resemblance, this display of the beginning of a writing before writing, signifies and celebrates the being of art as creativity in the service of Desire.

The implication of art, as this kind of signing practice, with Desire is metaphorised vividly by Matisse, as with Cézanne, through offering a sense of the artist's relation to nature as the source or impulse of his art. Not only is this pointed to in Matisse's remarks about his identification with the subject referred to earlier, but the mysterious origin of Desire, the absolute otherness of this compulsion to create, is pointed to in the following way when Matisse writes of the beginning of his career, 'I got on with my work as quickly as possible, driven on by something, I do not know what, by a force which I see today as something alien to my normal life as a man' (op.cit., p.171). This compulsion gained its coherence from its focus on the artist's relation to nature, to the other. And Matisse offers his erotic sense of this relation in an explicitly sexual metaphor; writing of the need for identification with the other as the pre-requisite for the creation of new signs, he presents this identification through the metaphor of sexual unity:

> An artist must possess Nature. He must identify with her rhythms, by efforts that prepare for the mastery by which he will later be able to express himself in his own language . . . become one with Nature, identify himself with her by penetrating the things – which is what I call Nature – that arouse his feelings (op.cit., p.121).

And again: 'The artist to a greater or lesser degree dominates himself, but it is passion which motivates his work' (op.cit., p.122). Possession, rhythm, mastery, expression, penetration, arousal, all founded in passion, exemplify the erotics of his relation with the other and what the practice of painting metaphorises. Painting, as a proto-writing, writes on behalf of the originary character of Desire; the marks on or in the surface of the painting point beyond themselves to the Reason for their inscription, where Reason is the suffusing of every emotion with a Desire for loss of self through absolute identification with the other that is concretised in the undeniable need to create the work of art.

It might appear that, as Matisse's metaphor of passion supports gender-specific terms, a specifically male erotics of the creative act (the artist's relation to nature, to other) is being offered as an expression of an inherent analytical maleness in the modern tradition, and certainly the artists discussed here were partially caught in the prevailing discursive conventions. However, passion as the concretisation of Desire, is relation itself, to be-in-relation-with-other(s), rather than a specific form of relation. Perhaps passion is the ground from which both the masculine and the feminine begin and to which they return; passion, rather than subsuming the erotic under a particular gender, metaphorises the space between. And it may be that post-modernity, through the intervention of feminist discourse, begins to realise this (see the later discussion of criticism for an expansion of this issue; see also Kozloff, 1974).

The practice of art and the works that it produces can read as metaphors for the erotic but finally impossible quest for unity with other through the partial loss of self. Matisse himself steps aside from the gender specificity of his metaphors when he writes of his relation to the other through an eroticised sense of rapport: 'Rapport is the affinity between things, the common language; rapport is love, yes love. Without rapport, without this love, there is no longer any criterion of observation and thus there is no longer any work of art' (Flam, 1978, p.147), and 'is not love the origin of all creation?' (op.cit., p.149), and this founding of the relation as the passion for unity, the impossible culmination of the rapport of love, is mediated for Matisse by colour, the life of which in a work of art is always a matter of relationship, of differences:

> I . . . used colour as a means of expressing my emotion and not as a transcription of nature. I use the simplest colours. I don't transform them myself, it is the relationships which take charge of them. It is only a matter of enhancing the differences, of revealing them (op.cit., p.116).

> Colour helps to express light, not only the physical phenomenon, but the only light that really exists, that in the artist's brain . . . colour can translate the essence of each thing and at the same time respond to the intensity of emotional shock . . . colour, above all, . . . is a means of liberation. Liberation is the freeing of conventions (op.cit., p.100).

Colour, which only has its significance in and through relationships, is the medium for the artist's inner light, the source of creativity which itself is a process of liberation, a liberation both from convention and also, therefore, from the self that lives through convention. It is a loss of the conventional self to the sought after metaphoric unity of the work of art, a unity which can only paradoxically be approached through the play of concrete differences on the surface, of fragmentation, of relations defining the possible life of the work.

If Matisse adds to and confirms the theoretic space of the modern tradition by giving coherence to the Language metaphor in the context of figurative painting and by radicalising the relationship between Desire, colour and painting, then Paul Klee not only confirms and extends this relationship but also writes in the possibilities of and provides pointers to almost all subsequent contemporary painting. Klee's notebooks undoubtedly form the most important body of theoretical writing by one artist in the modern tradition, and to do their richness any kind of justice would require an in-depth study. My concern here is to draw upon them to show some of the ways in which Klee offers a complex analysis of contemporary painting which complements, draws upon and deepens the value of his own painting practice to the Tradition. Klee exemplifies and develops to a high point the reflexive and inter-penetrating relationship between theory and practice first hinted at by Cézanne in his letters, and in the course of this development provides the theoretical spaces (and often the practical spaces too when his own work moves in these directions) for those subsequent turns in art practice which have brought the issues of action, time, energy/kinesis, and process to the fore. These latter may be gathered together under the trope of metonymy. Following Jakob-son and Halle (1971) here metonymy is the trope referring to the combination and association of signs in a chain of signifiers; it is concerned with the temporal/narrative/syntactic dimensions of writing and reading and is contrasted with metaphor whose syn-chronic function is that of the substitution of one sign for another (these terms are discussed in more depth in the subsequent sections on writing, reading and painting).

One of Klee's major contributions to the languages of contempor-ary painting is to have opened up and clarified their metonymic possibilities. He provided for the development of these in both his painting and his writing. But Klee never theorised the metonymic in isolation or as the only or the dominant feature of modern painting; rather what he did was to reveal, perhaps for the first time, the creative tension between painting's metaphoric and metonymic aspects by bringing the metonymic into view as intrinsic to the creation and re-creation of the work of art. This is done without any sacrifice of metaphor.

Of course Klee also articulated his own senses of and metaphors for the central underlying values of the modern tradition that I have already discussed in relation to the other artists, those of question-ing and celebration, Desire and otherness, the primacy of the idea, and the relation to Tradition itself; a brief look at his exploration of these can provide the back-cloth for a review of the significance of the metonymic in his work. As a profound dialectician Klee in his writing invariably works through the exploration of the creative tensions arising out of the relation between either opposites or differences; this occurs whether he is discussing the creative process itself where the tension is invariably some aspect of the relation between the 'inner' and the 'outer', or the relations within the work of art where he develops a wide variety of contrasts (such as endotopic/exotopic, dividual/individual, vertical/horizontal, and so on). Contemporary art for Klee is a search for and celebration of the essence of phenomena rather than their appearance or semblance, and this means discarding faithfulness to appearances in artistic practice; where appearances are retained they are always equivocated by and put in tension with reference to their other, Klee's rendering of, his metaphors for, inner essence. Many examples of this central commitment appear throughout his notebooks. One example is provided in volume two where three reproductions of contrasting rendering of flowers turn on the specific balance each displays between appearance and essence. These are followed by a succinct statement on Klee's sense of the relation between interior and exterior which also points to some of his other central concerns:

> The interior is infinite, all the way to the mystery of the inmost, the charged point, a kind of sum total of the infinite (the causal). Comparison from nature: the seed. The exterior is finite, i.e. it is the end of the dynamic forces, the limit of their effects, dictated by the causal. One may also call it the virtual, the objective. One could also say: erotic – logical – eros – logos (Klee, 1973, p.149).

Here Klee is turning upside down the everyday (and perhaps the scientific) sense that the exterior is infinite and the self is finite, and opens up art's space in doing this, in a way complementary to Kandinsky (with whom Klee was associated in the Blue Rider Group), for art is the exploration of the inner. Klee notes in his diary, 'wishing to render the things that can be verified I limited myself to my inner life' (Klee, 1961, p.461).

Art's work, then, is a 'making visible' of the inner whose being is implicated by Klee with Desire through the metaphor of eros. At the heart of the inner is the causal itself, the source or genesis of creation which, for Klee, is the ultimate mystery, so that works of art became metaphors for this origin and the process of genesis; if works of art for Cézanne where harmonies parallel to nature, metaphors for nature's harmony, then for Klee they are harmonies that parallel the process of genesis itself. And it is this which makes contemporary art different from yet continuous with the Tradition, for while the artist's dialogue with and study of nature remains a *sine qua non* for Klee, it is an inner rather than an outer dialogue, in that the artist's inner vision dialogues with nature's inner essence; in writing of the newness of this sense of the artistic relation Klee says:

> There is no need to discourage the joy of novelty; though a clear view of history should save us from desperately searching for novelty at the cost of naturalness. . . . Yesterday's artistic creed . . . precise investigation of appearance . . . the art of optical

sight was developed, while the art of contemporary unoptical impressions and representations and of making them visible was neglected (1961, p.63).

A sense of totality has gradually entered into the artist's conception of the natural object . . . a more spatial conception of the object as such is born. Visible penetration . . . intuitive inferences. But there are other ways of looking into the object which go still further which lead to a humanisation of the object and create between the 'I' and the object a resonance surpassing all optical foundations. . . . Intimated physical contact reaches the eye from below. . . . All ways meet in the eye and there, turned into form, lead to a synthesis of outward sight and inward vision (op.cit., p.66).

Klee offers here a strong sense that his and modern painting's subject is the relationship beyond the optical between the 'I' and the object, and that the work of art is a metaphor for the resonances of this relation. Painting writes into being, as it were, visual metaphors for that which is beyond sight, and in so doing constitutes the relation as a visible relation; but the ultimate concern is not with 'optical sight' or what Duchamp called the 'retinal' even though matters of visibility 'meet in the eye'. For art begins from and returns to the idea, which Klee also calls the spiritual function, and this beginning is always implicated with the word of logos.

In the beginning is the act; yes, but above it is the idea. And since infinity has no definite beginning, but is circular and beginningless, the idea may be regarded as the more basic. In the beginning was the word, as Luther translated it (op.cit., p.78).

And again in volume two:

The slumbering tendency towards form and articulation awakens in predetermined precision, determined with reference to the underlying idea, to the logos, or, as the translation runs: the word, which was in the beginning. The word as a premise, as the idea required for the genesis of a work (1973, p.29).

The word, then, puts into motion, acts as the originating motive force, for art here is already idea and is not a matter of pre-meaningful sensation. This beginning, as the word, also written of by Klee as an expression of art's spiritual function (1961, p.39), is not only a way of showing the continuity of contemporary art with Tradition, it also pre-figures Reinhardt's later rendering of art-for-art's sake in his 'art-as-art' thesis (Rose, 1975). Art's concern is the distillation of 'pure pictorial relations' where purity, as Klee wrote in 1928, is an abstract realm: 'Purity is a separation of elements pictorially and within the picture. Nothing may be added that comes from the outside' (1961, p.72). The credo of abstraction is contained in this sense of purity which, of course, also provides for a strong version of 'art for art's sake' that Reinhardt pushed with vigour in the 1950s and 1960s.

Klee makes it quite explicit that art is absolutely other in its specific manifestations of the idea or the spiritual to other dimensions of human being; his way of asserting the distinctive character of art's spirituality is through metaphor, for the power of creativity which is art's idea cannot itself be named, although its source can be approached. The difference art makes to the world, the way art is other to the world, is displayed precisely through the inner exploration and celebration of this source, and this is a process of 'formation' whose end is the work of art and nothing else: 'A picture of the object "nude man" should follow the dictates not of human, but of pictorial anatomy' (op.cit., p.449). Although art always constitutes a relation with nature it is always other to and a transformation of the latter for it is in its being a rebirth of nature and, as an acting again of the process of genesis, this transformation is a condition of its own life: 'The creation of a work of art must of necessity, as a result of entering into the specific dimensions of pictorial art, be accompanied by distortion of the natural form. For therein is nature reborn' (Klee, 1954, p.19).

Metaphor's necessity and its apparent firstness is guaranteed by the otherness of the source; the unity sought in the formation of the work of art, stands as metaphor for that source which can only be named as genesis, as in fact, process. For Klee, radically anti-formalist from the beginning, continually returns to this point: that whatever metaphor stands for (origination) we must see it as movement or formation rather than form. The search for the perenially elusive inner essence is constituted as a process of formation and this formation is always in some sense unfinishable for the source as process does not have a form. 'Genesis as formal movement is the essence of the work of art' (1961, p.17); 'Art is a transmission of phenomena, projection from the hyper-dimensional, a metaphor for procreation, divination, mystery' (op.cit., p.59). And because the work of art is genesis, but a movement which is concerned with space (the space of the picture surface), so space itself must be a 'temporal concept'; that is, the work of art's metaphors for the movement of genesis must have a temporal dimension. For if art is to exemplify creation, its metaphors must make reference to process, to becoming; much of Klee's theoretical writing is an address of the implications for painting practice of this tension between on the one hand a painting's attempted metaphoric unification of a single space and, on the other, the ways that this space can only be grasped temporally, metonymically. Thus for Klee, the process of formation was always higher than its end or goal (form), so that although formation determines form,

> form may never be regarded as solution, result, end, but should be regarded as genesis, growth, essence. Form as phenomenon is a dangerous chimera, form as movement, as active, is a good thing, active form is good. Form is bad; form is the end, death. . . . Formation is life' (op.cit., p.169).

Because genesis, formation, is ultimately the most profound mystery, it has the power to move us deeply and this is indeed the 'function' for Klee of the work of art, in that the strength of its metaphor for genesis will be shown in the ways that it awakens the consciousness of this power in the artist and the viewer. The work of art's potential is, then, that it can reveal that power of creativity that we ourselves are charged with 'down to our finest particles' (op.cit., p.463).

When taken in conjunction with the purity of pictorial relations Klee's insistence on the primacy of the process of formation as genesis over form provides the space within which abstract expressionism and other forms of abstraction were to emerge in the late 1940s and 1950s. The concept of action, crucial to the subsequent movement, is already latent within Klee's opening up of the relation between space and time in painting and his raising of the process of formation over form. To appreciate the importance of Klee's contribution we must move from the metaphoric dimension of the work of art to that of metonymy for it is in his analyses of the practices of formation that his dialectic of painting reveals the creative tensions that constitute the space of the modern tradition itself.

If painting seems to be and always has been in some way about our relations to and in space, then it is the virtue of Klee's work to have revealed this as, at the same time, a question of time as well. And this is already to put us firmly down in the realm of ontology for, even taken at their most concrete (as matters of measurement) we cannot avoid seeing the coordinates of space and time as in some way bound up with and defining the very possibilities of our re-presenting being. The modern tradition has from its inception equivocated the deep space illusion opened in the renaissance discovery of perspective. It thus re-opens the question of and makes problematic our apprehension of depth in a picture. The organisation of relations on the surface has to be approached in new ways if we no longer relate to the picture from one perspectival viewpoint; Klee's response to this is to re-affirm that the 'depth of our surface is imaginary' and to articulate space through using motion firstly, from 'fore to rear' (op.cit., p.53), and secondly, across the surface. Three dimensional space emerges when tone value or colour is added to a linear plane figure. Movement in the picture (we should perhaps say across and into the picture) is thus a conjunction of space-time. The function of the picture is understood as its relation to a respondent (the same processes have to be followed by both artist and respondent) and Klee writes of this function as

> the way in which the movement of the picture's genesis gets to
> the eye, and the way in which the movement inherent in the
> picture communicates with the eye and with the mind behind it.
> Our eye is so constituted that it must take time to explore what it
> perceives . . . (in a picture) it is first attracted to the region
> marked by the most intense developments of pictorial energy
> (op.cit., p.369).

In other words, as a matter of practice (that of painting and that of responding) the painting's space(s) only come to be temporally; there is no ideal space outside of the time that it takes to construct and perceive it. Space takes the time of both the artist and the respondent. Thus by focusing on the centrality to the work of art of the process of formation Klee is at the same time necessarily involved in constructing an analysis of the process of responding to, or what we might call reading, the work of art. The work's function is then to 'capture' movement (time), preserve it and make it available again for recreation in the process of responding so that one of the work's crucial tensions, the one that sustains the possibility of its continuing to live as a painting, is that between its state of absolute rest as a two dimensional object and the movement through which it is revivified:

> our works . . . stay quietly in place, and yet they are all

movement. Movement is inherent in all becoming, and before the work is, it must become, just as the world became before it was after the words, 'In the beginning God created', and must go on before becoming before it is (will be) in the future (op.cit., p.355).

For Klee the 'isness' of a work, *that* it is, is subordinated to its coming to be the-thing-that-it-is, because for him the-thing-that-it-is is itself an ever open and in principle unfinishable process, dependent upon the other-as-respondent. Thus if we speak of the 'being' of the work of art we need to remind ourselves continually that this being is not a state, is not a finished thing, but is always being-becoming-itself. And this being-becoming-itself is most concretely accessible in the very act of reading that constitutes the painting's space in and as time. Klee does not use the conceptual contrast between metaphor and metonymy, although metaphor is a basic constituent of his rhetoric. However it is my suggestion that his sense of the relation between the metaphors that define the fundamental telos of the work of art, those that show it as a metaphor for genesis and formation, and the movement through which these are constructed (itself exemplary of genesis) corresponds closely to the contrast relation between metaphor and metonymy proposed by Jakobson and Halle and used by others in a variety of textual analyses.

Klee's concern with movement in the work thus leads him to develop a way of understanding the relation between the artist, the work and the respondent, that places the metaphor of the work of art in a relation of tension with the metonymic processes through which the metaphor's sense is itself constituted. That is to say, the metonymic practice of reading, through its specific sequence of combinations, successions and associations, leads to and is itself constituted as metaphors for the parts of or the whole of the work. Metonymy is the work of combination whose outcome is a series of metaphors. Ultimately we may locate the significance of the work of art in its power to evoke the mystery of its own creative source, but this, and the subsidiary metaphors, can only be achieved as a matter of practice – the practice of reading as metonymic. The practice here is the necessary temporal movement which makes sense of the space that is the work of art, that space whose constitution or re-constitution takes our time. Just as the artist's work is temporal,

what the beholder does is temporal too. The eye is so organised that it conveys the parts successfully into the crucible of vision and in order to adjust itself to a new fragment has to leave the old one. After a while the beholder, like the artist, stops and goes away. If it strikes him as worthwhile – again like the artist – he returns. In the work of art, paths are laid out for the beholder's eye, which gropes like a grazing beast . . . the pictorial work springs from movement, it is itself fixated movement, and it is grasped in movement (eye muscles) (op.cit., p.78).

The artist's and spectator's work, as movement, are essentially complementary, but although paths are laid for the beholder, the latter preserves an absolute freedom to move along, across and off these paths. This freedom is an essential feature of the viewer's relation to the work for it shows the relation as one grounded in something other than control or domination; the work is an abso-lutely open invitation to share in the possibilities of re-creation, for no matter how the work is organised the artist cannot control the viewer's journey through the work. This provides a way of approaching the distinctions between the life of the image in illus-tration and publicity and the life of the work of art; in the former the illustrator's success depends on the way the respondent can be controlled by the rhetoric of the image, while in the latter it is the respondent's freedom which is celebrated; thus, that the respon-dent can and does find other pathways through the work than those which had the greatest significance for the artist in the course of creating the work, is a confirmation and celebration of the work's openness and the respondent's freedom. Works of art stand in this way as metaphors for non-violence.

The paths laid down by the artist in the course of making the work can influence or persuade the eye to move in one direction or way rather than another, but this persuasion can only work firstly if the respondent's freedom is accepted as a fundamental constitutent of the relation to the work of art, and secondly if the viewer's needs (Desire) find a way of engaging the work's 'rhetoric': 'the eye like a grazing animal, feels out the terrain, not only from top to bottom but also from left to right and in all directions *for which it feels the need*' (op.cit., p.359, my emphasis). Klee points to a variety of pictorial forms which seem to offer qualitatively different relations to the viewer in terms of the way they solicit the eye (op.cit., pp.358–65) and in his analysis provides diagrams which show how such eye work might proceed. The metaphor of the viewer as a grazing animal is sustained in this section as a way of showing the link between movement and the satisfaction of need (Desire). The animal is driven to eat but is free 'to wander anywhere in the pasture' to satisfy that need, and this freedom is activated and practically ordered through taste (style or an affinity for specific kinds of marks).

In an earlier passage Klee has already written of the relation between the organisation of movement and the viewer's freedom in the following terms:

> All figuration is movement because it begins somewhere and ends somewhere. In general the paths of the groping eye are free in space and time; that is, the eye is not compelled to begin at a definite place. Such constraint is imposed only by a particular pattern of movement which lays down very definite paths in a very definite order (op.cit., p.195).

A most obvious example of such a constraint would be the presence in a variety of Klee's own paintings of arrows to denote the direction of a movement; but even here the viewer can suspend the conventional rule governing the significance of a directional arrow and treat it as a mark integral to the relations of marks on the painting's surface. For Foucault, the work of these arrows displays how Klee's work confounds and abolishes the traditional hierarchising of figure and discourse in western painting:

> The gaze encounters words as if they had strayed to the heart of things. . . . Boats, houses, prisms, are at the same time recognisable figures and elements of writing. They are placed and travel upon roads or canals. They are also lines to be read . . . (it is) . . . a question of the intersection, within the same medium of representation by resemblance and of representation by signs (Foucault, 1982, pp.33–4).

Movement and the possibilities of making reference to it are central to Klee's understanding of the creative process and the work of art which is its outcome; for one of the founding tensions of both the creation of the work of art and the respondent's re-creation of it is that between the attempt to constitute a 'whole' (metaphor) and the 'parts' which enter into this attempted constitution. In discussing the temporal character of linear elements in painting, Klee notes that 'Distance is time, whereas a surface is apprehended more in terms of the moment' (1966, p.340). Yet the metaphoric moment in which the painting is somehow 'summed up' can only be arrived at through the metonymic movements through the work and this tension is one of the basic constituents of the work's concrete life. Klee speaks of this movement towards metaphor as a process of gradual integration in the brain of 'successively registered parts' (op.cit., p.358). The character of this process of integration will be specific to every act of viewing and in turn will be bound up with the specifics of each picture; thus one picture might encourage a continuous movement through a 'successive movement of values' while another might provoke leaps through 'strong value contrasts' (op.cit., p.360).

This back and forth between the 'whole' and our movement through is, as already noted, the very function of the picture itself for Klee; he writes of this relation too in describing his own theoretical work (and we must include his paintings as integral to this 'theoretical' work) as 'the organisation of differences into unity, the combination of organs into an organism' (op.cit., p.446). Here the unity sought would be the work as metaphor, while its achievement could only arise through the process of combination (metonymy); the circle is completed when we remember that this unity is always ultimately the unity of a process not a thing, the process of genesis itself: 'The way to form is more important than the goal itself, the end of the road' (1973, p.265). Cézanne's harmony parallel to nature is re-theorised and metaphorically transformed by Klee into both an echo and an exemplification of nature as genesis. In its humanisation of nature as becoming, art, by celebrating this process of becoming in and for itself, naturalises itself; it makes itself absolutely other to both its creator and its re-creator.

In the conjunction of his painting and writing, then, Klee offers us an oeuvre that exemplifies and develops a specific sense of the relation between theory and practice. And it is an exemplification that gathers the fundamental themes of the developing modern tradition and anticipates some of the directions that the tradition was to take after his death. The continuity between the analyses and comments of his notebooks and his own paintings (illustrated in profusion alongside his texts) is remarkable and yet the break between theory and practice is almost always absolute, for only rarely could Klee's painting and drawings be seen as illustrations of a theory. Analysis here is always in the service of painting in so far as it keeps as a central interest the preservation of the mystery of the process of genesis itself – the phenomenon which it is the function of the work of art to metaphorise and evoke; and while the analysis may serve painting it is performed on behalf of a painting which is itself first of all idea or theory. The practice of painting for Klee is permanently implicated with the word – with logos. This implication provides for Klee's elaboration of the relation between the creator and the audience of the work of art as both involved in complementary creative processes, which he metaphorises as a process of reading: 'No one can keep us from insisting that this temporal reading of a kind of pictorial writing be applied to our plane as well' (op.cit., p.83). His interest in the dynamics of the painting and viewing processes and his exploration of the tensions that constitute them provide for the first time in the modern tradition, an analytical ground for painting practice that comprehends the tradition through the tension of metaphor and metonymy. That is, while recognising the firstness of metaphor, Klee also saw that metaphor could only be reached through the work of metonymy; and it is the relation between the two, as the source of a work of art's potential significance, that fascinated Klee and provided the founding impulse of his own work.

In proposing that the modern tradition is above all a theorised tradition, that is a tradition whose members are radically self-conscious of their own relation to and difference from painting of the past and painting from other cultures, I have drawn on the writings of five artists whose own oeuvres (their paintings and their writings), as constitutive 'moments' of the modern tradition, open up a space for that tradition in complementary ways. Their work exemplifies a way of understanding both the relation of the modern tradition to its past and the continuities and synchronous relations that comprise its emergent life; they develop and begin to shape a region for the commitment to modernity. The continuity of the tradition is founded upon commitments to an idea of painting practice that is most directly accessible and vividly articulated in their work.

The wider movements that have contributed to the complexity of the modern tradition cohered around themes that were either articulated by the artists considered here, or were specific to the context and interests of each movement, and had marginal bearing on subsequent internal transformations of the tradition. Thus, for example, while surrealism, in any case an essentially literary movement in its emphasis on automatism and the role of the unconscious, is often cited as providing some of the grounds for the abstract expressionist painters in the 1940s, both Kandinsky and Klee provide clearer anticipations and justifications in both their painting and their writing for the practices of the New York School. Klee, who was marginally associated with the surrealist movement, had understood the value of the artist responding to what came to him or her 'from the deep' and incorporated it into his analyses, recognising the centrality of the unconscious in artistic creation (although his understanding of the unconscious and its role was removed from the Freudianism of the surrealists). And in making central the activity of creation itself as a process in time, Klee anticipated the later concern with 'action' that Rosenberg theorised for the New York School.

All the painters discussed put the implication of art with Language or writing-in-general at the centre of their concerns, either through metaphorising art as Language or through displaying the centrality to painting practice of theorising as an event of Language; and their explorations of the relations between art and Language enabled them to offer a re-vitalised sense of the respondent's relation to the work of art. That the respondent is now explicitly recognised as an active agent constituting and renewing the life of the painting is fundamental to the modern painter's sense of what it is possible for painting to do; it contributes directly to the sense of artistic freedom enjoyed and explored by the painter. Painting as a writing, a writing that unlike linear writing lives through its simultaneous re-presentation of several dimensions of being, depends for its renewal on a respondent-as-reader whose freedom it is to enter the work on any level which begins to satisfy the Desire for the other which art offers.

The sense of Language, and therefore of painting, writing and theorising, that underpins the modern commitment, is both reflexive and rhetorical in its call for an other (the creative respondent) to continue the life of the work. In this sense the writings of modern artists cannot be taken as attempts to explain the significance, or the 'real meaning' of their work, but rather may be seen as essential components of the practical theorising that painting is which write on behalf of a commitment to which specific works of art are the response. They contribute in this sense to the significance of the languaged space within which paintings' lives are possible; the specific features of these lives are dependent upon the relations developed with them by their audience. Modern painting has sought an other as audience who would recover the work of art as an occasion to re-member and re-create the process of creative genesis itself, a process whose telos is the Desire for, the search for, and the celebration-through-representation of its own beginnings.

And now, just as our experience of modernity has required our re-reading of Tradition, so modernity itself is re-inscribed through our emergent reading of post-modernity. If post-modernity says 'no' to modernity, the question is raised, following Bachelard's

'philosophy of "no" ', of the ways that post-modernity must include the modern. We cannot appreciate the significance of the
post-modern pronouncement of modernity's death until we have
tried to establish what, if anything, modernity gained for us and
contributed to post-modernity. For if the latter seeks to establish a
complete break with modernity it is saying that it has learnt nothing
from modern practice, that modernity is no part of its project. If that
is the case we are being returned to the Academy as the site for
work. But if the post-modern includes modernity, as it surely must,
then we cannot establish the difference the post-modern makes
until we recover its sense of the Good of modernity itself, of what it
was (and perhaps still is) to be absolutely modern, of what post-
modernity wishes to preserve within itself of modernity.

But before exploring these issues further the engagement of
Language by modern painting requires further excavation, for the
practical theorising reviewed here has displayed its centrality to the
modern commitment. Perhaps this is what post-modernity shows
that it has learnt from modernity. And it is from within post-
structuralist thought and critical practice that modern painting,
painting-as-writing and as already itself the practical deconstruction
of painting's languages can be re-thought. The following discussions of painting's implication with writing, reading, meaning and
signing provide too for a re-thinking of the critic's, the respondent-
as-writer's relation to the work of art.

The essential question today is no longer that of the *writer* and of the *work* (and even less that of the 'work of art'), but that of *writing* and of *reading*. Consequently we need to find a new space where these two phenomena could be seen as reciprocal and simultaneous, a curved space, a medium of exchanges and reversibility where we could finally be on the same side as our language . . . Writing is linked to a space in which time would have in some way *turned*, in which it would no longer be anything but this circular and generative movement. We might say that writing is genetic, that it is the most peripheral and most central phenomenon. . .

Can we still seriously reproach Mondrian for having done the painting of painting? Webern for having composed the music of music? Giacometti for pursuing only the sculpture of sculpture? No one would venture such insanities any longer, and everyone is well aware that what we still call 'art' henceforth passes through this reversal that places it in another dimension, where in a slight yet nonetheless decisive withdrawal, it lets itself be seen and understood as it sees and understands itself . . .

Writing takes place in and must pass into the ground (fond) of all forms, including those it activates as it writes itself; it must tell what it does even as it does it.

We are continually in the process of reading and writing, in our dreams, our perceptions, our acts, our fantasies, our thought – but we remain unaware of it insofar as we *believe we know how to read and write* . . . are we so sure we weren't taught to no longer know how to read and write *our life* from the day we were told that we knew how to read and write?

(Philippe Sollers, 1983)

5

Painting: Writing

Metaphorising painting as writing creates a double thrust for, in pulling painting directly into the thrall of an apparently utterly conventional practice of Language (writing-as-written-words), it also unhinges this same convention by pushing it towards and confronting it with painting. Neither painting nor writing can remain the 'same' in such a move, for painting could no longer be the outside of Language and writing could no longer be a mere copy of the spoken word. At stake in re-thinking painting's modernity, as the celebratory exploration of its own life in Language, are the very conventions of language use and theory which support both conventional understandings of art and also the structures of everyday practices themselves. Shifting the conceptualisation of these conventions onto the terrain of writing carries in its wake a train of radical consequences for the relation of theory and criticism to their topics, whether painting, art or culture generally. And it is the work of deconstruction that performs this unhinging of writing from its conventional ties.

The tension between the modern and post-modern in art practice and theory is curiously refracted within criticism in the relation between the discourses of the sign (those cross-disciplinary practices centring on the linguistically derived structuralism and semiotics) and what is loosely termed 'post-structuralism'. It is as if these discourses of the sign began to formulate in analytical terms, parallel to but always subsequent to painting and modern practice generally, the kinds of issues which were already at the very heart of the quest for modernity in art. From their base in linguistics (with its attempt to found a science of language) these discourses quickly totalised their field of inquiry to include the whole of culture itself in its differentiation from 'nature'; this programme, taking its sense of the limits of language as its own limits, obviously included the 'social' (all social and cultural phenomena), insofar as this was manifested in 'meaning', in 'significance'. Ferdinand de Saussure inaugurated this totalising impulse in his call for a general semiotics, a general science of signs, whether verbal, visual, kinetic or what-ever (de Saussure, 1959). And in this context, art, aesthetic practice and the aesthetic object, focused issues of Language that were unavoidable for analysis precisely because exploration and ques-tioning defined modern practice, and because this questioning centred on the artists' exploration of the languages of art and the latters' relation to the re-presentation of 'experience', 'life' or 'na-ture'. Art itself had now become a *practical* theorising and celebrat-ing of Language. Even though this practical exploration was entirely in the service of making particular works of art which live only in their absolute concreteness and specificity, the very reflexivity of modern practice, its self-questioning, gave it an exemplary character for the theoretical discourses of the sign. At the level of practice, embedded in the interpretative judgments of the specific works of art and entirely in the service of art, modern artists anticipated the issues that subsequently have been posed as the major dilemmas and problems for the discourses of the sign. And irrespective of whether the latter have actually, in their critical analyses, made the analysis of art central, it is art practice which has already circum-scribed their field of work: 'The poets were there before Saussure' (Hartman, 1980, p.267).

As the radical other to the traditional formulations of science/ analysis/theory/criticism, art has already defined their place of work. At their outside, their limit, and unbeknown to and repressed by these technical discourses, art, weak art, powerless art, in all humility, leads them wherever it goes. And the emergence of post-structuralism, that discourse which recognises itself as *coming after* the discourses of the sign, re-presents that rupture in the life of critical/theoretical practice when this otherness, this firstness of art is realised in its radicality. For post-structuralism treats as its un-avoidable self-defining problem the *quality* of its relation to the aesthetic object, the work of art as text, and takes very seriously the possibility that its own Desire to write and to write about art is so infused with and fascinated by the latter that it can finally establish no principled separation between itself and the object of its Desire – the work of art.

It is in this context that the sense of inter-textuality, discussed earlier, takes on significance, for post-structuralism writes for a critical relation to the work of art which knows that its own texts (and others' texts) are already under the sway of art, that the line between art and criticism, art and life, cannot finally be held because art, its texts, are indeed at work within life, within the general text. Post-structuralist responses to the work of art walk falteringly down this line, knowing themselves to be caught within the folds of the work and acknowledging that there is no final external ground from which the words of criticism can be separated from the words, the writing, the marking, of the work of art. If it has always been a necessary hypothesis of criticism that 'art is not as free-standing as it appears to be' (op.cit., p.233), then post-structuralism opens onto the question of how writing responding to the work of art does and might engage Language, how it desires to display itself, how it re-presents itself and its relation to Language in its response.

This post-structuralist responsive practice has been broached particularly in relation to literature and philosophy through the metaphor of 'deconstruction', which, largely through the exemplary writings of Derrida, gathers neither a method nor its antithesis, but rather a dispersal of writing practices that spiral around the question of limit, that of art, of criticism, and of writing. Deconstruction begins knowing that its work has already been begun within art itself – art as the exploration of its own limits – and that this work is not something which can be delegated to a scientific practice that can only work through an authoritarian control and a methodic distancing of itself from its object of knowledge. It is not so much that 'sign' as concept must be abandoned but rather that the assumptions underwriting its use and application within structuralism and semiotics must be bracketed. And this suspension of its status and its definition of the field of responsive practice is performed in the course of opening out an alternative space for writing where writing itself, the practice of writing, is the question and the limit.

Deconstruction has to dissociate itself from the scientific rationalism that informs the semiotic project, for the latter is unable to make its own writing a question for itself precisely because of its scientific commitment; rather than science, deconstruction associates itself with, finds itself already in the middle of, art, and, in this self-realisation, knows that its relating to the work of art, its own responsive activity, will be engaged in the play of words. It is this very play which, for deconstruction, enacts art's otherness to science, for it re-presents art as always many, as multiple, as fragmented, as heterogeneity. Beginning within art it can never finally escape from it to another site external to it, from which it might seek to contain it. In contrast, science's urge in establishing its own object of knowledge (art as an object *for* science) is to unceasingly map, to subjugate, its object according to its own interests. In echoing Hartman, de Man points to this alternative: 'Poetic writing is the most advanced and refined mode of deconstruction: it may differ from critical or discursive writing in the economy of its articulation, but not in kind' (de Man, 1979, p.17).

It is this entwinement of deconstructive practice with art, with writing, that requires a suspension of the senses of the sign that found the analytical practices of structuralism and semiotics, for the sign can no longer be foundational for writing practice in the way that it has been for the analytical discourses. Hartman, going back to the linguistic origins of the discourses of the sign, points us to what is at issue in re-thinking the possibilities of a critical relation to the work of art:

> Yet linguistics from the point of view of literature, is not a
> transcending form of analysis that orders all things well and
> leaves nothing over. It is a burdensome technical discipline
> seeking to master knowledge through knowledge. It creates a
> further set of terms or distinctions, that put new pressure on us,
> as if we had eaten again of the tree of knowledge. What is to be
> done with this superadded consciousness, these supersessive
> terms? Science may correct wrong ideas or remove vulgar
> superstitions; yet nothing, so it seems, can purify language by
> substituting for it an absolute diction. Though the scientific or
> mystical aspiration towards one language of Adamic or
> Universal character, crops up in every era, historically we inherit
> only the language trajectory of this purifying desire, a residue
> called literature that both represents and belies it (Hartman,
> 1980, p.142).

If linguistics and subsequently structuralism and semiotics gather themselves, as they have, under the metaphor of science, they write on behalf of a technical version of the purified language, the project for the one language, that could finally say Language, say art, say culture, say meaning, in the name of science. In pointing to the mythic ground of this hope for a universal language of pure knowledge, of Language, of Being itself, Hartman reminds us not only of its ultimate delusion but also that literature, that art, as Tradition, has already shown itself as Desire for purity, in its continuous manifestations of Language engaged in that impossible search for itself. But art's Desire seeks to show through its own work that it, art, is purely Language, and that Language is pure multiplicity, the pure possibility of heterogeneity. There is no gathering here under 'one', under some version of a final absolute 'saying', or a first principle, an 'a priori'; rather art is the keeping open of otherness. Discourses of the sign can only exceed themselves, become post-structuralist, through a radical equivocation of their commitment both to science and the sign which would place their own signing practices into question. Such a questioning would turn precisely on the status, the region, of critical writing as sign, of the sign as writing. If deconstruction is the work that has to begin this questioning that turns back on its own writing, it does so already from within the multiplicity of art, from a sharing and a showing of art's concern, knowing that the alternatives always end up doing some kind of violence to art in their attempts to subdue it through their versions of methodic control. It is precisely this sense of authoritarian control that was so carefully avoided in the discursive justifications of the painters reviewed earlier.

And yet post-structuralism and deconstruction are defined precisely in their relation to structuralism, to the analysis of signifying practices and structures and in no sense are they an abandonment of the sign. It is not, for deconstruction, a question of erasing structuralism and the sign and replacing them with a new method, an alternative set of concepts, but rather the necessity of re-thinking the sign from within writing which has been repressed not only in the discourses of the sign but also within the western philosophical tradition itself. This opening up of writing turns on the work of showing the discourses of the sign as founded upon a conception of the latter that privileges the spoken word, its apparent 'presencing' of the speaking subject, over other kinds of sign which are seen as derivative or secondary signs, at a distance from the presence of the speaking human subject to itself. This 'metaphysics of presence' works through an 'inside-outside' conception of Language. In this, following Saussure's formulation, the signs constituting a chain of speech or writing are made up of signifiers (words, sounds) that always point beyond themselves and *outside language* to their signifieds (things, ideas, images, concepts). The referent, the other of the signifier as bearer, is always a present thing, an extra-linguistic presence, transcendent of Language. It is this hypothesis of the transcendental signified, fundamental to the discourses of the sign, that meaning, significance, is *finally outside Language*, which requires deconstruction. And this has to be done from within a strategy of writing and reading that constantly equivocates, ambiguates, the textual practices that gain their security from their grounding principle, the hypothesis of absolute origin, and their particular hypostatisation of a 'presence' transcendent of Language; for every such presence turns out to be a signifier in a further chain of signifiers.

Deconstructive work seeks to open us to the ways that texts themselves provide for their own deconstruction in their very excessiveness. Every text through its figuration, its troping, its inability to erase the possibility of alternative interpretations, will always have exceeded its own founding assumptions. It is the play of Language itself, of writing, which already subverts the possibility of an absolute reading, a text's attempt to legislate for a correct reading. Now if this strikes at the heart of philosophical thought, practice and writing, in its absolute withdrawal from the possibility of securing truth through method, and in its radicalisation of interpretation, it also shows itself as a work, a practice of reading and writing, that approaches and shares with art practice the engagement of multiplicity, of openness, of Language's constitutivity.

As neither analysis, criticism, nor art, deconstruction seeks to share with art the space-in-between, to be the hyphen, that works constantly through and in its difference, performing a practice of reading-writing that follows and recovers what is already at work in the text: 'The incision of deconstruction . . . can be made only according to lines of force and forces of rupture that are localizable in the discourse to be deconstructed' (Derrida, 1981, p.82). Knowing, as Derrida says, that this work of deconstruction is engaged in producing, in practising, a new 'concept' of writing (op.cit., p.6), this very work takes it 'close' to artistic practice. It finds the engagement of writing already at work in art – the search for a new siting that constitutes itself as modernity. Derrida's readings of Bataille, Blanchot, Mallarmé and Sollers, for example, attend not only to the ways that literature has opened up issues such as re-presentation and mimesis, conventionally regarded as the preserve of philosophy, but also to the exemplary quality of their questioning of the practice of writing (Derrida, 1978b, 1979, 1982). And in attending to their example Derrida's own writing itself displays what it has learned from writers whose work exemplifies modernity's self-questioning through its engagement of Language. In hovering between art and analysis his writing shows the Good of art for analysis. This intervention in analytical practice, in philosophy, shows what analysis stands to gain from art:

> it is incontestable that certain texts classed as 'literary' seemed to me to operate breaches or infractions at the most advanced points, Artaud, Bataille, Mallarmé, Sollers. . . . These texts operate in their very movement, their demonstration and practical deconstruction of the *representation* of what was done with literature, it being well understood that long before these 'modern' texts a certain 'literary' practice was able to operate

against this model, against this representation . . . certain texts
. . . seemed to mark and to organise a structure of resistance to
the philosophical contextuality that allegedly dominated or
comprehended them (Derrida, 1981, p.69).

It is in this context that the relation between art work and art
criticism pointed to by de Duve has to be re-thought. While the
discourses of the sign have spawned a variety of analyses of modern
painting they have all preserved just that kind of analytical distance
between themselves and the work of art recommended by the rule
of method, by scientificity, which deconstruction puts into question
on behalf of another sense of writing. Just as we can now only think
the histories of modernity from within post-modernity, the sign's
possibilities in theorising art can only be considered through the
post-structuralist text. And the shifts in practice into the post-
scripts, the after-words, of modernity and structuralism are closely
inter-related.

If painting seems to have drifted out of focus here it is only in
preparation for better showing the ways that painting, writing and
Language mutually enfold each other. The inter-relationships between painting, writing, reading and signing are considered now
from the point of view of the practice of painting, from painting's
inside, and this is at the same time to open up a region, to show an
alternative sense of modernity to that of both formalist and vanguardist criticism.

The painter's signature in the corner of the painting, while not
ubiquitous, is a familiar enough feature in the tradition of western
European painting; such cryptic texts, sometimes accompanied by a
date, are taken as authentications of the work of art in the double
sense of affirming the identity of the painter by displaying a name
through a personal calligraphy. These signatures are as instantly
recognisable as their author's styles. But perhaps our very familiarity with this practice of identification and its obvious relevance in the
art-historical context of authentication has obscured an other significance. The signature, as a linear text, concretely exemplifies the
implication of painting with Language, for it puts the word into
painting in the most literal way. And as, since the renaissance and
up to the emergence of the modern tradition, space in painting has
been the play of illusory perspectival space, at the least the signature's assertion of the flat picture plane served to remind us of what
we already knew very well – that the space was indeed a constructed
space, the site of an illusion, and not a reproduction of the world as
'it really was' outside the painting. The signature faces us with the

paradox that the painting's image lies behind or beneath the signature, while the latter at the same time lies within that same image; in our act of reading the signature this apparently mundane convention affirms that the painting is other to the world and that the word is within, is already part of the image.

Thus when Picasso and Braque introduce words and letters into their Cubist paintings and collages, apparently inaugurating the practice of inter-relating texts and images, we have, perhaps without recognising it, already been prepared for this by our familiarity with the convention of signing. As with the signature these texts, and those that followed in the work of artists as concretely different as Duchamp, Schwitters, Klee, Magritte, de Kooning, Johns, Twombly, Kosuth, Beuys, Broodthaers and Kiefer, may seem to offer themselves initially as information. But such information in the context of a painting is always problematic precisely because of the ever-open need for the viewer's active interpretation of the relations between visual images and literal texts. It is this relation itself which, irrespective of the concrete information offered by either the literal or visual image, is always the interpretative problem, because it faces us with two kinds of signing practice which appear divorced from each other. It was precisely this separation which, as noted earlier, Foucault claimed that Klee had confounded in his painting.

Now if there are already linear phonetic texts 'in' paintings which raise the issue of writing's relation to painting, and if painting is 'in' Language, then *painting itself* may be the bridge across the void between linear writing and Language. It may be the very region within which writing's difference comes to reveal itself, and this possibility can be approached through putting a variety of inter-related metaphors into play.

Through the writings of the painters reviewed earlier painting was shown as a specific kind of practical theorising holding Language and world together in and through a relation to Language, and each painting, metaphorised as text, through its particular display, makes these relations possibilities for others, for those who Desire to engage it. But if painting as a practical theorising produces texts it is not only text; each work carries a surplus to which its text points and which shows its difference to all other texts. For painting the nature of that surplus is to be located in the specific ways that our seeing always seems to mean and know more than can be said in so many words. We speak of the visible but its plenitude always recedes from speech's or writing's grasp; we feel that we can know and name the visible world but its very visibility is always more than any text or sum of texts can say because it is the space within which we see; it contains all texts, but Language also contains all texts, so we need to recognise the way Language spaces, the way Language is in space and space in Language. An exploration of the relation between painting and writing offers a way of reading the relation of space and language.

Seeing, as an active making of meaning, a relating to a world, makes space foundational to the meaning of self's relation to other and world. It makes space for meaning. Our being together in space, the relations of nearness and farness, to the horizon and to the space we physically displace, is visibly organised in essential ways through the life of light and the interaction of colours, where this latter names a fundamental dimension of our opening on to the world. The world's availability is possible through the metaphors for light, its source and absence, that every culture rests upon. Thus it might be argued that, since the en*light*enment, in Western society, science as knowledge has been a dominant metaphor for light. That seeing always already means, and *is* relating, that we visibly relate to other and to the world through the colours that light makes available, where these colours themselves make reference to the unseeable source of light that makes them possible, makes the life of painting possible. And here the metaphor of light as source metaphorises Language itself as that which brings things to light. Painting's duality, then, pointing us both towards the world's visibility as lighted text and back towards Language as source, holds the two, Language and light, as one.

The critical issue in inter-relating painting and Language through writing is that of the difference between speech, writing as we know it, and, writing-in-general. Phonocentrism is the assumption, implicit or explicit, that the concrete origin of Language is to be found in the voice, in the moment of speech, and that writing as a subsequent and derivative emergence is a corruption of the fundamental character of Language as speech. Writing in this conventional view detracts from the primacy of living speech in which Language is said to have its original and authentic life; to show painting as sharing in this authenticity it would have to be metaphorised as speech (as it often is in art-critical writing) and not writing. And yet writing and painting open up the question of Language's relation to space in a way which speech cannot, for both reading a text and responding to a painting involve visibility itself: they engage space. But preserving speech as the only origin, as 'presence' itself, occludes the possibility of full presence for any other mode of being, whilst failing to 'account for' the necessity of space to Language. Where speech is preserved as the metaphor for painting, where criticism confuses speech with writing, this fatally weakens the power of the Language metaphor, for it brings us up sooner or later against the assumption which founds it, that Language has its 'origin', its 'real' life, in the 'living presence' of the voice, and that other dimensions of Language such as writing are derivative. This assumption would clearly locate painting as just such a derivative practice which must always ultimately depend upon and be subservient to speech.

Against this the possibility is explored that painting and writing are intimately inter-twined, and that writing (and thus painting) has always already been inscribed in the very possibility of Language. Preserving speech's firstness, by displaying a phonocentrism typical of the western philosophical tradition, raises the voice over the gesture or image and prevents us from recognising the possibility of the body's constituting work in textualising our own coming-to-be in Language. The inscription of human being-in-the-world 'through' the marks that trace the body's gestures as already a proto-writing implicates writing with Language, and thus, by affinity, painting with Language from the beginning.

And perhaps it would be better at this juncture to say 'writing-in-general' as Derrida does, rather than that system of writing which we know and practise, for when we are considering the very possibility of Language itself and its coming-to-be as writing-in-general, we must not replace phonocentrism with an ethnocentrism that treats all forms of writing as lesser or derivative forms of our own linear phonetic system of writing. It is not my concern, nor is it that of Derrida either, to locate some concrete historical origin of Language which would answer what are the impossible questions of when, where and how being-in-the-world as a possibility of Language 'arose'. Talk of origins, beginnings and priorities relates not to a given concrete occurrence, but rather to the requirement for the possibility of Language opening the space for relationality, for being-in-the-world in the first place (where the 'first place' names *that which has always already taken place*.) Every text or speech is a display, a re-presentation, of origin. There can be no 'presencing' of origin, only re-presentations.

As the sense of the relation between Language, writing and painting which is developed here is informed by and indebted to the work of Derrida (see especially 1968, 1973, 1974, 1976, 1978a, 1978b, 1979,-1981, 1982) the following remarks may show the importance of his work to the unfolding of the painting-writing relation. Although his general interests may seem to be at some distance from painting, I want to show how his founding concerns and the play of his writings offer a way of seeing painting's fundamental relation with

Language. The difficulty of his writing, which stems in part from its reflexive character (it is about the very practice that Derrida is himself engaged in) should not be allowed to detract from its importance and relevance to understanding the ways in which the work of art signifies.

Writing out of the phenomenological tradition, his work circles around perennial philosophical issues and, in particular, what he understands as the 'metaphysics of presence'. For Derrida, every western philosophical tradition rests upon and has had to make assumptions about being, about the 'presence' of the phenomena it inquires into; in order to carry out its analytical work each philosophy in some way 'fixes' presence through a, usually hidden, metaphor. In recent philosophy these hidden metaphors fixing presence have typically referred to the thinking subject, to some rendering of the Cartesian ego, as a thinking subject that strives to be fully self-present to itself in the act of thought (exemplified by philosophical reflection itself). It is part of Derrida's thesis that the particular senses of presence which each philosophy relies upon typically involve phonocentrism; that is to say, the absolute self-presence of the subject to itself, the point beyond which philosophical reflection cannot go in its analysis of conscious being, is invariably located in the act of speaking. The closest the thinking being gets to absolute self-presence is in the act of speaking; it is in this sense that the voice is given an ontological primacy in these 'metaphysics of presence'. They are metaphysical in that they rest upon hidden assumptions, unexplicated metaphors offered as absolutes, which fix being itself and allow for the construction of a philosophical edifice which gives a specific form to being as it is erected upon these metaphorical grounds. Each fixing of being offers, then, a version of origin, of what is 'first', of that which philosophy cannot go beyond in its search for knowledge. This absolute point is the fixing of being as a particular sense of presence for each philosophy.

Now Derrida's concern is to step back from any such hypostatisation of being or presence and to explore the hidden metaphors which make fixing possible and necessary for every discourse. His writing is thus elusive and difficult to engage precisely because it is on the move and is seeking to avoid the undisclosed theses of origins which pull discourses back into the realm of metaphysics. As it is 'presence' itself which is the fundamental hidden metaphor of the tradition, his writing is an explicitly metaphorical attempt to display the way in which thinking-as-writing might proceed without such attributions of presence.

Central to his critique of presence is the term (not yet a concept) – 'differance' – a neologism holding together the meanings of both 'differing' and 'deferring' (Derrida, 1973). In the context of Language, for example, speech may be a means for differentiating some thing from Nature, bringing it from the realm beyond meaning into meaning; Language as speech makes the difference between Nature and meaning or significance, it differs the phenomenon from its origin in absolute otherness. Speech here seems to desire to represent the thing-in-itself in Language, to differ it completely from its site outside Language and bring it to full presence within Language. But for Derrida this desire to re-present the phenomenon in its full presence is an impossibility, so that the very movement of the speech which seeks to grasp phenomena 'in themselves' can only be approached as a paradox; and this is where the sense of 'deferring' in 'differance' comes into play. For each act of differing, of bringing some thing out of nothing into meaning, is also necessarily a putting off, a delaying, a lacking. In this continuous process of deferral it is the 'thing-in-itself' which is forever deferred, never achieving full presence in speech; on the one hand, the phenomena can only come into being, into meaning, in our signifying practices through which we differ them both from that absolutely other realm outside of meaning, and also concretely from each other within the system of differences that texts enact and live within, while on the other hand the full presence of these phenomena is continually deferred. Language is that differing/deferring which gives phenomena their only real life while withholding it and them fully from us.

If the coming to 'presence' of any phenomenon in Language is constituted as a re-presenting of the 'thing-in-itself' from beyond Language, this suggests that every origin in Language is always a repetition of some thing which has always already been. And yet, and here the paradox deepens, that which has always already been could not have the simple status of a present that has gone past, a past present, for that would require an absolute origin, something that was absolutely given to us in full presence in Language, and this is precisely what Derrida seeks to step away from. There can only ever be representation; and this has fundamental implications for the post-modern stance. In offering us this paradox for approaching the coming-to-be of meaning in Language his writing works through a sense of Language that places metaphor at the very centre of its life, for every re-presentation of phenomena in and through writing or speech in Language is fundamentally metaphoric. Metaphor is not here founded on some ultimate and absolutely firm sense of the literal or real, but rather what we understand as the literal lives in and through the space and work of metaphor. The presencing which is a re-presencing is a movement of metaphor bringing some 'thing' from one realm into another and holding the two together in its creative con-fusing, while holding them apart at the same 'moment' through its deferring work. We might say that Language 'languages' through metaphor.

Now this movement away from 'presence' towards metaphor, enabled by the metaphor of 'differance' itself, also moves us away from the voice's primacy, of speaking and hearing as the origination of meaning, towards writing as 'writing-in-general'. The bracketing of 'presence' itself and the proposal that what we are faced with is the perennial deferral of presence through a relay of metaphors, also raises the issue of relation and this is crucial for the work of art. Relation, as that which holds two beings together and apart, is clearly nothing positive, but rather an empty fullness hiding Nothing with something that is no-thing, for without a sense of relation a sensible world would be incomprehensible. So, works of art and deconstruction, as the exploration and celebration of relation through their equivocation of our empirical assertions about the presence of things, open us to the metaphoricity of Being. Through confronting the illusions of literalism we are thrown into the play of writing itself.

Relation then (like the work of art) is never fully present, and is always deferred through metaphors for its presence. Whenever the presence of a work of art is asserted, its 'thereness', we need to consider the metaphors which are used to show this presence; for this showing is not a capturing of the work-in-itself but rather a display of the writer's metaphoric relation to the work – it is the constitution of that relation itself in and through metaphor. Thus the critic, Kozloff, says of some of the early paintings of Frank Stella: 'These pictures were so palpably "there", in one's own space, that their expressive opacity was all the more intolerable. For paintings so aggressive in their presence, there seemed to be surprisingly little visual material to work with' (Kozloff, 1970, p.266). Here the metaphors for the paintings' attributes, their palpable thereness, expressive opacity and aggressive presence, are, from within the sense of presence and relation offered here, rather metaphors for the writer's constitution of a relation with them; as phenomena that are not things but works of art they are represented, textualised, in this specific metaphor through which the respondent evolves a relation with them, and this is a process which turns them typically from nothing into something, into things of a particular kind (aggressive and so on). The specifics of their thingness are nothing other than the construction of relation itself. The painting is a space inviting the play of differences, a play which can be engaged by another through the marks which, precisely as such play, refuse presence; the movement of engaging the painting by the respondent is the constitution of metaphors for and in this play.

The phonetic writing and the phonetic alphabet which western culture inhabits are bound by definition to speech. Derrida's thesis is that this specific form of writing, phonetic writing with its serial character, is taken by philosophy and the social sciences to be the model for all writing, for what he calls 'writing-in-general', and it is precisely this 'privilege of the phoné' (Derrida, 1977, p.7.) that he opposes. But the phonetic model of writing, he proposes, remains an unrealisable ideal, for *no writing* can ever be the simple exteriority of interiority (speech). This is so because even phonetic writing relates to speech through a double absence, the absence not only of the referent (which it shares with speech) but also the absence of the signatory (op.cit., p.40). Pure phonetic writing, a writing that reproduces speech in the form of writing, for Derrida 'does not exist' (op.cit., p.39) because no practice of writing can remain faithful to the phonetic principle. This infidelity he locates precisely in writing's excess, or surplus, over speech; he says of writing's infidelity to the phonetic model:

> one can also remark its massive phenomena in mathematical
> script or in punctuation, in *spacing* in general, which it is difficult
> to consider as simple accessories of writing. That a speech
> supposedly alive can lend itself to spacing in its own writing, is
> what relates it originarily to its own death (ibid.).

Far from being reproduced in phonetic writing through a simple exteriorisation, speech faces its own death in the 'spacing' which makes writing possible. Spacing in writing, pointed to in the gaps between letters and words, punctuation, symbols for space, and so on, is not a simple mirror of the temporal gaps between the sounds of speech. Writing can never be faithful to speech because it lives, as speech dies, through spacing. Writing, as Derrida points out in his discussion of Saussure, can thus never be an 'image' or 'representation' of the spoken language because the phoneme is 'the *unimaginable* itself, and no visibility can *resemble* it' (op.cit., p.45); the grapheme, the mark in a system of phonetic writing, can have no 'iconic' relation to its phoneme.

Spacing, then, defines writing as inscription but it has a curious quality for it is an image of nothing; we cannot formulate spacing as a sign or signs because it has no signified, no referent; it is always itself absence:

> Spacing . . . is always the unperceived, the non-present, and the non-conscious. . . . Arché-writing as spacing cannot occur as such within the phenomenological experience of a *presence*. It marks the *dead-time* within the presence of the living-present, within the general form of all presence. The dead time is at work (op.cit., p.68).

And yet, although, as Mallarmé puts it, the place 'where the "whites" indeed take on an importance' has no presence, it is always at work; in the context of painting we can think very concretely here of the way 'white' may be read as a signifier of a 'full emptiness'. In drawing, the 'white' space which surrounds the marks of a pen, pencil or inscribing instrument is both presence and absence. The same might be said of the 'empty' spaces in Cézanne's late paintings, or, taken to its apparent limits, of the history of 'all-white' paintings from Malevich to Rauschenberg and Ryman, which can be read, among other things, as metaphors for the work of spacing itself – white as an absent present in the emergence of significance itself. And by a reversal, black as the absolute other of white, Reinhardt's 'black' paintings signify that empty plenitude necessary for the emergence of spacing itself: the positive absence of a space before spacing.

Perhaps too all those forms of painting referred to as 'expression-ist' also raise a similar issue, for expressionism is often articulated as the exteriorising of an interior state in a way similar to the way writing is shown as an exteriorisation of speech in the phonocentric model. But the painting itself, this supposed exteriorisation, this 'expression', is always absolutely independent of the inner state to which it is a response. The painting is always an excess over the internal state; in the very work of spacing that painting a picture involves is carried at the same time the death of the 'inner state' that is 'expressed'. The resulting work of art is absolutely other to the inner state. Painting, like writing, can never be 'faithful' to the inner feeling because its life as the coming-to-be of spacing is the absolute other to interiority (speech, thought, feeling and so on). It is the very dichotomy itself of interior and exterior which is equivocated if we carry Derrida's analysis through on to the terrain of painting. We can no longer think of expression as a simple process of something being pushed out, but rather have to see it as the institution of another kind of life whose relation to the 'inner', always assuming that we can locate this inner space, is absolutely problematic. Expression can no longer be an iconic rendering of some prior given state – the re-creation of a prior creation, the re-presenting of a past presence. Spacing is, then, that which, precisely as lack, as the absence of a presence (the living speaker), gives writing and indeed presence itself its possibility. In developing the sense of painting's implication with writing-in-general the transposition of the work of spacing to painting is crucial at the most general level. The work of spacing points us to the ways that painting's marks are tied to Language as writing-in-general. It also begins to reveal the weaknesses of the critical use of the metaphor of painting as speech rather than writing. However the western system of phonetic writing is only one form within writing-in-general, which would include the pictographic, the hieroglyphic and the ideographic, so that these systems of writing when taken together require a general concept, what Derrida calls the 'graphie' or the unit of a possible graphic system, and this, in its turn, 'implies the framework of the *instituted trace*, as the possibility common to all systems of signification' (op.cit., p.46). Thus writing-in-general points to the need for the 'trace' which would be the very possibility of the durable institution of a sign and which would also include speech as the arena where the sign's durability is practically instituted and affirmed. The possibility of writing and speaking is regionalised through the instituted trace, the possibility of sign as duration of the same.

Trace is, then, nothing 'real', nothing positive, it is not a mark, natural sign or index, *it is the movement of differance itself*. If the sign of phonocentric writing is unmotivated, if the relation of signifier to signified is absolutely arbitrary as Saussure argued, then the other, the signified or referent (i.e. the world the sign seems to show as beyond itself), is 'announced as such' (op.cit., p.47). The trace is where this relationship with the other as absolutely other is formed, for it is, as neither natural nor cultural, the becoming-unmotivated of the sign, out of which the oppositions emerging in the metaphysics of presence are derived. The science of the operation of the trace is what Derrida institutes as 'grammatology'; it is the 'science of writing before speech' (op.cit., p.51). In some ways, then, Derrida turns round the problem as I have formulated it earlier for, in grammatology, the question is not how writing as text might be the concretisation of Language but rather 'how language is a possibility founded on the general possibility of writing' (op.cit., p.52).

Perhaps this introduction to Derrida's discussion of the trace as 'differance' has taken us far enough to open up a space for a specific kind of association between painting, writing and Language, the possibilities of which have already been alluded to in the concept of 'writing-in-general' which includes not only phonetic writing, but, as noted, pictographic and ideographic writing. And indeed Derrida himself provides for this very possibility.

In his reading of Saussure he shows that for Saussure's linguistics with its phonocentrism there is no figurative writing (op.cit., p.32). As long as writing keeps some kind of natural figuration through resemblance to what it represents it is not yet writing for Saussure; writing only emerges for Saussure, and therefore for linguistics, structuralism and semiotics too, when the relation of resemblance is replaced by the unmotivated sign:

> the concept of pictographic or natural writing would therefore be contradictory for Saussure. If one considers the now recognised fragility of the notions of the pictogram, ideogram etc., and the uncertainty of the frontiers between so-called pictographic, ideographic, and phonetic scripts, one realises . . . the unwiseness of the Saussurian limitation (op.cit., pp.32–3).

Derrida wants to re-open the sense of writing to include those forms of marking which began as relations of resemblance to what was represented, most obvious in the case of pictographic script; his concern is as much with that form of writing that 'speaks its meanings pluri-dimensionally' (op.cit., p.85) where meaning is not 'subjected to successivity, to the order of a logical time, or to the irreversible temporality of sound' (ibid.). We can immediately recognise painting as one such pluri-dimensional site of meaning. In fact, in his subsequent discussion of Rousseau, Derrida notes that for the latter the first writing is the pictogram – a painted image or representation of an image – which, as a natural writing, is the only universal writing (op.cit., p.283), for the diversity of scripts 'appears from the moment the threshold of pure pictography is crossed'. Pictography, as resemblance, preserves one sign per thing and is the least 'economical' form of writing, whereas the hieroglyph, in which picture and character come together, depends on the fact that only a single figure is used to 'signify several things'. Writing pushes painting into absolute insignificance, preserving it only as a subliminal trace, a lost memory, in the 'analysis' and 'rationality' 'proper to the alphabet and to civil society.' Here we find 'Absolute anonymity of the representer, and absolute loss of the self-same' (op.cit., p.92). By reversal and by extrapolating from Derrida we may say that the original work of painting, which made the pictogram possible, stood for the absolute primacy of the representation itself as the painted mark or set of marks and for the faithfulness of the image represented in and for itself: in the 'beginning' was the painting and the painting was both in-itself and for the other. Derrida himself says,

> There was a natural universality of a sort in the most archaic degree of writing: Painting, as much as the alphabet, is not tied to any determined language. Capable of reproducing all sensible being, it is a sort of universal writing. But its liberty with reference to languages is due not to the distance which separates painting from its model but to the imitative proximity which binds them. Under a universal appearance, painting would thus be perfectly empirical, multiple, and changeful like the sensory units that it represents outside of any code. By contrast, the ideal universality of a phonetic writing is due to its infinite distance with respect to the sound (the primary signified of that writing which marks it arbitrarily) and to the meaning signified by the spoken word. Between these two poles universality is lost, I say between these two poles since, as I have confirmed, pure pictography and pure phonography are two ideas of reason. Ideas of pure presence: in the first case, presence of the represented thing in its perfect imitation, and in the second, the self-presence of speech to itself. *In both cases* the signifier tends to be effaced in the signified (op.cit., p.301, my emphasis).

What Derrida faces us with here is the opposition of two 'ideal' poles: on the one hand the perfect empiricism of a universal painting language that would achieve pure representation, that would capture the 'things-in-themselves', and on the other hand the absolutely phonetic writing, a writing that was a pure representation of speech. But both remain fictions, or rather they are 'ideas of reason' and not achieved or achievable practices, for both rest on the need for pure presence, on the need for the absolute effacement of the signifier by the signified. And because we already know in the case of painting, as indeed painting itself knows and has always known, that such a pure presence is always its other, we can say that from 'the beginning' painting has always been performed in the acknowledgment of the impossibility of absolute representation; and this would include the moments of *trompe l'oeil* and super-realism. To say this is also to say that every form of figuration, of resemblance, of naturalism, has owed its life to its other, what we might term its 'abstract', qualities. In the absence of full presence painting has always worked through transformation of the 'things themselves' into their other; all painting is thus metaphor – it is and is not the thing it represents. Resemblance is the re-sembling, the constituting and transforming work of metaphor.

By extension, we can note that the recognition that painting owes its metaphoric life to its 'abstract' qualities has been one of the central themes of the modern tradition. While painting may always have known this inchoately, only in the modern tradition has this theme been an explicit and central topic of the theories of artistic practice; the writings of painters across the range of modern movements offer a diversity of metaphors for their commitment to the primacy of 'abstraction'. And this is so for all kinds of contemporary work, both figurative and non-figurative. Although non-figurative painting, commonly called 'abstract', by definition does not seek a relation of resemblance to specific and concrete phenomena in the world, it still represents; its images re-present, are metaphors for, an enormous range of subject matter, such as our experiences of and response to time, space, change, identity, difference, possession, loss, the sublime, the abyss and so on. Through its images, its content, all art represents, though it may not resemble.

Because painting's re-presenting is not a 'pure representation' but metaphor, when writers on art or painters themselves claim that particular works of art reveal something 'in itself', the 'essence' of a thing, or a 'primary structure', as if these were the bedrock of being, then each concept should be heard as a metaphor rather than a claim for a work's literal description; thus the English artist, Kenneth Martin, working broadly within the constructivist and kinetic traditions says, 'By arriving at the primary structures of forms and acts, one approaches an understanding, a consciousness, of that of our own make-up' (Martin, 1975, p.23). 'Primary structure' here is a metaphor for the artist's limit; the work of art marks the furthest point attainable in the artist's work to metaphorise the relation between being and consciousness as a certain inscription. Such terms are not, in other words, independent of the specific features of the artist's own relation to the phenomena in question; they represent that relation and not the 'thing-in-itself'.

Painting, as metaphor, then transforms things into their other, and it is this other which is gathered here as the language(s) of painting, as proto-writing, each moment of which makes reference back to its possibility in writing-in-general. This writing circumscribes everything we may designate as inscription, a metaphor which represents being-as-writing; writing, for Derrida, moves to replace or stand for Language, for all those activities for which Language has been a common metaphor:

Now we tend to say 'writing' for all that and more: to designate not only the physical gestures of literal pictographic or ideographic inscription, but also the totality of what makes it possible; and also, beyond the signifying face, the signified face itself. And thus we say 'writing' for all that gives rise to an inscription in general, whether it is literal or not and even if what it distributes in space is alien to the order of the voice: cinematography, choreography, of course, but also pictorial, musical, sculptural 'writing'. . . . All this to describe not only the system of notation secondarily connected with these activities but the essence and the content of these activities themselves (Derrida, 1976, p.9).

In this passage Derrida concretely distinguishes the 'literal' pictographic inscription, which we regard as a primitive writing, from pictorial writing, the writing of the work of art, but gathers them both together under inscription which finds its sense, as does Language, in writing-in-general. And we have already seen that every writing concretely recognisable in the mark has always been already begun in the instituted trace; the mark, as a representation, refers back to the trace which, as the formation of form, has never been present. Thus, for example, what we refer to as the expression on someone's face is the mark (the signifier) of a 'meaning' (the signified) which is already the very possibility of writing itself; our body is a gesturing that de-scribes its own being in space. Here de-scribing is paradoxically both an originary constituting or inscribing of that being and, at the same time, a pointing behind itself to its other, its possibility in the trace which is always already writing. Each painting, then, is an inscription which de-scribes and re-presents the passage from the absent trace, the formation of form, to the mark, the coming-to-be of meaning, significance in the mark. And this mark is, as with every mark, both an originary inscription and a secondary re-presenting where what it re-presents is the trace or differance, which in its differing and deferring movement both brings phenomena into their being in the system of differences that Language provides and, at the same time, perenially defers their full presence as things. Every 'moment' in the language of painting is a metaphor for this double life, the life that is both original and derivative, both itself as mark and its other as trace. Insofar as the painting, as mark, is always between two ideal poles of pure representation of the thing and pure representation of speech, and insofar as painting *has always already known this*, then painting can perhaps be written of as originary concrete writing, the

118

writing before the pictograph. It holds within itself and re-presents the tension between these two movements whilst eschewing a commitment to either, for *its* commitment is precisely to hold, to question and to celebrate that very tension. Painting is here a proto-writing, a *first* writing, a writing before writing that, as a display of the body's possibilities as gesture, re-presents the future of writing within itself.

The gesture of painting, as it has been variously lived in the modern tradition, constitutes a form of re-presentation which is other to that of words, of verbal images, as we conventionally live within and use them; and yet it is nevertheless intimately inter-twined with the originating and the continuing life of Language, metaphorised as the inscription of Being, as writing-in-general. We can still preserve painting as other than the word because word is typically bound in our culture to the phonocentric view of Language and writing; and it is a feature of the word as sign that it is absolutely conventional. Words signify because there is a silent contract that preserves the relative stability of their meanings. Words not only provide for repetition; they have their very life in and as repetition. Now if the word as repetition is contrasted with the painting, perhaps we can see the gesture of painting as re-collecting the origins of re-presentation itself, a beginning that has already begun in and as repetition: the modern tradition as an archaeology of (re-)marking.

Although painting as re-presentation is already a marking which is both originary and secondary, it stands for the Desire to be absolutely in-and-for-itself. It is central to its life to seek its own unrepeatability. It marks *for* that moment of re-presentation before it has laid itself open to and become repetition, where image and mark have not yet been held apart by a *logic* of representation (see Derrida, 1978b, p.240). The gesture of the mark signifies before it has been held by the web of convention that signs apparently require; it is thus a signifier before signification as we know it has been instituted, and so opens the way for repetition while preserv-ing itself from it: 'is not a mark wherever it is produced, the possibility of writing?' (Derrida, 1976, p.302). Style in painting reminds us of this, for while each mark is particular, concrete and unique, at the same time it refers us back to that no-thing that it repeats – the painter's bodily institution of the possibility of signifi-cance itself.

Painting's always primitive gesture, then, is to institute and point to the possibility of re-presentation as repetition; it is re-presentation as it were, before the pictograph, the hieroglyph, the ideogram, or the phonetic alphabet; it is a writing of the hand before handwriting that writes on behalf of what always already came before it – the trace, while handwriting is deliberately forgetful of the trace and writes on behalf of that which follows it – its referent or signified. The very openness of painting, the way it requires its reader to suspend the conventions of re-presentation and actively explore its own possible being as writing, preserves the wildness of originary marking – which means that state before gesture, mark, image and word have been separated as a system or logic of re-presentation.

Perhaps modern painting's interest in the art of other cultures, especially in so-called 'primitive' art is founded in part on the emergence of a strong sense of its own 'primitiveness', of its excavation of that primitive moment of the origin of signification itself in the mark that exemplifies and performs the 'rupture with totality itself.' (Derrida, 1978b, p.71). This embrace of alternative traditions displays the Desire for the recovery of an other side of painting's life to that which was to the fore in the explorations and celebrations of post-Renaissance painting. Art, as the celebration of the creation of significance itself, is placed unequivocally before art as the skill or craft in rendering some inner truth, or as the means for 'expressing' an 'impression'.

This founding marking is one site on which significance or meaning erupts without a signified and which cannot therefore be a conventional signifier. It differentiates itself and its producer from the seamless web of natural being, of the absolute self-presence of being to itself where being, as this full self-presence, has no need of re-presentation. And yet this seems already to point to a way in which painting might be repetition: if modern painting on each and every occasion of its performance is a reminder of this origin, it could be said that each painting is a repetition of it. But this might be called a re-memoration or rehearsal of the origin rather than a simple repetition of it in the way that a word is concretely used on separate occasions to signify the 'same' phenomenon. Now if the work of painting in our culture can be seen, at least in part, as a continual re-membering and celebration of the eruption of significance itself, then the mark that each painting is and contains is what makes the difference between itself and what it constitutes as its other, where this other can have a variety of references. For 'other' may refer to what the mark seeks to avoid (repetition), or it may refer to its concrete topic (what its 'content' refers to), or it may refer to the other as collaborative audience, and so on.

The mark, in other words, is the offer of and the opening up of relation itself in the ways that, in the process of its emergence, it is the making of the difference in specific forms between itself and these others; it constitutes the possibility of a series of specific relations in the ways that it is accomplished. Thus, for example, in different ways early Renaissance perspective or impressionism inscribe for the first time ways of viewing, a way of relating to, landscape and nature that may now routinely inform our mundane vision; these specific relations to nature were not possibilities prior to the works which instituted and then codified them. And it is when such relations have been codified, have become convention, usually towards the end of or after a movement or style, that we may genuinely speak of concrete repetition in painting's re-presenting. Works at such a stage may still partially be re-memorations and celebrations of re-presentation prior to repetition, but increasingly they seem to celebrate the conventions themselves, rather than the reason which rendered them possible in the first place. Adherence to a logic of re-presentation will inevitably and by definition go hand in hand with a falling away in the questioning dimension of the work, in the ways in which the painting is an exploration of and for re-presentation itself.

The mark, as the making of difference itself, utters itself as utterly concrete and thus as prior to repetition; but by virtue of its life as mark, as a re-presenting, it inscribes the possibility of repetition. It provides for writing as copy (simulacrum) while witholding itself from repetition, where the copy attempts to persuade us that one mark can stand for, can perfectly replace, an other, its predecessor; the history of the emergence of phonetic script is the history of the success of such copying, for here it is a necessary condition of a mark that it be perfectly reproducible. What non-reproducible marks, works of art, seek to remind us of is the other world before this original deception. It is not so much that every work of art cannot be reproduced, for clearly concretely that is not the case, but rather that such reproduction, as copy or by extension forgery, is not the production of a work of art, but a display of an attempted absolutely literal re-presentation. The copy seeks to become not a work of art but pure re-presentation. Now if we see all forms of writing, pictographic through to phonetic, as resting upon a forgetting of this original deception, the deception that all writing must, in order to signify its other, forget in obliterating itself as a work of marking, then painting, against this, attempts to keep open a memory of what marking is in itself.

Thus the work of art as re-presentation is not the repetition or copy of specifics, but is rather the showing of a certain affinity between a mark and its other through a process of questioning of re-presentation itself. And affinity here refers first of all to the predecessor of the work, namely to the Tradition itself, for what each work displays and performs is a relation to Tradition: it is always a repetition of Tradition. Each work dissociates itself from Tradition in its very concreteness, in its difference from each preceding work (it is not a copy), but associates itself with the Tradition in what it exemplifies about, for example, the Desire to paint in certain ways, and in this way it makes the space between itself as a specific mark and its predecessors an absolutely full space or significant space. The work of art works precisely in and as the relation that it makes possible for another, its viewer, to construct. It is the possibility of relation.

There is a complicity of marks that is bound up with marking itself; a mark re-presents this complicity 'before' it re-presents something other than marking (that which we typically regard as its content or referent, be it figurative or 'abstract'). A work of art's affinity with Tradition, the way it associates itself with other works of art, is a work of marking whose primary work is to utter itself in a way that invites an other to repeat the work of marking. But here the invitation to repeat is on the one hand to the respondent to collaborate with it in its reconstruction of the work of viewing, and on the other to others to become artists, to produce works that utter themselves. It displays the possibility of re-presenting that which can be done again and again, not as copies of itself, but as further exemplars of the possibilities of re-presentation in, for and as itself. Each painting in its affirmation of its own concreteness is thus a re-presentation of the work of marking that, in this very affirmation, asserts its absolute unrepeatability; it celebrates its re-presentation of marking as the eruption of significance which inscribes it, metonymically, into a tradition of marks, while refusing on the one hand to repeat or copy its predecessors and on the other hand the possibility of its own future perfect re-presentation or repetition in a copy. Every work of art is an originary re-presentation.

Painting in general is thus repetition of the unrepeatable, for it repeats that original mark whose concreteness, unrepeatability, is its meaning: re-presenting the un-re-presentable. And each mark in a sequence of marks (and Tradition is, among other things, a sequence) refers to and is associated with its predecessors even though it is not yet a repetition or re-presentation of the specific character of any of its preceding marks. What a specific mark re-presents here is its relation to and its difference from its predecessors, and in this performance of the affinity of differences the

Tradition is metonymically constructed.

Painting, then, inscribes itself as a relation to writing-in-general and to other specific forms of writing, and through the specificity of its re-presenting it displays its meaning 'pluri-dimensionally' (Derrida, 1976, p.85), that is, through a form of re-presentation that is non-consecutive. It is re-presentation before writing's transformation into linear sequencing. Derrida suggests that this 'pluri-dimensional' quality 'corresponds to another level of historical experience', to that of the 'linear scheme of the unfolding presence' (ibid.). Linearisation, as the rendering of the verbal, finds its limits, as we have seen, in spacing, in the way phonetic writing is constituted through its other, the significant absences of spacing. And what painting does is to make spacing itself its own concern: it is an exploration of and a writing on behalf of spacing, the mute absences that nevertheless signify the very possibility of linear writing. Perhaps the self-conscious 'all-over' quality that is intrinsic to much painting in the modern tradition is an explicit making reference to the 'pluri-dimensionality', to the forms of spacing, at work in each work of art:

> *Spacing* designates *nothing*, nothing that is, no presence at a distance; it is the index of an irreducible exterior, and at the same time of a movement, a displacement that indicates an irreducible alterity (Derrida, 1981; p.81).

6

Painting: Reading

All writing, and painting-as-writing is no exception, pre-
sumes, provides for and opens on to its readings. And the
preceding exploration of painting as a re-presentation of writing, of
Language, in a Tradition of re-presentation, calls for complementary inquiry into the practice of reading: the work that any
respondent is involved in already in opening up a relation with a
painting. This is unavoidable in any consideration of modern painting for central to its practice has been the challenge to the respondent, the reader, to turn back upon his or her own assumptions
about the very practice of reading and relating. If modern painting
faces us with the question of writing, of itself as an inscription of
Being, we can only enter this inscription through a practice of
reading in which the inscription is instituted as such.

The general thrust of work sharing the modern commitment
solicits a specific engagement of the work of art by another, a
respondent. It calls for a reading of a very particular kind, for the
reading will be pulled towards, if it is to grasp the painting's writing
on the latter's terms, a necessary deconstruction of writing as we
know it, that is – phonocentric linear writing. The very act of reading
the painting will require a putting into question of *itself-as-reading*; it
will be a reading in the process of dissolving itself. The modern
tradition seeks to re-open the question of what literacy is and
performs this illiteracy through demanding that the respondent
become illiterate again, where illiteracy, as a bracketing of phonocentric writing, seeks to disclose the possibility of writing-in-
general as lying elsewhere. To participate in the life of the modern
tradition we have to become illiterate.

And yet this is always an ironic illiteracy, for we perform this
bracketing of phonocentrism in the full knowledge of its power.
Perhaps the virtue of modernity in the arts lies in the difference that
the achievement of this knowing illiteracy, this literate illiteracy,
makes, for it is by definition a transformative process. In a culture

founded on the necessity of a minimum literacy to support its own absolute literality, the illiteracy of modern painting, its undoing of literacy, serves to remind us that literacy as we know it is only one possibility of being, and one that rules out as illegitimate or inferior those forms for exploring and celebrating Being which practise another form of writing. In discussing Artaud's theatre of cruelty, Derrida quotes Artaud's cryptic self-description, 'I am writing for illiterates' (Derrida, 1978b, p.188). Substituting painting for writing in Artaud's sentence provides us with an aphorism for the modern tradition of painting: it insists that we suspend the values of literacy and the literal which uphold that sense of the relation between representation and Being that modernity itself seeks either to displace or, at the very least, through its relativising of the literal, to step back from. Illiteracy here could never be a simple return to some supposedly primal state, for it is always a sophisticated ironic illiteracy that knows what it is doing in the very process of trying to forget both *how* it knows and *that* it does know.

The cubist deconstruction of some of the conventions of the illusionary pictorial spaces of realism and naturalism exemplifies this in its double movement: its constitution of new possibilities of pictorial space is at the same time a decomposing of taken-for-granted conventions of reading and a throwing back upon the respondent the responsibility to re-new reading as an originating practice; in this way it transforms the relationship to the painting by re-minding the respondent of his or her responsibility to actively constitute the relation as a practice of reading. This re-minding also necessarily involves a transformation of everyday senses of Language for the 'language of cubism', as manifest in any particular painting, is seen to be a language that preserves the absolute openness to the viewer to re-create its form and being, as well as having characteristics specific to each painting. It is a language which is constitutionally uninterested in legislating for its own reading, as indeed are most of the languages of the modern tradition; in the act of putting reading into question they equivocate mundane senses of Language as the bearer of specific messages or information. The 'conventions' of cubism (or any other 'ism') are not concerned to elicit 'correct' readings from a viewer.

To become illiterate would not be the accomplishment of a negative state but would rather be the achieving of a movement of being in which writing and reading as we know and live them mundanely are put into question in the course of a questioning that seeks to disclose, and, in this way, to celebrate other possibilities. Where cultures, such as ours, are under the sway of the literal, an art which writes alterity into being stands as the text for otherness; its practice is to exemplify and preserve the sense of what is other to that culture, and this is indeed the practice of modernity: 'To overthrow the power of the literal work is not to erase the letter, but only to subordinate it to the incidence of illegibility or at least of illiteracy . . . illiteracy can quite well accommodate the most profound and living culture' (op.cit., p.188). The wrench is required to produce an ironic illiteracy in which the painter or the viewer equivocates the power of the legible and begins an erasure that rubs away its previously unquestioned ties with its referent. Being is no longer unequivocally legible as the simple referent of a phonocentric linear writing, for that it might be and might always have been other than this simple referent may be precisely what the alternative paintings and texts of modernity seek to explore, remember and remind us of.

The loss of culture is a threat and its unlearning can be a painful process; but art provides us with occasions where we can re-enact this unlearning in relative security because we know that it is we ourselves as artists and audience who have initiated and constructed the whole process. We can only sustain and live with the awe-ful implications of Gregor Samsa's reverse journey through the evolutionary process out of culture towards originary dust because we can withdraw our absolute trust in Kafka at any moment. And so with painting: when Picasso confronted our culture with its other face in the *Demoiselles d'Avignon*, when Giacometti's sculptures offer the brittle armature of being-there as the materialisation of shadows, when Rauschenburg turns the culture against itself by investing its discarded shards with a poetics, we stay temporarily within the works' terms as willing witnesses of the deconstruction of our culture. Our thoughtful acquiescence in our own un-doing is grounded in an erotic trust in which we submit to the artist's advances. For this trust is also grounded in the Desire that the work of art seeks to exemplify – Desire for that which is other to what is. The work of art strips away the veneers of culture as part of its exploration of and Desire for other possibilities. But these can only be grasped through engaging the work on its own terms and according to the specific exploration of re-presentation it puts into play.

And sharing the terms of the work of art means precisely reading and engaging the specific language(s) through which the work's re-presentation 'takes place'. If painting is a pluri-dimensional proto-writing, the reading it calls for would be one which suspended all the affirmations and securities involved in reading the phonocentric text; the move into illiteracy unseats the hold of the

literal, the linear, the 'Natural', the quotidian, through its engagement of metaphor's archaic work. The problem then becomes that of
offering a sense of the practice of reading painting that frees itself
from the restrictions of the linear phonocentric conception of reading, that is open to its own self-dissemination by modern painting's
way with Language. The respondent, trusting self to the play of the
work, putting self in the care of the work, on finding the work
illegible within the conventional terms of reading, of pictorial narrative, either has to engage the work's own subversions of convention
or step outside its frame. Modern painting insists upon the respondent's willingness to place the self's conventional securities within
Language into question through a deconstruction and renewal of
the work, the life, of reading.

In the deconstructive poetics of painting-as-writing metaphor's
contribution was central and it can act as a bridge in approaching
reading too. The potential of metaphor always exceeds the narrower
framed and limiting concerns of, say, scientific linguistics/semiotics,
and analysis of rhetoric or a literary poetics, for, as seen, it points to
the emergence of significance, of meaning, itself. If modern painting, too, involves an archaeology of significance then the respondent is drawn into this excavation through the play of metaphor.

The perennial openness of the work of art to interpretation is
bound up with its resistance to our looking, with the way it stares
back at us and throws our looking back upon itself. Paintings
confront us with our own ambiguity, through the tension of the
references both outwards towards the world and us, and inwards
towards art itself. The openness or ambiguity of the literary phonocentric text, the text based upon repetition and linearity, can be
contrasted with the ambiguity of the painting through differences in
the way the reading metaphor 'works' in the two cases, for in the
latter case the text is pluri-dimensional and not linear: the words of
the linear text conventionally efface themselves in the service of a
signified 'beyond' the text, whereas in a painting it is the marks
whose preservation the work is finally about. The fixed seriality of
the phonetic text provides a departure point for the contrast and also
points us to a companion term – metonymy. The relation between
metaphor and metonymy has already been encountered in the
reading of Paul Klee's writings.

The structural linguists, Jakobson and Halle (1971), use a contrast
between metaphor and metonymy in their study of the speech
defect of aphasia. Metaphor is treated as a process of substitution
according to likeness which, at the most general level, can be
accommodated to the understanding of metaphor here. But

metonymy conventionally refers to the process by which a quality or part of a phenomenon stands for the name of the whole; in this sense it is traditionally a specific kind of metaphor. Jakobson and Halle, however, modify this meaning considerably to comprehend the two basic ways they found that 'meaning' emerged in their study of aphasics. Metaphor as substitution is preserved, but metonymy is developed, not as a subsidiary form of metaphor but as a contrasting polar alternative to metaphor. Further, the concept of metonymy is used to describe the process of combining terms in an utterance to produce a phrase or sentence. For them the two fundamental modes of constructing meaning in any text or speech are: substitution through similarity (metaphor) and combination through association of qualities (metonymy). So they shift the meaning of metonymy to refer to the combining of terms each of which can make significant reference to the others through associatable qualities. In their understanding metonymy is the process of combining terms through association: it is the way that units of an utterance (words, phrases) are combined, put in a specific order, which affects the possible associations that we, as readers/hearers, can find between them. Metonymy is thus absolutely dependent on context and is itself the making of context.

In the process of *making* sense, of reading, we discover associations between combined units/terms; each unit holds the potential for an association with those whose context it shares, and it does this through the ways we may find within it a reference to a part, an attribute, a quality of the unit or units with which it is combined. Each makes reference to something outside itself. The trace is again at work. Some of the traditional sense of metonymy is thus preserved in Jakobson's and Halle's transformed use of the concept. But whilst the concept of metonymy is understood as referring to the process of combining associated units or elements in the production of meaning it is not treated here as a polar opposite of metaphor but rather as its essential complement. I treat their cryptic proposals as suggestive rather than as rigid guidelines for a methodic approach. The possible relevance of their analysis to visual phenomena is thrown out as an after-thought by Jakobson and Halle, and while others have followed their suggestions in the analysis of literary forms, they do not appear to have been developed in the analysis, structuralist or otherwise, of visual phenomena. The English writer and critic, David Lodge, has critically developed the metaphor/metonymy opposition in his analysis of modern writing; he uses it in an inventive exploration of the cycle of contemporary literature, showing literary discourse, through an examination of a range of writers, as a movement back and forth between these two poles (Lodge, 1977). But how might the two contrasting terms be relevant to an exploration of the practice of reading a painting?

Following their study of aphasics, Jakobson and Halle suggest metaphoric substitution and metonymic combination are the fundamental processes involved in the creation of linguistic sense; the lack or the impairment of one or the other of these two processes results in a speech defect in which the very processes of interpretation and meaning-construction are themselves disrupted. Thus for them discourse itself (speech and literature) develops through these two possible semantic modes. Whilst in their analysis these are 'pure types', in practice most discourse is a mixture of the two with a tendency towards one or the other; they note that, in 'normal verbal behaviour both processes are continually operative, but careful observation will reveal that under the influence of a cultural pattern, personality, and verbal style, preference is given to one of the two processes over the other' (Jakobson and Halle, 1971, p.90).

The basic tendency of poetry is thus metaphoric, while prose tends to metonymy, although both obviously contain the other. Thus, for example, a radical form of naturalism in prose which was committed to minute and detailed description of phenomena would work, through the continuities it provided for its compounding of associated details, essentially metonymically. Poetry, on the other hand, with its typical concern, within the particular economy of rhythm that it has chosen, for transforming our understanding of phenomena through substitution of identities according to similarity or contrast, exemplifies and elaborates the metaphoric dimension of sense-creation. Given that reading is always a matter of connection (of relating elements), the linear text works through two basic forms of connection of meaning, connection through recognition of substitution, and connection through recognition of association of contiguous elements.

An individual, as speaker or writer, exhibits his or her particular speech/writing style, verbal predilections and preferences through the idiosyncratic manipulation of the possibilities for inter-relating the metaphoric and metonymic dimensions. And in noting similar tendencies to either metaphor or metonymy in contrasting literary forms, Jakobson and Halle also make a passing reference to the visual realm when they propose that the predominance of either metaphor or metonymy occurs in 'sign systems other than language' (op.cit., p.92), mentioning painting and film:

A salient example from the history of painting is the manifestly metonymical orientation of cubism, where the object is transformed into a set of synechdoches; the surrealist painters responded with a patently metaphorical attitude. Ever since the productions of D.W. Griffith, the art of the cinema, with its highly developed capacity for changing the angle, perspective and 'focus' of 'shots', has broken with the tradition of theatre and ranged an unprecedented variety of synechdochic 'close-ups' and metonymic 'set-ups' in general (ibid.).

The reference is left to stand in these cryptic terms and, as Lodge shows, very few analysts have taken the fundamental polarity of metaphor and metonymy out of the context of linguistics for under-standing either literature or the visual arts; in their undeveloped statement even the examples are suspect. For example the diagnosis of cubism as fundamentally metonymic and surrealism as metaphoric can only be proposed within their oppositional sense of the concepts. The complementary sense proposed here where each is 'present' and needs the other would always find metaphor as the founding 'moment' of the work of art, but this would be a founding secured through the work of metonymy. Thus cubist painting, while explicitly drawing attention to the metonymic work through which objects were deconstructed and re-combined in the painting would still stand as and would contain metaphor. Likewise the metaphors of surrealist painting, substituting a surreality for the mundane world, could only be constituted and read through the metonymic work of the association of the elements within the work.

Precisely because the semantic space of the painting is pluri-dimensional and that of the linguistic text is linear, the terms of Jakobsen and Halle cannot be applied as they stand. However, while the linearity of written texts may appear to require a very different kind of reading to that of the picture, even the 'empirical fact' of linearity in a text may not determine an absolutely linear reading. Kolers, reporting on his own and earlier studies comparing reading pictures with reading texts, notes, after reviewing evidence on sequential scanning as the basic form of reading, that 'mere sequential scanning is not by itself an adequate description of reading' (Perkins and Leondar, 1977, p.145). Buswell's study, carried out in 1935, showed that the reader of a text

is sensitive to many features of the array he is reading, sampling the array and constructing a representation of it in his own mind. The constructive act need not proceed serially, the eyes and the mind faithfully mirroring the text; rather the inputs are highly variable and can be remarkably free from sequential constraints. (op.cit., p.161).

Clearly the conjunction of eyes and mind can make reading an extraordinarily flexible process. And because reading the text need not necessarily preserve the 'syntax of the message on the page', the reader of a linear text and a picture can share an important characteristic:

they can proceed without immediate regard to syntax but do have to have regard for the semantic or interpretable component . . . (the) means of achieving this interpretation or understanding can follow idiosyncratic or personal rather than formal rules (op.cit., p.155).

In a study of forty subjects' viewing of Hokusai's *The Wave*, Buswell challenged the belief that pictures are seen whole by showing that they are seen, 'by means of a series of scanning, information-selecting movements of the eyes' (op.cit., p.154). Subjects' eye fixations on the surface of the picture were not distributed homogeneously, although there was a concentration of fixations on a particular region of the painting – that of greatest perturbation and irregularity. Although over the course of viewing there was a general agreement as to what was looked at there was great individuality in both sequence of looks and manner of looking. This work does support at the most concrete level the use of the metaphor of reading for viewing the picture and it shows that the process of reading anything is an idiosyncratic practice. This suggests that a work of art, as something other than mere visual information, will be met by the uniqueness of the viewer's interpretative reading style. The painting's pluri-dimensional space can and will be read but not according to a set of rules. Rather what we can provide is an interpretive context in which both the sense and the openness of this process are preserved.

Fundamental to this pluri-dimensionality is contiguity itself – the inter-connections between all of a painting's contiguous elements. The viewer is free to explore the connections between the smallest elements, such as brush marks, or to combine these into larger elements such as colour areas, tonal areas, forms of 'objects', areas defined by their contours and so on. Thus, in reading the relationship between two or more areas divided by, for example, a line, the significance attached to the relationship at any moment of viewing may depend upon which side of the line the eye approaches the relationship from. The way the painting's space lives for us at that point is already bound up with the kind of journey we have begun to construct through it and with the relative 'weights' of the continuous elements we are focusing on. One example of this would be Klee's contrast between the 'endotopic' and 'exotopic' or postive-negative treatment of relief applied to linear figures containing intersections; endotopic refers to that which is contained within the contours defining form. The rule he gives for constructing this 'inside-outside' contrast is also a rule for reading it: 'in handling boundary contrast always stay on the one side of the line' (Klee, 1961, p.51). But he adds that

> The movement of boundary contrast is brought out in different ways. Sometimes we have an endotopic treatment aimed to produce contrast on the boundary, and sometimes an exotopic treatment. Sometimes the endotopic centre receives a special new emphasis. A conflict arises between endo- and exotopic. Then we have a sort of mesh of forms (op.cit., p.50).

Thus not only may the basic contrast apply, but in some paintings the endo- and exotopic contrast will be deliberately equivocated by the artist, and the viewer will find that the reading of the form is ambiguated at such points whether it is approached from within (endotopically) or from without (exotopically). The form's sense or significance is produced metonymically through the way we associate and combine the elements within it with those outside of it.

This kind of contrast of contiguously related elements could clearly be extended endlessly, for the kind of elements which can be read contiguously can be continually re-combined. The issue of contiguity in both the creation and the re-creation of the painting defines the very life of the work of art itself, for our sense of the painting as a whole is dependent upon the particular continuities of contiguous elements that constitute our reading of it: that is, the way we 'make sense' of relationships between its parts. But no reading is a simple sequence of movement through all the contiguously related elements of a painting for our eyes may jump from one part of the painting to another, may rest on one element and ignore others and so on. The relation that we have with it will always be constituted in part by the specific combination of contiguous elements that contribute to it. And in most if not all painting the inter-relation of contiguous elements is absolutely central to the painter's interests, for it is through these relationships that the painter seeks some unachievable finality or 'unity'. The contiguity of elements in a painting is always bound up with meaning and seems to direct us to the kind of phenomena that are classically gathered together under the term 'form', for the so-called formal elements of a painting's composition (those that are read as producing a final 'unity', as, for example, a harmony of balanced rhythms) are inter-related contiguously. It is they that influence the ways our eyes are drawn through the painting. Meaning is thus always to some extent dependent, as in the linear text, on the specific configuration of contiguities that provide for our relation with the work of art.

Every positional contiguity in a painting (the relation between any contiguous elements) is thus always potentially what Jakobson and Halle call a semantic contiguity too: its latent significance awaits the re-creative work of the reader in the way that a string of metonymic associations in a sentence awaits the reader's attribution of sense. Metonymy here does emphasise context much more explicitly than metaphor, for, while metaphor, both in the painting and the text, directs us away from an element to its other (it could direct us to somewhere else in the painting or it could point outside the picture altogether), metonymy emphasises the continuity between elements; it is the process of association in which we might say 'Ah! This mark is associated with that mark in terms of their colour contrast, and they, in terms of their shape, direct me across to that line which divides two tonally related areas, which, in its turn . . .', and so on. Kandinsky notes this process in discussing 'structure' in drawing and the importance of combination, contiguity, and separation:

> The flexibility of each form, its internal, organic variation, its direction (motion) in the picture, the relative weight of concrete or of abstract forms and their combination; further the concord or discord of the various elements of a pictorial structure, the handling of groups, the combination of the hidden and the stripped bare, the use of rhythmical or unrhythmical, of geometrical or non-geometrical forms, their contiguity and separation – all these things are the elements of structure in drawing (Kandinsky, 1964, p.51).

Patrick Heron, too, commenting on Braque's *Intérieure*, emphasises, in defining his sense of what it is to read a picture, the metonymic process of constituting meaning as a process of associative movement through the picture:

This is what I mean by 'reading' a picture. The significance of each part of the picture that my eye visited altered according to the direction from which it was approached . . . Every line operating within the strict economy of this design defines it in at least two directions simultaneously, describing and terminating whatever lies to the right and left of it. The reading which is momentarily the strongest will be the one relevant to the side from which our eye approaches. But the other meanings are latent, and the eye has only to swoop back from another direction to that first reading to be submerged in a second or third (Heron, 1978, p.31).

Reading for Heron is the eyes' metonymic journey through the work, a journey ever-open to self-transformation. The metaphoric dimension is the product of this journey – metaphors are the conclusions, the moments of stasis, of the journey, for they represent conclusions about the significance of the work or elements of it, however temporary such conclusions may be; these arise through substituting or contrasting the identities and similarities of elements within the painting with other elements either within or outside it. Ultimately the work lives through a play of differences, the tension between the work itself and its others, and any reading, as a process of movement and stasis is a dialectic of metonymy and metaphor.

Jakobson's and Halle's contrast thus opens up reading as process, as practice, as movement. While metaphor may refer to the more radical confusing in which significance 'takes place', metonymy directs us to the combinatory practice through which that occurs. And of course seriality, the way words follow each other in a fixed sequence in the process of sense-making in phonetic writing, speaking, reading and hearing, is a 'given' feature of language's concrete life. Sequencing defines the context of each unit of the utterance and gives it a role within the utterance as a whole through the ways that the units (words, phrases, sentences, etc.) are associated. Seriality preserves the context-bound character of meaning and refers to the metonymic side of Language at the level of practice.

Even the 'avant-garde' in writing, from Mallarmé on, where the conventions of language use are, along with the reading subject, put to the test, has not produced texts which are 'able' to dispense in any absolute sense with the serial connection of word and word. One kind of subversion of this convention has been the loose-leaf novel whose pages can be assembled according to the order of the reader's choice, and both William Burroughs and B.S. Johnson produced variations of this. The writer's choice is between the creation and juxtaposition of minimal sequences to which meaning can be 'attached', and silence. Similarly, as Kristeva has shown (Kristeva, 1980, pp.159 et seq.), while the sentence, as the conventional limit of the unit of sense, may be suspended, as in Sollers' 'H', the text still lives through the sequencing of words as the rhythm of a represssed subject or subjects.

Part of a text's hold over the reader lies in its requirement that the reader follow the text's sequence to re-create a work's 'meaning'. Metonymy provides for the text-reader relationship as process; and in writing or speaking, if not reading, this association is all but fixed. Can this feature of reading as metonymic process be transferred to the respondent's relationship to the painting?

A painting requires the respondent to order, serialise, the active practice of looking at and engaging the work. But, even though this may concomitantly require a dis-ordering of existing ways of making sense, as might be the case with the initial appearance of 'new' painting, this serialising is the viewer's own work. Unlike the conventional linguistic text a painting opens onto an infinity of possible reading sequences and this openness is both the power and the problem of the painting's relation to conventional other images, reading and art itself. Whether we call a picture art or something else may depend in part on the character of its openness to the 'work' of looking. Art is in tension between the two ideal poles of complete openness (as, for example, when we stop to 'admire the view' and we are responsible for the choice of theme, content, duration, etc.), and the attempt to produce a text closed to all but one reading, as in the case of the picture as diagram containing non-linguistic signs such as arrows to programme its own reading. Art secures its own space through the specific balance between openness and closedness that it displays. Its space is preserved where the aim of the closedness (the ways the painting limits the respondent's freedom) points back to the painting itself, and through it to art itself. In celebrating and exploring controlled openness, painting is essentially about the quality of the respondent's responsibility for re-animating it. And re-animation, as a practice of reading, coheres around the inter-play, the inter-weaving, in the reading itself of the respondent's metaphoric and metonymic work.

In this work metaphor is the key, for it is itself the link, the builder of a relation, between Language, art and textuality. Metaphor is the term of relation itself, while metonymy, as developed here, is a metaphor for the *practices* whose products are metaphors: metaphor as the bridge that is the outcome of theoretical practice, and metonymy as the metaphor for that practice. The painting, as an always incomplete whole, and its separable 'moments' (marks, regions, spaces, figures, and so on) are metaphors while the practices through which the painter or the respondent arrives at them are its metonymic dimension: 'Art comes into being not through correct reasoning but through uniting contradictions of reason in the ambiguity of a metaphor' (Rosenberg, 1969, p.226). This coming-into-being, the moments of practice, makes reference to the metonymic associations and combinations whose end is metaphor.

Metaphor, as the creative con-fusion of two realms, itself metaphorises the emergence of significance as relation and, following Derrida, this movement of Language, the coming-to-be of metaphor, points us towards the movement of differance. Because metaphor names the grounding of significance itself, the possibility of meaning as relation, we cannot get outside it through some kind of meta-metaphorics, for every attempt to do so is itself limited by the metaphors to which it trusts its analysis. Philosophy itself, as the dialectics of truth in our tradition, can no more escape metaphor than any discourse, and its own 'truths' achieve whatever temporary stability they can through hidden metaphors, often metaphors for an 'absolute origin' of 'presence'. Derrida also points to the metaphor of light (and its own indebtedness to the sun) as fundamental to philosophical discourse, producing what he calls a 'heliocentric' metaphysics (Derrida, 1978b, p.127). Philosophy here is an emergence from darkness into light, the light which reveals; it is always indebted to the source of light – the sun. Oppositions of appearing and disappearing, visible and invisible, present and absent, are possible 'only under the sun' (Derrida, 1974, p.52).

But the sun itself is metaphorical for it can never be properly or fully present in discourse (metaphor is required precisely because things can never be brought in their full self-presence into Language):

> the sun is never properly present in discourse. With every metaphor there is no doubt somewhere a sun; but each time there is the sun, metaphor has begun. If the sun is always and already and always metaphorical, it is not completely natural. It is always and already a lustre . . . if the sun is not entirely natural, what can remain in nature that is nature? This object which is the most natural in nature has in itself this capacity to go out of itself; it joins with artificial light, it suffers ellipse and eclipse, has always itself been other: the father, seed, fire, the eye, the egg and so on, all of them so many further things

providing the measure of good and bad, or clear and obscure metaphor (op.cit., p.53).

The truth of the being that is present, that which may claim to know about the being of things, is then 'fixed by passing through a detour of tropes' (op.cit., p.55). There is no direct immediate access to things, for their absolute presence is always deferred through the tropes of discourse, the most persistent of which is the metaphor of the sun's light which lets things appear for us.

It is significant that it is the hidden metaphor of light (sun) which underwrites philosophy and discourse itself. For if light is a 'first' metaphor it provides the region in which metaphor shows itself; if metaphor en*light*ens us about beings it can only do so through its own indebtedness to the metaphor of light. At this level it might be said that metaphor exemplifies the work of light, and is this not precisely what painting itself does? Perhaps we can say that painting's way may take us to the coming-to-be of metaphorising itself in its own celebration of the life of light. Even the blackest of black paintings (think of the many different 'blacks' in Reinhardt's late paintings) exemplify the good of light, by relying on it to display their exploration and celebration of the limits of opacity, density, disappearance, no-thing. If light is a necessary and a founding metaphor, if it makes the metaphor of truth itself possible, then painting, as a writing-before-writing, takes as its first hidden subject textuality's, 'being's', indebtedness to light, and in this way it draws us towards the question of our own very origins. Not only is painting itself metaphor; more strongly, it is the exemplification of metaphor, for it is done on behalf of no other end; it does not write first of all for another truth, a metaphoric truth about things in themselves, but rather it is an acting out and displaying of the life of metaphor itself where this life is the life of light, the very possibility of relation, the only life we have.

If, as Derrida proposes, 'Concept is a metaphor, foundation is a metaphor, theory is a metaphor, and there is no meta-metaphor for them' (op.cit., p.23), then perhaps painting itself as a practice and not as a concept is one such meta-metaphor or proto-metaphor, this gesture within writing-in-general but *before the concept* is one such meta-metaphor or proto-metaphor precisely because it is both prior to the word and utterly exemplary. If we treat metaphor as a word inscribed in a chain of signifiers, or other metaphors, as indeed Derrida does, the meta-metaphor could only emerge outside that chain, beyond the phonocentric linear script, and this other space is exactly that which painting itself continually institutes as a matter of practice. It reminds us that the word as metaphor is dependent upon something other than the word, and it can say this other (light) mutely by withholding itself from phonocentric linearity. And yet, while it may be a meta-metaphor for metaphor, it is still, like music, within Language but before all philosophy, all analysis. And perhaps there are further clues to this in the way Derrida describes metaphor's place at the 'origin' of Language:

> But above all, it is metaphor *itself*, the origin of Language as metaphor in which Being and Nothing, the conditions of metaphor, the beyond metaphor of metaphor, never say themselves. Metaphor, or the animality of the letter, is the primacy and infinite equivocality of the signifer as Life. The *psychic* subversion of inert literality, that is to say, of nature, or speech returned to nature (Derrida, 1978b, p.73).

If painting, as a 'first' writing, as the re-memoration of the gesture that inscribed the possibility of meaning, is before the word, and thus before the word metaphor *as metaphor*, it is the beyond-metaphor of metaphor; it exemplifies the filling of the space between Being (and) Nothing. Although he does not take it in this direction Derrida's very metaphors for this process do indeed point us to painting, for what is painting if not the 'animality of the letter' or the 'psychic subversion of inert literality'? Painting's wildness, its refusal to subordinate itself to the economy of a code, its pluri-dimensionality, its openness, its otherness to nature, its resistance to our looking, are nothing if not displays of the animality of the letter and the subversion of literality.

Of course metaphor's centrality to the life of Language has been recognised since Aristotle as a, if not the, fundamental trope; the vast body of contemporary literature analysing the work of metaphor attests to the agreement, across a range of analytical perspectives, about metaphor's importance (see Ricoeur, 1978). But it is the radicality of Derrida's writing, working in the rift in the western philosophical tradition opened by Heidegger, that holds in suspension conventions of analytical work on behalf of an other practice of writing. The current philosophical interpretation of metaphor as 'a transfer from the sensible to the intelligible' (Derrida, 1978c, p.13) is precisely what is in question in Derrida's traversal of this play of metaphor.

Through reading as this metaphoric-metonymic practice the respondent engages the painting in a process of questioning that draws him or her into the erotic play of the question of origins, of the implication of art, Language and Being. The work of art as the source and site of reverie can act as a bridge to this pre-philosophical and post-ontological region; but access to this other realm of questioning can only come through the concrete reading of the work, through the ways in which the respondent creates and discovers, or in Ricoeur's word, 'invents', a path through the work (Ricoeur, 1978, p.306). This process of invention calls for an analytical understanding, a critical response, that is sensitive to the ways that the work of art opens onto 'first' questions. In undertaking any concrete analysis the onotological questions are typically bracketed, hidden, until we reach the point where the significance of the work's ambiguity forces us to move into that other region where the subversive life of metaphor and its hiding of the trace opens onto originating significance. How might a respondent's invention of paths through the painting open into the realm of the painting's ownmost, its self-absorption with the re-presentation of textuality itself? The interplay of the metaphoric and the metonymic in and as the reading *is* the constitution of the painting's region, its own specific opening, for any respondent. And the openness is such that any element of the painting can be read either metaphorically or metonymically according to the particular aspect of the painting's languages that the respondent is engaging.

Max Raphael points to this in his remarks on the duality of even the smallest element in the painting which can be both metaphor (a whole in itself) and metonym (part standing for a whole and associatively contributing to it):

> each spot of pigment simultaneously performs various
> necessarily inter-related functions. Furthermore, each spot has
> the tendency to go beyond its mere local function, to become an
> autonomous form with its own relative significance, such that
> the smallest part not only serves the whole but also, in a limited
> sense, is a whole (Raphael, 1968, p.12).

In the context of reading, Raphael's sense of simultaneity requires qualification for, at any moment of reading, the spot of pigment is either being 'held' as metaphor or functions within a metonymic chain; simultaneity can only refer to an abstract characteristic of a spot's function and not to the *practice* of painting or reading.

The work of art points us in complex ways to its context and preceding 'moment', to what motivated the work. This engages the question of the work's other. A preceding 'moment' is crystallised in the artist's Desire to paint and to paint this particular picture in just this way, but the crystallisation that displays the Desire makes reference to a variety of complexly inter-related phenomena (those defining the artist's and art's existential situation). Through the artist's specific creative practices the painting is produced and stands as a metaphor which puts itself in a dialogue with its own motive, this complex other; it puts itself in a relation to what it is not. And this relation is only possible through the conventions which the painting either shares with others or invents to offer to them.

A picture's references (its resources for dialogue) are thus many and complex. In the course of viewing, a picture's internal relationships will be used to construct external references, and in their turn the constructed external references will be fed back into what was earlier called the work's inter-textuality, for all references, internal and external, engage other texts. Referencing *is* the practice of textualising.

Responding, as an alternation between the metaphoric and metonymic dimensions, can only be contexted through the *languages* of the painting. Trusting ourselves to the painting *is* the work of finding and placing ourselves within the specificity of its language(s). Matisse showed us that signing was specific to the particular painting and in this sense each painting may be a metaphor for the re-invention of painting itself, but at the same time each work also engages and places itself in relation to Tradition and its others through its languages. Thus within any work a variety of languages may be held as a play and a tension of inter-penetration. Some of these, such as for example the language of the play of marks, may seem to be specific to the painting, while others will be languages that all painting confronts. Two such languages exemplify this interplay, and the relation between them has been a continuously significant issue for modern painting. This relation has also been a recurring theme in critical writing though such writing has not necessarily formulated the issues through the language metaphor. One language is that of the re-presentation of space in depth; the life of this language produces the possibility of the respondent reading a sense of depth, of spatial illusion, of some phenomena in the painting advancing and others receding. A contrasting language is that through which the painting's flat surface plane is organised; it points to the way the respondent follows the marks, colours, shapes, figures, or whatever, on the surface, at the picture plane.

If we take the re-presentation of space in depth and the organisation of the surface as the sites of two interacting languages, whose work the respondent re-creates in engaging the painting, then the painting's life, its being-viewed, may partially turn on the Desire for engagement which the work installs in the respondent through this interaction. By equalising or holding together these two languages the modern tradition, encouraged by formalist critical emphasis on their interplay, has required that we re-read Tradition itself in these terms; we cannot stand outside the equalising tension of these two languages to re-create past modes of responding, for this interaction now partially defines for us what the life of painting is and has been. Moreover this tension is a way of bringing metonymy's power to our attention for the first time, for while painting before the advent of the modern could readily be understood through its iconography as metaphoric, as pointing beyond itself to its other message (concerning a supposedly given independent reality be it nature or idea), the assertion of this tension requires the respondent to recognise the fact of and the processes involved in viewing itself. Through its disruption and partial replacement of some of the conventions of painting practice, modern painting has made the engagement of painting itself a problem; the respondent, in beginning to engage a work, and confronted by the tension of the two languages, finds that the engagement itself requires an address of his or her own reading. He or she thus comes to recognise the constitutive character of responding itself, where the constitutive process as process occurs metonymically. And the subsequent metonymic journey through the work will involve constant movement between the two (and other) languages.

The respondent's concrete relation to the painting, as an erotic theoretic practice, is defined through the associated processes and moments of its reading where metaphor names the moments of rest, arrest, reverie and subsidiary conclusions within the journey; metaphors here are our 'conclusions' about the painting and its internal life that arise at the beginning, during and at the end of our reading. But metaphors, in the course of reading, are produced through the work of metonymic association; metonymic work as process is itself a metaphor for the practice of reading.

The interaction of these two languages of painting offers one possible way of organising the sense of painting and viewing practices. Both have metaphoric and metonymic aspects in that both can be read as a relation between the process of associative movement through the painting (metonymy) and the sequence of 'conclusions' about it (metaphors). But each language has a tendency towards one rather than the other. The language of spatial illusion tends towards metaphor in its concern with the representation of depth; here the painterly construction of space is a metaphoric feature of the painting as a whole. The language of surface organisation tends towards metonymy in its concern with the associative inter-relationship between elements on the surface where these associations are grasped through metonymic traversings.

The attempt to put one of the two languages completely out of play occurs only rarely (as, say, in the blue paintings of Yves Klein) and, whether or not the attempt 'succeeds', it confronts us precisely with our conventional reliance on norms from the language of spatial re-presentation in relating to painting. Rauschenberg's re-definition of the painting surface in the mid-nineteen fifties as a 'flat-bed' within which elements could be juxtaposed for reading laterally rather than in terms of approach and recession was a radical equivocation of the language of depth re-presentation (see Steinberg, 1972). His work is itself a deconstruction of reading conventions which begins to explore the metaphor of painting as a writing-reading practice in the most radical way. Jasper Johns, too, in asserting the frontality of the painting's surface and making it coincide with the limits of its image, as in his flag paintings, re-constitutes the painting as object, and confronts us with another kind of text in which the language of spatial depth re-presentation is radically equivocated, if not entirely eliminated. But wherever a painting works in more than one colour, as both Rauschenberg and Johns's work did, there is always the possibility of the respondent re-constituting it partially through the language of space re-presentation, for the life of colour itself provides for the coming and going of the surface marks.

But through its address of the surface as a whole modernity has brought the surface into a more equal if not dominant role in painting, and this invites a re-reading of the whole Tradition. Because modern painting opens up the tension between the two languages as central to the life, to the reading, of painting, the emphasis on the language of the surface organisation is a way of re-engaging the spaces of the Tradition. The rule of the modern is in part that convention of the relation between the two languages, where the language of surface organisation moves the language of spatial re-presentation away from its hold over mundane vision (the illusion of naturalism, of perspectivism) and reminds the 'content' that it is other than 'what is'. It displays the difference between the painting and the external world to which it refers and asserts that the painting is *not* the world. And the interaction of the two languages, the tensions it generates, defines, in part, our reading of both figurative and non-figurative painting. The two languages are themselves metaphors for the ways our relation to a painting develops and each has both metaphoric and metonymic moments.

Whether or not there are concrete external references, references to things already 'known', already in a 'code', as in all conventionally understood figurative painting, each work of art works, in our viewing of it, as a metaphoric-metonymic interplay.

This reciprocity of metaphor and metonymy, irrespective of painting 'style', is brought out by Kenneth Martin in his comments on the kinetic dimensions of art:

> The kinetic nature of art – the word used here to embrace the motion of making, movement as a compositional or constructing process, depicted motion and actual motion – is a correspondence with that of life.
> Repetitive pattern, meander, the journey in the landscape painting are all related . . . Composition is to be seen as the means of expression by kinetic equivalents for the conscious or unconscious organism of man just as was the first drawing of a line to make an enclosed space (Martin, 1975, p.16).

Thus art itself always makes reference to movements and 'kinetic art' specifically explores and celebrates this aspect; movement as process, rendered in the work of art through metonymically associated elements, is itself a metaphor for life itself – life as process. We read composition itself, developed metonymically (the meander), as a metaphor for the re-textualising, the re-presenting, of wild organic processes.

But if we move from the concrete practice of reading towards questions of the picture's 'significance' we are returned to the space of metaphor. The wild act of inventing, metaphor's creating and discovering moment of fusion, demands that we attend to it as a product, as something that is new. We need to ask *what* this metaphoric process of fusion discloses; to remain with metaphor and metonymy as a pair of structural complements, as concepts of form, and to understand metaphor's ultimate meaning only in terms of its complement (metonymy as process) would be to recognise only the 'howness' of metaphor, that is to say, *how* it works in and through a specific process, while eschewing the question about the significance, the value, the power, the Good of its disclosure. It would be to note merely that metaphor is historical, while passing over the difference that this transformative fusion makes to ourselves, to textuality itself. Attentive to this difference, we can begin to recognise metaphor's originating wildness, its violence, for it is metaphor which makes all the difference in the world. And we are returned here to the way metaphor glosses and defers origin, for meaning is founded, the world and our relationship to it is disclosed in new ways, in the metaphoric 'moment', in its covering of the movement of differance itself.

The responsibility of response and of analysis is to treat the exploration of painting as a necessary first move in the attempt to follow the ways in which the work of art points beyond itself, into re-presentation and textuality itself. Once we have developed ways of exploring how a painting 'means' we are drawn towards the question of the significance of the fact that it does mean, and it is at this point that our relation to it, the concrete ways through which we have engaged it, itself displays something other than itself. Our relation to the work of art stands for, is a metaphor for, something other than that relation. The goal of our journey through the concrete complements of metaphor and metonymy is to open up that region where the work's metaphoric relation to Being-as-text is disclosed.

Reading the work of art is always a struggle to hold together the tension between significance and Desire: to recover our and the artist's Desire to invest the relation to Being with a certain significance. Reading is always implicated with Desire, is always erotic, and remembering this should prevent the critical re-presentation of reading practice from falling into a technics of reading, into another formalism. Far from wanting to legislate for a single method, the elaboration of the interplay between metaphor and metonymy as the practice of reading proposes that the endless variety of critical practices can be drawn into the play of art's relation to Language.

Modernity, moving into its own after-history, seems to realise itself, and needs us to fulfil this realisation, as a recovery of another kind of writing and reading. It brings us to the point where we realise it in these very terms. But if the point of modernity's labour has been to draw us into the play of painting-as-writing through teaching us the necessity of its reading, then the post-modern, modernity coming to a grasp of itself, begins to undo this work. For if modernity has taught us to read the specific character of its illiterate writing, post-modernity immediately becomes suspicious of its own (modernity's) achievement, of our ability to read modernity's codes. Apprehensive of our reading skills and not wishing to be gathered as a vehicle for a new literacy, post-modernity begins to put into question exactly that which we thought we had learned from modernity. If modernity has become increasingly legible, if its languages have come 'closer' to us, if criticism has provided a comfortable context for reading the 'new', then post-modernity's need, if it is to be absolutely modern (to know its own modernity) is to seek the limits of the readable: to become unreadable again. For only by doing so can it show that it has grasped the significance of the modern tradition itself. When post-modern painting appears to appropriate or cite from the repertoire of earlier modern painting (as in Chia's quoting of Futurism or Baselitz's references to German expressionists like Kirchner) we are being drawn along the path towards un-meaning. For post-modernity, in maintaining modernity's deconstructive urge, finds that its overwhelming need is to confound just that which we were beginning to take-for-granted – our ability to read the modern from a position of comfort.

Just as modernity undid the signing conventions of re-presentation that were so dominant in late nineteenth century Europe, so post-modernity seeks to deconstruct those categories of practice and criticism, the languages of modernity, which have already begun to harden into styles, habits, mannerisms and critical conventions. Painting, turning again back upon itself, keeps up its running critique of the sign, signing, re-presentation, and in doing so continues to confound the discourses of the sign and of criticism, by remaining the absolute other to their method. Painting's challenge to these discourses is now explored in greater depth.

7

Painting into and out of Meaning

Painting inscribes, signs, itself as the erotic undoing of signs as we know them, and in this undoing takes us through signs, as we saw in the discussion of writing, to differance, to their possibility in the trace:

> no element can function as a sign without reference to another element which itself is not simply present. This inter-weaving results in each 'element' – phoneme or grapheme – being constituted on the basis of the trace within it of the other elements in the chain or system. This interweaving, this textile, is the *text* produced only in the transformation of another text. Nothing neither among the elements, nor within the system, is anywhere simply present or absent. There are only, everywhere, differences and traces of traces (Derrida, 1981, p.26).

In its very practices modern painting splits, sunders, the sign as relation between signifier and signified, as vehicle and referent, the essential relation for linguistics and semiotics, and takes us into the swirling play which is the underlife of signs – a commingling in which each contains a trace of another(s). For unlike the discourses of the sign the signified, the referent, is never radically other, is never a transcendental signified, outside signification, but only takes place, its place, in another chain of signifiers. And to make a chain, for there to be a chain, a relation, each must contain something of the other within itself; this overlapping and imbricating is tracing, the trace of the one (signifier) in the other. In the discussion of reading, metonymy, as combination, as association, displayed this inter-tracing of the elements (signifiers) in a chain. The signifier brings no signified to full presence nor does it exist itself in isolation as a 'present' thing. And modern painting displays this as its own concern and as the confounding of theories of the sign.

This subversion of the sign was seen at work in the earlier reading

146

of the exemplary artists in relation to figuration. Just as Matisse made explicit the crucial problem of reference, the relation between a painted signifier and its signified, by showing how a sign's life was specific to each painting, so Klee, in opening us to the metonymic dimension of making and reading practices drew us into the play of tracing. Cézanne had already equivocated conventions of resemblance in offering his elaborate (and finally wild) marking schema of colour combinations as art's harmony parallel to nature, drawing us into the work and interplay of the signifiers as the 'first' meaning of a painting. And Kandinsky radicalised this foregrounding of the signifier by eliminating painting's references to objects 'in the world'; this forced a re-consideration of what painting's signifieds might be. Duchamp, through his inter-twining of the linguistic text with the image, his insistence upon the unavoidability of Tradition and the absolute openness of interpretation, and his opening of irony as a necessary dimension of practice, confounded all those empiricisms, formalisms and materialisms bent on preserving the sign as a relation between a material signifier and a material signified that was somehow for the eyes alone. As if eyes were or ever could be alone! The exemplary practices of these painters, focusing modernity's critical issues, could have been added to through readings of others' work, but the depth and force of their subverting of the sign are sufficient to show the challenge that painting was making to theory and criticism, immersed as these latter were, and still largely are, in positivist senses of writing's relation to its object.

And it is painting itself from its own ground and on its own terms that invites its respondents to approach it through the metaphors of writing, reading, and signing. On entering painting's region we find that our journey through is not a linear trajectory (formalism/vanguardism) but rather a scattering, a fragmentation, and a dispersal of more or less legible paths in the region of Language. This very dispersal seems to show art's multiplicity, its refusal of the One, its denial of the metaphysical urge to find a place for everything within a universal schema of Reason and sense.

The falling away of modernity into modernism locked practice into just such a search for the One, for the reduced essence, for the absolute statement, so that having finally gathered painting to itself, it could then bequeath it to history and move on. But just as the last rites of modernism were being celebrated (it was hailed as a triumph for critical reasoning if not for painting) over the 'terminal' works of minimalism and conceptualism, painting itself, confounding all criticism, from within the terrain of modernity, burgeoned in a renewal of its quest. Modernity as multiplicity reasserted itself through a re-address of its relation to its past, both recent and distant; this re-turn to Tradition necessarily relativised abstraction and foregrounded figuration which had never ceased in spite of its critical marginalisation. Painterly exploration was being re-invented in a terrain where abstraction and configuration confronted each other with neither as the dominant partner. This is the terrain of post-modernity. The market pendulum, the demand for the 'new' has certainly encouraged this re-centering, but it hardly accounts for the extraordinary outburst of creative energy and commitment among painters themselves working in very different cultural contexts. And both market and criticism are followers when shifts occur on this scale.

This resurgence of the experienced potential of painting amongst painters, their sense of the continuing vitality of painting and its still open possibilities left criticism suspended over a vacuum of its own construction. The last thing modernist and vanguardist criticism could comprehend was painters' re-invigorated need to make 'non-abstract' paintings. And this need, this public re-generation of painting's possibilities defines the post-modern paradox and takes us back to de Duve's question. For this re-emergence of the question of Tradition, of the possibilities of painting's languages, in spite of reminding us of the multiplicity of modernity does have modernist abstraction as its justified and theorised past, its partial origin. Figurative imagery may predominate in the post-modern project, but it has to be a figuration that in some way preserves the gains for painting won by the early modern artists. Just as modernism did not erase figuration, neither can post-modernity eliminate abstraction; for how can the continuity between post-modern practice and its at least partially abstract past be understood without grasping and preserving the value of abstraction in the emergent figuration? What is the Good of modernity's past for painting's supposed self-projection out of modernity?

Various hypotheses suggest themselves in this situation. Either modernity is dead, in which case re-emergent figuration is completely other to modernity, it is an absolute rupture with it and is making painting on another site; or post-modernity is still within modernity, in which case we need to re-theorise modernity to see how it could provide for such radical differences and shifts in practice; or, a third possibility, modernity never really existed except as a by-product of what was essentially a theoretical/critical literary practice – it was a chimera of critical reason in which the moment of abstraction was an absolute and practically meaningless deviation from painting's true figurative and traditional academic path.

The interpretation of painting's involvement with the question of Language, its exploration of writing-reading-signing, and its self address as an inscription of Being-as-Language, pull us towards the second hypothesis. For the impossibility of an absolute rupture was exemplified by modernity itself. Neither the first nor the third hypothesis can be sustained because they require a notion of absolute rupture: in the first hypothesis post-modern painting cannot be absolutely other to either modernity or Tradition, while in the third hypothesis, abstraction, as we have seen, was never completely other to Tradition, for despite its radicality it preserved itself as painting and foregrounded form; further it is clear in relation to the last hypothesis that post-modern figuration, far from being other to modernity, is very much involved in modernity's project. And this involvement hinges crucially on its address of painting's relation to its own past, to Tradition, to writing-in-general; painting explores this relation through practices of re-presentation that suspend the conventions of making and responding that had defined modernism and its formalist support. It is the second hypothesis within whose terms the present formulation has been developed, for it is within modernity as multiplicity, as the celebratory engagement of Tradition through the questioning of its languages, that both abstraction and figuration have co-existed in complex ways. By relativising modernism modernity itself is a renewable force. A reconceptualising of modernity in other than modernist terms shows how its very engagement of Language-as-writing has itself precipitated this renewal of painting at the level of its 'subject matter'.

If modernity is recovered as the celebratory exploration of the question 'what is painting?' (see Lyotard, 1981) – on the terrain of Language, of writing – an exploration in which Tradition is sustained by and is the bearer of languages of painting, then the project of modern painting *is* this growing realisation. Modernity begins to know itself as a space for practice in and through the work of self-questioning which has included *modernism* but which is not exhausted by it. This emergent self-consciousness, legible in the works themselves, this modernity-coming-to-itself as a matter of practice, defines the post-modern tradition for painting. Modernity in painting realises itself in its self-transformation into post-modernity. And this showing of the post-modern situation as absolutely modern holds modernity as the tension of life and death. For modern practice knows that a work of art as soon as it is made is dead, is already part of the past; and yet this joining of the work to Tradition is itself what keeps Tradition alive. The death of the modern is repeatedly enacted and infinitely postponed; and the question without an answer 'what is painting?' is thus kept alive and open.

The shifts, transitions, differences, constituting modern painting practice themselves traverse and are traversed by the critical issues of signification; it is painting's engagement of the sign and of the work of signing that *is* the elaboration that defines the movement of painting within and as writing-reading. Concretely, at the level of practice, that of both painting-as-writing and responding-as-reading, painting works itself out as a practice of signing that puts the sign itself into question. The other side of a science of signs, of linguistics, of semiotics, and on behalf of another relation to Language and Being, painting deconstructs the life and times of the sign; in its very practices it confronts the sciences of the sign with their other, with that which in its very excessiveness to calculative thought finally denies science its object of knowledge. The problematic character of painting's treatment by semiotics will be drawn out in greater detail after considering some of the ways that modernity's and post-modernity's confrontation with meaning bear upon the painting's possibilities as signing.

The 'history' of painting's modernity becomes a necessary detour, a detour in which painting increasingly allowed itself to be pulled 'forward' by reductionism, on the way to 'itself' in post-modernity (where 'itself' can name no identity but only the ceaseless traversing of multiplicity). This detour, which is also a field, can be mapped through painting's equivocal relations with the signing of meaning. If the transition into post-modernity marks a shift towards modernity's self-realisation, then this shift can be seen through the ways painting changes its conception of itself as a signing.

Throughout this text painting has been implicated with 'first' questions, questions of ontology and metaphysics, of Language and Being, and has been shown as a celebratory exploration of them. Several interchanges in the pluralogue showed paintings as working in the space between meaning and Being, as providing metaphors (works that mean through what they 'say') for Being and for the thereness of things, of experience, and metaphor was shown as precisely about the work of relating. Modern painting's practical engagement of meaning produced works which were metaphors for relation itself. But perhaps this reading of painting as relation, encouraged by what modern painters themselves said about their work, is already a post-modern reading? Perhaps we can find already inscribed in modernity from the beginning alternative possibilities, the pre-tracing of the post-modern?

If modernity in painting invited us to approach it through the metaphors of writing and reading it did so through displaying itself as a concern with origins – its own and those of Language; origin here refers to the very constitution of meaning itself in and as a creative act. The painter's task was to explore the origination of meaning, the coming-into-being of painting as meaning, through making works that radically questioned conventions of meaning in the Tradition. And this had to include a positive hope for a belief in meaning, in the absolute value of seeking metaphors for the meaning of Being. Modern painting, working with a phenomenological sense of truth as disclosure, was to be the making of signs for Being itself. It was as if the painting could open us onto, give us a glimpse of the 'thing', of Being itself. Painting and art here were indeed tied to the Logos: painting as a saying of Being.

The search for the purity of the Absolute has been a consistent theme across different areas of modern practice; modernism, albeit under the banner of abstraction took this search for the pure origin, the real meaning, the absolute essence, of painting to its limit via formalism, but it could only do so because it found this urge already inscribed into the beginnings of modernity itself. Selecting this out as the 'real' meaning of modernity, modernism pursued it with the utmost rigour. As 'signifier' the telos of the painting was to carry us to its signified, the being, the essence of art itself, and this in turn was to point to its own possibility within Being. But the painting's life as a sign or bearer of signs, as signifier(s) with signified(s), was already complicated. For the signifying work seemed to open onto a plurality of signifieds: it had to point forward beyond itself to the being of art; it had to point backwards to Tradition; it had to point outside itself to the specificity and difference of the artist's vision (declining often into style); and it had to point beyond itself to the being of whatever was re-presented concretely (an 'object' or 'being' in 'nature' or phenomenal experience). But above all, and first of all, in Merleau-Ponty's word it had to be 'autofigurative', to be a sign of itself, or, through being a sign of itself, to be at once a sign of all its other referents. And yet, confounding all this 'positive' signifying work, the painting, done on behalf of no-thing, for no other end than itself, had 'at the same time' to be a 'sign which refuses to signify' (Rose, 1975, p.111). As the in-itself-for-itself, on behalf of nothing other than itself-as-art (and thus on behalf of art and Tradition as no-thing), it could never become a positive sign; rather it is the unbecoming of the sign, the becoming unsigned of the sign.

Somehow all the apparent signifieds (Being, Tradition, Vision, World) are undone, are dispersed in the very movement of writing-reading in which a certain referent seems to solidify and take shape, 'take place'. The respondent as reflexive constituting reader discovers that in trusting to and succumbing to the play of signifiers no privileged signified can be established; the privileging of one signified over another is immediately subverted by the trace within it of another signifier which inserts it into a further chain of signifiers. Each painting as text opens onto the multiple play of signifiers for which there is no right, final, privileged reading, but only readings. As with the painter's painting of the picture, the respondent stops, disengages, not as a result of a cracking of 'the' code, but rather through practical contingencies, exhaustion, or the waning of interest and Desire.

If modernity began as a renewal of the search for Being through an attempted reflexive grasping of art itself, where Being was the One which was 'present' in every presence, the One that each painting sought however fleetingly to present in its very presence, then post-modernity is the displacing of this hope, this Desire for the fullness of Being. Modernity in its lapse into modernism certainly clung to this metaphysics of presence, for painting was the search for its own formal essence. The painting's signifiers were to signify this essence.

But the transition into post-modernity is marked precisely by a different reading of painting's signing work. In this shift, modernity, as the exploration of ways of re-presenting, of signing, something outside itself, begins to realise itself, to recognise itself as forever caught in the play of re-presentation: no more 'presences', only re-presentations. As the multiplier of re-presentation, post-modernity, denying a presence beyond re-presentation, immerses itself in the play of signification on behalf of re-presentation itself. For there is nothing else: no truth (only truths), no essence (only differences), no wholes (only fragments), no boundaries (only intertextuality), no masterpieces (only the gesture of their refusal) . . . only re-presentation (of that which is always already in re-presentation).

If modernity celebrated the coming-to-be of meaning apparently *ab nihilo* in the difference each painter's vision made to Tradition, it accomplished this through its commitment to the Good of sharing, through the re-socialising of painting's languages. Modern painting began by believing in the revelatory power of Language, so that painting was a passive exhortation to the other to join the painter on this site of the renewal of Language. As the coming-to-be of Language, painting exemplified the coming-to-be of the meaning of signing, of the social itself. Painting in avant-garde terms was to assist in, was to exemplify, was to be an agent in, the emergence of new social forms, in spite of and perhaps because of the very difficulty pointed to by Klee: 'We still lack the ultimate strength, for there is no culture to sustain us' (Klee, 1961, p.65).

This need for the other was typically founded and supported by the universalist metaphysics found in manifestos where the 'one way', the absolute and exclusive justification sponsored a painting practice that was always open to the lapse into style through repetition; the recommended search for a new language often terminated once the artist, supported by the shared terms of a programme or manifesto, had established his or her stylistic difference. Repetition ensured a style's, a language's, sociality. Modernity discovered that any re-presentation could be read, could and would be meaningful, in a culture founded on the Desire for Reason, the search for meaning, for the Logos; but specific languages, each painter's difference, soon exhaust their revelatory power through the lapse into the comfort of repetition. And each new difference reminds us that there are only differences, no one right way, no single sublime, no final saying, only differences whose possibility was inscribed into modernity from its inception. And if modernity knows only a fractured sublimity, that there is no absolute, no pure essence of painting, but only a multitude of crossing paths, then it comes to recognise that the cult of style, the establishing and pursuit of a 'single' difference, can only result in a repetition which turns into the absolute denial of modernity itself. Modernity ironises its own commitment by negating itself through its decline into style.

Post-modernity is the dawning of the decadence of style, of repetition, which is why it is both a going beyond modernism and a recovery of the originating Good of the modern commitment itself. Part of the radical promise of modernity in its emergence was its commitment to the undoing of style, where style was the lapse into the false securities of mannerism, habit, convention. Style, as the corruption of vision, is marked by the disappearance of self-questioning within the domain of the signifier, that is, at the level of the painter's making of his or her 'own' language; for to be absolutely modern required that continual searching for the new language that was adequate to the painter's experience of the 'present'. And within this experience primacy was to be given to the defining and opening experience of the self-transforming Tradition of painting itself. To stay within the terms of a stylistic difference, a difference which may indeed in the beginning have been a result of an artist's vital process of self-questioning, is to lapse into patterns of repetition which consign the work to the pre-history of modernity. To habitualise, to conventionalise, to systematise a difference, is to re-introduce the Academy into modernity's body, for what it allows is the containment of the painter's vision through the rules of signification established in making a difference in the first place. In the rigidification of a style the signifiers of its language channel and limit the painter's vision in such a way as to provide only for variations within the confines of an established language.

It may be considerably easier for us retrospectively to re-construct style as one of the major threats to modernity in the light of the post-structuralist critique of 'presence'. For if modern painting in its earlier stages sought a truth to experience (modern experience, 'the present'), a truth to the 'things themselves', to the 'being', the 'thatness' of things, it may often have been partially caught within a metaphysics of presence. Artists and respondents may have worked with a sense of the work of art as offering something in its essence, as giving us a glimpse of the being of something. To establish a painterly difference in this context could have been seen as the opening onto some phenomenological truth; repetition of this difference (what I am calling the lapse into style) might well be supported by a conviction that this very making of difference was an opening onto Being itself. To live and practise within this difference would then be a continuing self-confirmation of the belief in painting's ability to carry the artist and the respondent into its realm of truth. And perhaps we can see the consequences of this belief wherever we find only variation and repetition of the signifiers over a long period in a painter's oeuvre; very often such work will be protected by a rhetoric making claims for the ability of such work to open us to the sublime, to Being.

The New York school of abstract expressionist painters and much of the succeeding modernist abstract painting exemplifies the problem, for the repetition of the signifier defines the later work of many of its members. The work of both Rothko and Newman, for example, became increasingly academic (by remaining within a limited play of signifiers and combination rules that allowed for infinite variation within repetition). And in this local context the radical transformations in Guston's paintings are instructive. For Guston had made doubt central to his practice from his earliest years. His oeuvre displays a restless movement, a ceaseless quest, in which doubt precludes from the beginning the possibility that painting was the search for the one 'right' difference. Doubt continually worked to prevent, to subvert, the securities of a lapse into style: 'The trouble with recognisable art is that it *excludes* too much. I want my work to *include* more. And "more" also comprises one's doubts about the object, plus the problem, the dilemma, of recognising it' (Ashton, 1976, p.132).

It was from within this doubt that figuration began to re-emerge as he moved out of the abstract expressionist aesthetic, raising for the respondent the issue of whether figuration had ever really been absent even in his 'abstract' work. Similarly, it is doubt which precipitated his subsequent but temporary withdrawal from paint- ing into a period of intensive drawing in which his re-address of 'things', of figuration, precipitated his leap into a radical but abso- lutely personal figuration. And whilst this later painting contains many traces of his earlier work, going right back to some of his earliest painting imagery, it exemplifies his willingness to question the ways that he was succumbing to his own signifiers and to try to recognise the ways that they were continually working to control, contain, and limit his vision.

Guston's later figurative painting, a figuration in tension with abstraction, by keeping alive modernity's self-questioning at the same time inscribes a post-modern practice in its equivocating of the relation between signifier and signified. Whilst the hooded figures, the boot soles and other imagery may refer us beyond the paintings to the cultural text itself we can find nothing 'out there' which enables us to 'de-code' them. They assemble a 'meaningless' text – meaningless that is in terms of the conventional relations between signifiers and signifieds. The paint seems loaded with a meaning that is beyond our meanings; the paintings disconcert in this very painterly undoing of the comfortable securities of re-presentation which we mundanely inhabit. We are insistently thrown back upon Guston's own paintings, his oeuvre, and behind them the Tradition itself, as our only resource; and when we do this these very resources equally insistently return us to each painting in itself as the dissolving of signification. In the very work of celebrating painting as painting his late paintings keep alive the question 'What and how does painting re-present?'. We are confronted by a qualita- tively different void to that pointed to in the rhetoric surrounding Rothko's paintings and another sublime to that of Newman. For with Guston lack, absence and sublimity are already caught within the web of re-presentation; far from being elsewhere, beyond the painting, beyond the text (some transcendental signified), the lack is a condition of the text itself, of our insinuation within its folds, and its insinuation within us. For Guston and for post-modernity paint- ing is no longer and has never been an occasion for going some- where else, a means to another end, but an exploration of the ways we are in the thrall of re-presentation itself, of how we can never escape from the signifiers to a realm of pure signifieds. As an absolute rejection of the aesthetic categories of the formalism that dominated late American modernism and the hegemonic sensibility that it fostered, Guston's work, through its self-doubt, its self-parody, its self-mockery, thrusts irony (previously the preserve of Duchamp-inspired artists like Johns and Morris) into the very centre of painting's site.

And his painting, together with a wide range of post-modern work, marks a break with modernity's earlier concern with the question of meaning, with the belief that paintings were signs taking us nearer to things in themselves, to their inner meaning. Modernity's demand to be read, through the interplay of metaphor and metonymy, as writing, as the inscription of Being, required the active participation of the respondent. But the very entwining of painting with Language and writing already equivocates this apparent Desire for meaning, for presence, by showing painting's and by extension Language's condition as re-presentation. If one of modernity's central achievements was its assertion of and its drawing of attention towards the primacy of the play of the signifiers as its very condition, then it has to be asked whether post-modernity is precisely the ironising of modernity's journey through signification. Perhaps post-modern work, recognising modernity's achievement in showing the need for an actively constituting perceptual/critical respondent, begins to reverse the journey, to take us back through it, but this time ironically.

If the outward journey was a deconstruction of the subject's (painter's and respondent's) relation to Language, then at the journey's 'end' (the collapse of modernity into modernism and the demise of the latter through the repetitions of style) painting discovers for itself that there is no 'one' end, no truth, no one over-riding privileged vision outside of Language for which it is ultimately responsible. Rather the subject is shown as inescapably caught within Language, writing and re-presentation. Modernity's search for meaning, for the revelation, the glimpse of the absolute, turns back on itself and on its being-within-Language to confront, to show, the very problem of this withinness: how to find and show the limits of this withinness in a world saturated by meaning.

Post-modernity faces the uselessness of attempting any 'final' 'saying'; and to do this it has to re-constitute painting's meaning as unmeaning. This subversion of meaning from within, this undoing of meaning, seeks the meaningless in the heart of meaning. But unmeaning here is not something beyond, the other side of, Language, it is rather the very condition of being-within-Language. Art is about and for the Nothing that Language is: and art work searches for that Nothing, the no-where that haunts every signifier. This Nothing is not the absence of a presence, a simple negative, but is rather the condition of Language itself, its essential lack. Ruptures, breaks, shifts, tears, rents, incisions, openings, apertures, halts, hesitations, stutters, closings, boundaries, inter-faces, conjunctions, frames, lines, hyphens, punctuation, all mark the zone within which the Nothing that intervenes as difference, as the in-between, is at work – unmeaning masked by meaning.

Post-modernity admits both modernity's uncovery and celebration of the power of the signifier and that we are, within modernity itself, in the thrall of and fascinated by the signifier, held in our reading by the very metonymic erotics of combination. But with this admission painting's task as the archaeology of the conditions of unmeaning is re-opened. Just as modernity had celebrated the radicality of the subject's constitution of meaning as writing-reading, so post-modernity realises the conditions of this quest through its commitment to the meaningless. So whilst post-modernity is in essential continuity with modernity in its radical stance towards the languages of Tradition (which now include those of the modern tradition) it marks its own difference in its turn away from meaning, away from the metaphorisation of Being. For modernity privileged metaphor over metonymy precisely because its works were to be taken as metaphors for states of affairs, states of being; the metonymic work (of writing-reading), whilst essential for the work's constitution, was subordinated to the metaphor, to the way the work could be taken to stand for its other (its many possible signifieds). Post-modernity deconstructs metaphor, the very site of meaning's coming-to-be, in its attempt to stay with, to follow, the constant scattering of meaning, its dispersal, in the inter-penetration of the signifiers. It not only finds the threat to meaning in this dispersal, but delights in it and exploits it. It can no longer, if indeed it ever was, be a case of a signifier having an unequivocal relation to its signified; an expressionist brush stroke can no longer be read as an unambiguous sign of some presumed preceding extra-linguistic state of the artist (anguish, anger, joy, or whatever), but is first of all an inscription in a text, a text within an archive of texts, standing absolutely independently of what within express-ionism it might be taken to 'express'. And, in any case, the 'state' of the artist (feelings. . .) is already always textuallsed; we can know of this state of being only through the texts which bring it before us, bring it into meaning. In whichever direction reference takes us we find the referent already a signifier in another chain. It is only through staying with the signifiers, through its play with the play of signifiers, that post-modernity can encounter the ruptures and make the incisions that carry it away from meaning into the anasemic swirl, the no-where of spacing-tracing.

Now this site of practice is in a very specific relation to its own modern past as well as to Tradition generally, for what it wants to do, has to do, is to re-work the gestures of painting from within another site – to equivocate the 'meaning' of the gestures on behalf of non-meaning. Those gestures which, in their origination within modernity, sought to display their relation to their object (painting) and their subject (the painter) as a true authentic relation – painting as truth-to-being – have to be equivocated, for, as signifiers they already contain traces of other signifiers, of what they are not. For post-modernity no painting can be taken as a capturing of the 'presence' of some-thing, but can only be a re-presentation of re-presentation(s), a simulacrum, a metaphor for the original copy. To find non-meaning at work in the heart of that massive weight of meaning through which modernity sustained itself (the meaning of cubism, of orphism, of suprematism, of productivism, of expressionism, of dada (yes, even of dada), of futurism, of surrealism, of abstract expressionism, of post-painterly abstraction, of pop, of super-realism, of minimalism, of conceptualism, of modernism itself. . .), to find, in other words, its own complicity with, its own pre-figuring within modernity, the post-modern has to re-explore, to appropriate, to ironise modernity for its own ends. And also for the Good of modernity too – to return modernity to Nothing.

Modernity's markings, gesturings, figurings, imagings, abstractings, spacings, colourings, drawings, patternings, formings, all the differences through which it sought to sever itself from what had preceded it, from convention, become the necessary focus of post-modern work in its search for difference. And since convention, that which modernity sought to escape, embodies meaning, the original thrust of modernity itself was indeed into non-meaning. Modernity too sought non-meaning, Nothing, on behalf of Being; it displayed painting as a practice whose sole concrete concern was with that realm traditionally named by philosophy as the metaphysical, or, more precisely, the ontological. Now if the goal, the point, of the absolutely concrete practice, the making of paintings, is always and only ontological, is always a re-making of a re-marking of re-presentation itself, of difference itself (what Heidegger earlier named as the ontological difference – the difference between Being and beings) then any work's engagement of a specific language is always a detour, but an absolutely unavoidable detour. We can only approach, be drawn into, the play of difference from where we are within Language. So the modern painter's generation of a language, a language perhaps specific to a single painting, is the detour carrying us towards the undoing of meaning. and the post-modern recovery of its origins within modernity, this re-appropriation of modernity's marks and traces, far from being a simple taking over of the original rhetoric of justification, only works through a radical transformation of painting's earlier conventions. No gesture can any longer mean what 'it did' in the context of its emergence and original difference. The very irony underwriting the re-appropriation not only renews but also preserves painting from the modernist threat of death, thus traditionalising post-modernity itself; in re-opening and rejoicing in the possibilities of painting post-modernity traditionalises itself and shows itself as anything but a negative irony. But in this very transformative work it confounds the art-historical significance, the meaning, of the earlier originating gestures; it seeks to erase the steady accretion of layers of meaning which have subsequently pulled the works of modernity into a clearly theorised, historically comprehended pattern. Its project is to return painting itself to a state of resistance to meaning. In a culture which not only can but must assimilate everything to meaning, which must conventionalise and rationalise in order to preserve itself, this is a difficult and perhaps despairing project.

Now this reading of the relation between modernity and post-modernity has already put the discourses of the sign to work through showing the primacy that modernity generally gave to the signifier. The terms of linguistics and semiotics have so far been used as an adjunct in this exploration of painting's work; and as with writing-reading I am suggesting that it is painting itself which confronts us with the problem, that of the sign. The sign as problem is not something grafted onto painting from the outside but is generated from within modernity's concerns as the terrain within which its transformation and renewal of writing and reading would be worked through. But this working through confronts the discourses of the sign with radical problems. It puts them into question on their very own ground because it faces their terms with questions which they are constitutionally incapable of dealing with.

8

Painting Signing-on and Signing-off

Ineluctable modality of the visible: at least that if no more, thought through my eyes. Signatures of all things I am here to read, seaspawn and seawrack, the nearing tide, that rusty boot. Snotgreen, bluesilver, rust: coloured signs. Limits of the diaphane (James Joyce, *Ulysses*).

Within the comparatively brief life of semiotics (it occurs within, and is itself a response to, modernity) the aesthetic object has been at the centre of its interests. Creating a new site for analytical-critical practice between the human sciences, linguistics, philosophy and criticism, its very transcendence of disciplinary boundaries has produced widespread disquiet within the methodological confines of particular disciplines; and yet, and this may be a significant problem when it seeks to grasp both art practices and art works, it displays a very similar stance towards its object of knowledge to these other disciplines. No general assessment of the potential of semiotics or its radical implications for the human sciences can be attempted here, although many of the issues that arise through relating semiotics to painting do bear directly on the practice of these disciplines. Descombes' lucid account of the place of semiotics in contemporary French philosophy opens onto many of the issues which the present inter-weaving of painting, Language and modernity engages (Descombes, 1980). And Barthes's writing is exemplary in this context, for his work, moving across the spectrum of cultural analysis, both espouses and then goes beyond the semiotic sign. Exemplifying the post-structural turn towards writing and the play of signification, his later writing shows, from within criticism, what it is to be absolutely modern in its undoing of his own earlier semiotic (see the trajectory of his writing from *Writing Degree Zero*, 1967, through *Elements of Semiology*, 1969, and *Image, Music, Text*, 1977, to *Camera Lucida*, 1982a, and *Barthes by Barthes*, 1982b).

Apart from what it shares with other forms of art painting raises specific problems for semiotics, and various writers have offered programmes for analysing painting or analyses of specific issues (see, for example, Schapiro, 1969, Bann, 1970, Matejka and Titunik, 1976, Damisch, 1979, and Marin, 1979). The writings considered here were selected because they open most clearly onto the fundamental themes of this text – the inter-relation at the level of practice of modern painting with Language and writing in a post-modern culture, and the problems this raises for theorising, for theoretical understanding, and for the respondent as critical reader.

Can there be sign, a signifier, without a referent? This is the challenge which modern and post-modern painting throw down to semiotics, philosophy and the human sciences. And this challenge can take different forms. For, if painting is auto-figurative, is about itself, it is a signifier of itself. How can something be both signifier and signified? What would mark the difference? And if modernity is a 'starting again' of the practical exploration of Being-within-Language, and if both Being and Language are the other side of a specific language or languages, then Being is certainly neither 'thing' nor concept, for it is our own very possibility. Can Being, Being-as-writing, be a referent, a signified, if it is no-thing? Can semiotics countenance a sign without a signified? And, pushing further, if post-modernity is precisely the attempt to deny meaning, the inscribing of non-meaning, the lack, the void within meaning itself, its signified could only be Nothing. What is it to be a signifier of (and for) Nothing? All these questions are utterly un-reasonable and wild questions, but they serve to show painting (and art too?) as absolutely other to the rational. Painting comes to itself, into its ownmost, only at this level, in the region that is no-where; it has already signed itself off the semiotic map. Every attempt to recuperate painting for science (semiology, linguistics, the human sciences) that fails to approach art on art's terms, in art's own region, succeeds only in rehearsing and re-presenting its own method without ever touching or being touched by painting. Can practices, methods, discourses, whose very urge and thrust is to subdue phenomena, to convert them into their own things, find a way of relating to, of sharing, of loving, that which is their absolute other? No! For these practices painting and works of art can only be vehicles for displaying the strength of method to overcome anything, to pull back everything into the system of meaning on their own terms. But what happens to painting, to the painter, to the respondent, when semiotics treats them as objects of knowledge?

Eco's general conceptual schema for semiotics leads us into work which engages painting more specifically (Eco, 1976). Promisingly, Eco argues that 'the aesthetic text represents a sort of summary and laboratory model of all the aspects of the sign-function' (op.cit., p.261). Following Jakobson he notes too that a message or text assumes an aesthetic function when it is both ambiguous and self-focusing (op.cit., p.262). This obliges the respondent to recon- sider the correlation of content and expression. The text directs the attention of the addressee primarily 'to its own shape' (op.cit., p.264). Rules broken on the planes of both the signifier and the signified produce an ambiguity in the respondent requiring an interpretative effort to engage the 'unexpected flexibility in lan- guage' (op.cit., p.263). But the finding of this unexpected flexibility turns the work of art into an object of knowledge, or rather it becomes a vehicle for producing 'further knowledge' of the cul- ture's, the language's, codes (op.cit., p.274). Indeed the virtue of aesthetic texts for Eco is that they will provide semiotics with vehicles for clarifying many of the problems left unsolved by 'tradi- tional philosophical aesthetics'. The work of art is related to as an object for analysis, a means to the solving of problems by one discourse (semiotics) abandoned or unsolved by another (philoso- phy). We are here thrown not into art but into the politics of discourse, the politics of knowledge appropriation. For whether and how the work of art may be a source of knowledge (a knowledge specific to art and not semiotic, psychological, sociological, psychoanalytic, biological, physical, or any other knowledge what- ever) cannot be decided by fiat from within one sense of knowledge (here, semiotic) which fails to put its own sense of knowledge in question.

Semiotics thus reconstitutes the work of art as its own object of knowledge and then traverses and dissects it according to its own concepts and methods. For semiotics this means 'finding' (consti- tuting) the 'rational', the codable, in what was previously taken to be non-rational (the unspeakable residue, the 'je ne sais quoi' of the work of art) (op.cit., p.265). The semiotic rule is to de-code every- thing. But what this hides is the originating hypothesis and consti- tuting work of semiotics concerning the universality of coding. The empiricist would argue that the codes are already 'there' indepen- dently 'in' the phenomena being analysed; but perhaps it is semio- tics itself, through the ingenuity of its method that constitutes the codes: perhaps what is taken to be a phenomenon that is coded throughout all its 'levels' is rather a phenomenon constituted through the elaborate analytical coding practices of the semiotic method. Without this assumption of universal and absolute codedness semiotics could not operate, for, with meaning as its own territory it has no way of marking or knowing its own limits. Semiotics thus cannot allow anything to escape its conceptual sway, even though Eco will allow the 'addressee' a certain inventive freedom. The text, the painting, is already completely encased in and traversed by meaning, for the respondent's ' "open" experience is made possible by something which should have (and indeed has) a structure at all levels' (op.cit., p.276).

Yet it is precisely Nothing which escapes this ubiquitous structuring. The work of art confronts us with the question of whether Nothing is something we can have (semiotic) knowledge about. We might ask of semiotics, what is the code for Nothing? Because, for semiotics, there is only being, only meaning, because it recognises no difference between Language and languages, it cannot comprehend the absolutely un-reasonable Nothing, the abyss between Language and languages, between Being and beings, between writing and speech. How can lack be a referent?

Perhaps this is resolvable in those analyses which specifically treat painting. Bryson has offered a semiotics of painting which seeks to confront a theoretically moribund art history with the possibility of re-siting its practice. Although not developed in relation to specifically modern painting it is clearly proposed as the basis for a general methodology capable of addressing all painting (Bryson, 1981, 1983), and it is centred on the sign, the material sign:

> painting *as sign* must be the fundamental assumption of a
> materialist art history; the place where the sign arises is the
> *inter-individual* territory of recognition; that the concept of the
> sign's meaning cannot be divorced from its embodiment *in*
> *context* (Bryson, 1983, p.131).

This introduces three of Bryson's fundamental themes: signing as a material practice; the importance of understanding the practices of both painting and viewing; and the contexted character of both making and viewing paintings. In the latter case it is the 'social formation' itself which is the all-embracing setting for these practices.

The complexity of Bryson's analysis provides a strong challenge to the conventions of art historical practice, for he shows the necessity for art history of constructing a theory which can comprehend painting and viewing as always socially contexted languaged practices. Painting and discourse inter-twine; and painting can only be recognised and given meaning as such through discursive material practices within a specific social formation. Certain global concerns and grounding concepts organise Bryson's theoretical field. Western painting, founded upon the centrality of oil painting, supposedly denies syntagmatic movement; it addresses visuality in an impossible and mythical 'guise of stasis' (op.cit., p.121). The centrality of this hypothesis of stasis to Bryson's argument is crucial for it supports one of several organising dichotomies; the Gaze polarised by the Glance. Western painting solicits the Gaze through producing works which seek to be both instantaneous and timeless, outside 'real time', outside the 'durée'. They exemplify for Bryson the Dream of Essential Copy (op.cit., p.121). Oil painting (glazes notwithstanding) has been used as an essentially opaque medium and this has provided for what Bryson calls its work of 'erasure'. It is the work of the body itself, the body which produced the painting, which is erased through successive layers of over-painting; the 'body of labour' absents itself from Western painting (op.cit., p.164) because the marks of production (mostly erased or buried) cannot be referred to their 'place in the vanished sequence of local inspirations' from which they emerged. The final surface which is presented to the respondent has erased the work of its own production through painting's commitment to and attempt to display an 'eternal moment of disclosed presence'. Seeking a synchronic instant of viewing, 'that will eclipse the body, and the Glance, in an infinitely extended Gaze of the image as pure idea' (op.cit., p.93), Western painting hopes to eliminate the 'diachronic' movement of 'deixis' (ibid.). And this points to a contrast basic to Bryson's argument; deixis is a linguistic concept ('indispensable for the analysis of painting' (op.cit., p.87)) for utterances that contain information about their locus in the text or chain. Over and against Western painting, Chinese and Japanese brush drawing/painting displays its ability to make reference to the 'body of labour', its preservation of the performance of the drawing; the work of production is displaced 'in the wake of its traces' (op.cit., p.92), whereas the alternative temporality of western painting is 'rarely the deictic time of painting as process' (ibid.). This marking, as the congealing of gesture into trace, then solicits not the Gaze but the Glance; and the Glance, against the Gaze, proposes Desire as that which can 'never be sated' (op.cit., p.121).

Bryson's analysis touches at several points the explorations of the present work; the contrast of the Gaze and the Glance, for example, resonates strongly with the contrast of metaphor and metonymy in the discussion of writing-reading, as does, at a more general level, his insistence on the necessity of implicating painting with language. But, in spite of his interest in theorising practice (particularly the practice of reading the painting) and his critique of de Saussure's failure to conceptualise practice, the value of his work lies in its potential for re-juvenating art historical theorising rather than in its re-presentation of painting as a site of the Desire for practice for both painter and respondent. Answerable only to theoretical interests painting is used as a vehicle to develop a theory of the relation between social formations and cultural production; however subtle or potentially illuminating to its own theoretical peers particular points of his strategy may be, the work contexts itself not within painting but within the theory of materialism. Painting is appropriated for the needs of this theory. And it is as an intervention in materialist theoretical practice that the work must be judged, for painting is radically elsewhere.

The dilemma all theorising faces in theorising art can be formulated thus: if painting (art) is radically other to theory, it cannot be assimilated to it, but can only be an occasion for theory to display itself while missing painting altogether; on the other hand, if painting (art) is merely one kind of knowledge among others, one 'thing' among others, a potential object of knowledge, then the only point of a theoretical treatment would be to flesh out its own system, to complete the theoretical system by including painting and showing the all-inclusive power of the method. In the first case, as a matter of practice (for the artist and a few respondents) art makes all the difference in the world, while in the second case art makes no difference at all (it might just as well be pigeon fancying).

Now if art makes a difference how can the theory display what it has to learn from art? Perhaps art might even be the undoing of theory. But which theorising, materialist or whatever, could bear to contemplate the awe-ful implications of this? As we have seen, of the discourses which treat art as topic only post-structuralism has been willing to suspend the need for theoretic mastery and control on behalf of an alternative sense of relation to the work of art.

It is not a question of asking Bryson's text (or any other text) to do something it did not set out to do, but rather of asking about the sense of art, of painting, that the text re-presents. If art makes no difference it can be *used* as a mere illustration of a theory; if it does make a difference, if it is other to the theory (*for* another kind of re-presentation to that of theory), the theory needs to find ways of showing what it might learn, what it has learned from art. If, as a matter of practice, painting is ontological, if it is about Being-as-writing, about Nothing, about, in other words, *the very ground on which theory seeks to secure itself*, then theory will not engage art but only itself, unless it finds a way of preserving and responding to the firstness of these 'abouts'.

It seems that Bryson's diagnostic materialism needs conceptual dualities, binary oppositions, to construct its object of knowledge (connotation/denotation, deictic/non-deictic, Gaze/Glance, material/non-material, Western oil painting/Japanese brush drawing, and so on), and art history's object of knowledge is reconstituted through these polarities. But art practice is somewhere else, busy working in-between. Even 'empirically' there are radical problems arising from working within such dualisms. For example, *does* Western oil painting, or even any major period or genre within it, eliminate deixis? It may be that many of the gestures of production constituting the pre-history of an oil painting are indeed buried, but the surface itself will inevitably point to these and is itself constituted as the inter-relating of deictic markers. It is hard to think of a 'major' painter, even those cited by Bryson, whose surfaces eliminate deixis (we need think only of Titian's 'Flaying of Marsyas' to recognise a virtuoso preservation of the body's labour). Indeed the absolutely flat, traceless surface may only characterise those paintings which, *precisely because of this*, display a falling away from painting's inner desire to both re-present the painter's relation to some-thing – to put some-thing in place of nothing – and, in so doing, to preserve and not erase its life as painting (at least its final life, the life of the surface that appears).

And this has been a central theme of modernity in painting (something in the light of which modernity invites us to re-read Tradition itself) – the recovery of the life of the painting through our engagement of the re-presenting marks. We have learnt this from the divisionism of impressionism, through Cézanne's colour patches, Pollock's drips and dribbles, to Clemente's slurries. Stages of a painting's genesis may indeed be buried or scraped away (just as the Japanese calligrapher may have scrumpled up many drawings before leaving us with the one which he or she wished to bequeath) but the very life of the final re-presenting surface, what the painting 'is', is unavoidably a display of the body's labour. The practice of water-based media (whether Japanese, English, or whatever) does indeed relate differently. Typically such media enter the ground rather than rest upon it; but this too has been frequently explored within the Western tradition, from the early renaissance fresco painters, through the life of water colour painting, to the acrylic soaked canvas practices of Helen Frankenthaler and Morris Louis. Japanese painting is certainly not alone in soliciting the eyes' movement, the Glance (or rather Glancing), through its preservation of the labour of marking, of the inter-weaving of gestures as the life of its production.

A painting's life is only sustainable both in its making and its reception through a continual interplay between the gazing and glancing that are the responses to the surface work; and insofar as modernity has required the reflexive exploration of painting itself, as a matter of practice, one of its accomplishments has been to confront the respondent with the tension between image (presence, stasis) and deixis (movement, gesture). And in this it has taught us to review Tradition itself in these very terms, to recover painting as this tension.

Clearly the essence of painting for Bryson has to be located in the gesture's mark because it secretes a trace of time and of the energy of labour, which, for him, is the material 'origin' of every cultural and social phenomenon. In this conception the Good of painting lies in this preservative ability, its exemplification of the production of significance through the transformation of matter. But matter, material life, remains wholly other, some 'thing', outside Language, and entering the latter only as discourse, where discourse is 'language *as it circulates* within the social formation' (op.cit., p.84); and painting, embedded in social discourse (op.cit., p.185), interacts with social formation. Now this takes us to the heart of the issue of Bryson's theoretical practice and interests for, if painting is treated as (a) language, we find at the root that a theory of reflection describes the relation between language and some language-independent social formation.

The catch-all 'social formation' glosses the crucial analytical issues because it is re-presented both as a language-independent 'thing' and also as the term for a process which is constituted by discursive practices, amongst which is painting. Painting as an intelligible social practice is analogised with language, where language consists of intelligible sentences (grammatically correct). But 'Those sentences which do not reflect the material conditions of the social formation cannot circulate within the social formation' (op.cit., p.84). Painting and language can finally do no more than reflect the material conditions of a specific social formation, where both the latter are beyond Language, transcendental signifieds. The social formation stands as an encompassing but analysed 'thing' enforcing (determining?) reflection in all acts of intelligibility.

The reflexive question arises, treating modern painting's own explorations as exemplary, of what this theory of reflection and determination would do to the life and status of Bryson's own text. How can the practice of writing escape the same determinations and reflective relationship? Or is it claiming some privileged exemption, the privilege, for example, to innovate? Is the labour of production of the material signs of writing in a relation of reflection to its 'place' in the social formation? Is the writing of materialist art theory ensnared by the very binary oppositions that contribute to Bryson's analyses of painting, and, if so, with what effects on the claims to authority (to theoretical mastery) that the writing seeks to make?

If Bryson gathers modernity to the tradition of western oil painting, seeing Picasso as a further exemplar of the erasure of deixis on behalf of the 'presence' of the image, there are other formulations of painting as sign which approach modern painting differently. Burnham offers a structuralist analysis of art grounded upon the language analogy (Burnham, 1973). Following on from Lévi-Strauss, Burnham proposes that art is a mythic system which relates the radical dualism of nature and culture posited by Lévi-Strauss in particular ways. The myth of art is one kind of reconciliation, a mediation of the two poles of nature and culture; if, as Lévi-Strauss suggests, religion is a humanisation of natural laws and magic is a naturalisation of human actions, then 'Art is simply another case of the conjunction of religion and magic, a language expressing the effects of both through its own internal logic' (op.cit., p.48). Successful art for Burnham is that which integrates successfully both effects as 'equally as possible'. As a language mediating the nature-culture opposition, the goal of art is to 'separate man from the undifferentiated consistency of nature, bringing a certain order to the environment as it is conceived' (op.cit., p.55).

In analyses of some forty three contemporary works of art (from Turner to Buren), together with a more detailed structuralist analysis of Duchamp's *Large Glass*, Burnham attempts to show how art as we know it is disappearing because 'the old separations between nature and culture no longer have any classificatory value' (op.cit., p.81). This is largely a result of the development of contemporary science which replaces those conceptions of human beings' relation to nature which informed Classicism (especially the Western ideal of constancy – the normal condition of things being inertia). And the supposedly linear career of modern art, seen by Burnham as a sequence of successive stages of avant-garde movements culminating in conceptualism, has been for him a movement towards a sense of art as a conceptual system whose surface ideas rest upon an inner logic, a structural relationship, which, when revealed (by, hopefully, his analysis) gives us the essence of art as a sign system. Modern art is the tradition of the successive discarding of habits or conceptions of perception through 'formal transgression' (the suspension or transformation of such phenomena as perspective, local colour, shape relationships, figure-ground constructions and body-object associations) based on literary or plastic innovations, and 'historical transgressions' which disrupt at the level of structure the myth that art progresses in time from stage to stage (op.cit., pp.47–8). Duchamp is cited as the first artist to employ 'historical transgressions' as a matter of strategy and this is repeated in the work of the linguistic conceptualists. Their work undercuts for Burnham the works of 'formal transgression' which still live within the myth of art as an historically progressive practice; conceptualism realises the end of art by treating art as in essence a proposition. 'Historical transgression' through its demythification of art opens up a site for the emergence of an artistic practice which would be 'much more essential to contemporary life' (op.cit., p.180).

Burnham's work brings to the fore the inherent tendency in structuralism to eliminate the work of art as a source of continuing value and interpretative interests through transforming it into a source of 'rationalist knowledge'; the claims made by structuralism, specifically that the 'meaning' or 'significance' of a phenomenon is carried by its inner structure (as laid bare by the analysis), produce it as completely 'known'. Once this knowledge of its inner structure is produced the phenomenon's other dimensions are no longer of interest and it becomes a merely historical curiosity, rather than something to which we may return again and again and whose significance changes dialectically in relation to the historical processes in which it participates. Thus Burnham's schematic analysis of Cézanne's *The Basket of Apples* (op.cit., pp.72–3) and his passing comments on Cézanne provide us with no reason for continuing to look at the works of Cézanne other than as exemplifications of that moment in the history of modernism when the implication of a 'literalist' picture plane (that is, a pictorial surface that claims no innate powers of illusion but depends upon the ordinary consistency of paint application to provide the naturalistic metaphor (ibid.)) is first examined. Cézanne's work signifies an art proposition whose significance for us now is as a 'formal transgression' of some traditional conventions of representation, and once structuralism has revealed this as the conceptual structure of the work it has, as far as the goal of structuralism goes, exhausted the work. Any more detailed examination, structuralist or otherwise, of the organisation of the surface or of the relation between the work and nature, or the work and the viewer, would be subsumable under the structure derived by the analysis. Structuralism, in other words, can offer us no reason for preserving the work other than as an index of a significant moment in modernism's history. It exemplifies in extreme form that predominant form of contemporary thought and art criticism which consumes the phenomenon that it takes as its topic.

This analytical or critical consumption of the phenomenon and its relativisation of all other kinds of relationship to the phenomenon exemplify the fundamental violence of instrumental modernity. Modern critical thought cannot allow space for the other; whether or not its own methods or concepts are internally dialectical it cannot develop a truly dialectical relationship with the phenomenon which would allow the phenomenon an existence independent of itself, of its own terms and methods. Yet this dialectical relationship is exactly what art above all needs. Because structuralism violates, takes apart, and disposes of the phenomenon it is constitutionally incapable of putting itself in a learning relationship with its topic. Structuralism could never learn anything from art because, far from approaching it as an other, it seeks to contain and subdue its otherness. Posing as a neutral metaphysics-free method structuralism presents itself as the one speech that can contain all others by revealing their hidden inner structures. In the case of painting this means reducing it to speech (the privilege of the phoné), and showing it ultimately as a conceptual relationship (op.cit., p.44). Painting reduces itself to the spoken word and the literal text replaces the painting; image and painting thus become footnotes of history. Once art has revealed its own underlying logic we can all turn to something else.

This kind of conceptualism both falls under the sway of a rationalism that is incapable of hearing the ontological questions as anything other than questions of logic, and also lives as a phonocentrism that privileges that form of writing (phonetic writing) which is already subordinated to speech; and phonocentrism here is also an ethnocentrism that privileges the writing of western culture over other forms of writing.

In putting the ontological out of play structuralism also excludes Desire and its implication with Writing-in-general. Structuralism and semiotics as method cannot conceive of the work of art as the erotic expression of Desire, as exemplifying a commitment to that which is its other, art as the desire for Being-as-writing. Their sense of Language renders it incapable of preserving this realm. Thus, Burnham in his structuralist analysis of Duchamp's *Large Glass* simply notes in passing Duchamp's self-transformation into Rrose Selavy and his equation of eros, art and Language. When Duchamp, in his notes for *The Green Box*, refers to the *Large Glass* as a 'World in yellow', Burnham, following Schwartz, notes the revelationary import of this, given the connotations of yellow as a symbol for eros, or the creative force (op.cit., p.160), but does not pick this up or develop it, for Duchamp's significance for Burnham is rather, that he has 'arrived at a semiological theory of modern art as early as 1912' (op.cit., p.170).

Burnham's Desire (and structuralism's too) is to produce the one correct reading of the *Large Glass* and this can be seen in his need to go through the particulars of the *Large Glass* and to translate them into an already comprehended language of symbols. The *Large Glass* is not, for Burnham, a plunge into the undoing of meaning; it is not read as a new text that takes on old texts and forever defers translation of them and itself by setting up its own anarchic 'meanings' which are absolutely specific to it. Surely its invitation to us is to stay entirely within its text, and, through a metonymically associative reading, to *create for ourselves* an absurd logic for it? Yet for Burnham its reason is a code which can be deciphered and its real message revealed. Because the work of art for structuralism is nothing in itself, is not the in-itself-for-itself, it can have nothing to do with Desire, it cannot be either celebration or a display of eros.

The invocation of Desire is not a reduction to psychological or psychoanalytical issues but is an expansion on to the ontological plane of the kinds of questions it is necessary to ask about the work of art in which every kind of analysis is implicated. Every analysis needs to address the ways in which its concepts either do or do not provide for this realm of questions, for it is art's very life to draw us towards them, to open us to them. Each work metaphorises the artist's failure to satisfy or capture the Desire from which it sprang, and the successful failures are those which give us a glimpse of this realm through the tensions which give them life and which we read in our relation with the work.

Painting seeks, then, to keep open a space for Desire, for Desire concretising itself as passion, as the scattering of the reasonable through the eruption of unreason, but an unreason tied to Tradition, directed unreason: we are returned to Rimbaud's reasoned deranging. Now if the discourses of the sign can only offer us structures of the reasonable, if they are defined by their need to construct a model of the reason in unreason, a structure of differences, their diagnoses of culture, while unable to place art as their absolute other, may nevertheless point to the tears, cracks, and fissures within the culture, within the rational, the reasonable, the 'ideological', the quotidian, where art is at work. Art may be found by de-fault; Baudrillard's writing opens onto this possibility (1975, 1981, 1983a, 1983b, 1983c).

171

Addressing painting in the context of a revision of Marx's political economy, his own work describes a trajectory out of political economy, through a critique of the emergence of the economy of the sign, towards the post-modern culture founded on communication and information. Through this we are returned to the problem of post-modernity in painting. His earlier work re-presents modern society reproducing itself through the production and consumption of signs: the essential commodity is the sign whose signifier, exchange-value, is continuously privileged over its signified (use-value). Every cultural phenomenon is consumed first of all as sign, and modern painting is no exception. Baudrillard offers a reading of the dynamics of painting within the modern economy, an economy founded on signing, that ties painting as signifier into the consumption of signs.

For Baudrillard modern painting realises itself in, is defined by, its quest for authenticity, the concrete marker of which is the painter's signature in the painting (1981, p.103). To be authentic is to produce paintings, an oeuvre, which mark their difference to all other paintings. The signature, and thus the painting, is no longer simply 'read' but 'perceived in its differential value' (ibid.). The painting is read first of all as its difference to paintings by others, and as the member of a series (the painter's oeuvre) whose significance (exchange-value) is precisely its difference, within modern painting as a system of differences, to other oeuvres. Today, where painting is no longer the 'restitution of appearances' (was it ever just this?), of some transcendent reality, the oeuvre is defined by its originality and originality is difference: 'Value is transferred from an eminent, objective beauty to the singularity of the artist in his gesture' (op.cit., p.104). This marks the beginning of modernity:

> The modern oeuvre is no longer a syntax of various fragments of
> a general tableau of the universe, 'in extension', where
> continuity and reversibility are active; rather it is a succession of
> moments. The oeuvres . . . are only able to follow one another in
> order then to refer, by virtue of their difference and their
> discontinuity in time, to a quite different mode, to the *subject-
> creator* himself in his unlikeness and in his repeated absence. . . .
> Once legitimacy is transferred to the act of painting, the latter
> may prove itself untiringly: by this very fact it constitutes a series
> (ibid.).

The referent of the work of art as signifier is thus first of all the series of which it is a member; all other referents (world, experience, nature, Desire, other painter's paintings, and so on) are not only inessential but irrelevant. The 'meaning' of a painting is thus tied to the 'constraint of seriality'. And the inauthentic, be it forgery or, crucially, the artist's own defection from the gestures constituting the difference of the series, threatens not only the series but the system itself: 'Today only the artist may copy himself. In a sense, *he is condemned to do so* and to assume, if he is logical, the series character of creation' (op.cit., p.106).

It is painting itself, or rather two paintings, which explore and reveal this limit. Rauschenberg's *Factum I* and *Factum II*, ironising the gestural qualities of abstract expressionist painting, are two supposedly identical abstract paintings. The doubled canvases confront the question of authenticity and seriality: they are both the same and different (painted at different moments with small differences of paint handling, having different owners, and separate exchange-values). And yet we cannot know whether one is the copy of the other, and each first of all 'means' – signifies – the other. 'Subjectivity triumphs in the mechanical repetition of itself' (ibid.; in italics in original). Any attempt to turn painting 'back' towards 'the world', to painting's exterior, to insert a 'new' referent, other signifieds, has, first of all, Baudrillard suggests, to come to terms with this deeper level of coding, for 'what is signified . . . in contemporary art is . . . a certain temporality that is that of the subject in its self-indexing (and not the social individual of biographical data)' (op.cit., p.107). The respondent's construction of the artist's difference consists largely of reading the variations and repetitions that constitute the difference (what I have earlier called 'style'). And it is the systematic of repetition that confounds the ideology of art's criticality (the avant-garde justification for modernity), for this systematic gesture of authenticity, of spontaneity, nostalgically marks a lack (the lack of the integral spontaneous subject) in a culture where the subject is 'crushed by the technical habitus' (op.cit., p.108). But this marking by its very systematic of repetition is inversely homologous to the systematic of the full technical world; its systematic seriality reflects the systematics of the world which contains it. This contradictory character nevertheless preserves art as ambiguous but defines its limiting condition, for art 'can only signify the world on the basis of a structural affinity that simultaneously marks the fatal character of the *integration*' (op.cit., p.109). Baudrillard does allow a tiny hole, a chink, in this all-encompassing power of signification – the symbolic; although repressed by the sign's positivity, the symbolic continues to haunt the sign, for in its total exclusion it never ceases to dismantle the formal correlation of signifier and signified.

Subsequently Baudrillard (1983a, b, c) accentuates the disappearance of 'reality' through formulating the system (modern culture) as a 'simulacrum'; in a system dominated by the electronic media of communication, the production of meaning dominates and the model for this production is essentially cybernetic, that of information and the genetic code. Through the simulations of communication and information the real is transformed into the hyperreal; the society (western capitalism) that developed through explosion, a centrifugal movement, having nowhere else to go, turns back upon itself: implosion of meaning. 'The very definition of the real becomes: that of which it is possible to give an equivalent reproduction. At the limit . . . that which is always already reproduced' (Baudrillard, 1983a, p.146). As a hyperreality, reality itself becomes 'esthetic', for with the confusion of the imaginery and the real, 'esthetic fascination is everywhere' (op.cit., p.150). With production reproducing itself artifice, and so art, is everywhere, and therefore nowhere: the death of art. Metaphor and metonymy are abolished in digitality (op.cit., p.152)

We are faced with a diagnosis of absolute limit, of the terror of the sign, for there is nowhere else to go other than to another level of simulation. Baudrillard's earlier pointing to the symbol as the sign's other seems to have been absorbed by the over-production of meaning; but what about Desire, what about the 'silent majority's' destructive inertia, its 'refusal of socialisation', what about its resistance to the social, to simulation (Baudrillard, 1983b)? The silent majority, as the unmeaning of politics, is the last hole in the hyperreal system.

As with the previous writers considered, art becomes an occasion for displaying the authority of the writing, its ability to subdue its topics, its other; and we need to ask again whether the theoretical reason under-writing Baudrillard's rhetoric has exhausted its topic (here, for us, painting and art). In Baudrillard's world of all-encompassing simulation, of hyper-reality, where does *his* writing stand? Can it free itself from the rule of simulation? And if not, what does this do to its own attempted critical intervention? What privileges his critical voice while art is shown as succumbing? What would be the Good of writing if it knew itself to be caught within the surrounding information systems? What Desire underwrites Baudrillard's own writing? Can it preserve some subliminal Hope or is it condemned to self-mockery? But perhaps there are escape clauses, fissures, lacunae, in his end-game rhetoric. . . .

To find nothing in art that is beyond theory's grasp and scope, no excess, is itself excessive, for it finally puts the theory itself beyond the conditions of simulation which contain all other practices, art included; theory seeks to display itself as the exceeding of simulation. And the reduction of art practice, painting, to a condition of seriality, of difference and repetition, has all the marks of another formalist or essentialist reading, a re-presentation of the 'presence' of what painting 'really is' (seriality). What Baudrillard has to take for granted here is the absolute loss of any referent, any signified, other than a work's reference to its place within the series, the painter's oeuvre. His argument relies on the absolute and necessary subordination of reference to the signified – 'series'. But what if there were other signifieds working at the same or a deeper level than the 'series?'

In the previous discussion of modernity I also proposed difference as a fundamental constituent, but it was Tradition itself, it was the Desire to re-member and celebrate Tradition, that provided for painting's identity with itself; and this is profoundly different from reducing and restricting identity to identity with a single oeuvre. If we can respond to a work only in terms of its identity with the series of the individual artist's work how could we possibly recognise it as 'art', as 'painting', in the first place? The Desire to re-member Tradition, to celebrate painting itself, is precisely what exceeds theoretical reason, what exceeds the restriction of reference to the single oeuvre. Tradition is The Series, transcending the specific condition of modernity (which Baudrillard seeks to diagnose) and confounding any attempt to show modernity as emerging from an absolute rupture with its past. And if Tradition itself, Tradition as already a web of signifiers, must become a crucial referent, may there not be others equally important? Might these not include Writing-in-general, Desire, Other, Nothing, all those non-concepts which provide the space for both painting and theory (Baudrillard's included) 'in the first place'? Are these not the signifieds beyond the ontic but within Language, within textuality, which act to subvert the proposed homology between modern painting's system and the surrounding system of sign consumption? Once again the terrorism of theory, in subjugating art to its reasonable rule, seeking to keep art within reason (just as Baudrillard himself proposes that information plans to keep the 'masses' within reason (Baudrillard, 1983b, p.97)) operates a radical limit on painting through its appropriation. From supposedly secure grounds, in a region apparently free from the ligatures of the sign, of simulation, theory pretends to capture what art 'is', and shows it as a surrogate but failed form of critique, a pale shadow of itself.

And yet (there is invariably an 'and yet') Baudrillard may well have shown us what has been proposed earlier as the decadent form of modernity, modernity's empty shell, the decline into modernism. For what is the painter's supposed condemnation to copy himself (Baudrillard, 1981, p.106) if not the lapse from vision into style? And this challenge that modernity still throws down is precisely what is picked up in post-modernity where style is itself the question; post-modernity, as modernity coming-to-itself, is the ironising of style as the condition of modernism, the ironising of 'isms'. Baudrillard's constitution of post-modern culture as a hyperreality of simulation does insinuate unavoidable questions for a painting practice in a critical relation to modernism.

Learning the lesson of the decline into style, post-modern practice would have to keep as its goal something other than the production of an oeuvre as series gathered through stylistic repetition. Continual disruption of the series, the subversion of identity, putting the 'one', the style out of joint, re-open the space of post-modern practice; this realigns it with the emergent modern question of what it is to be absolutely modern. The painter has continually to confront what it is to begin again (and again, and ag. . .) and the consequent ever-present threat of artistic exhaustion (remembering Rimbaud's abandonment of poetry): the impossibility of re-inventing self and the history of art when confronting each new blank canvas. Post-modernity re-presents both the Desire for this and the realisation of its impossibility. But this realisation occurs, post-modernity is generated, within a very different culture to that of nascent modernity. And Baudrillard's shift of the problematic of culture onto the terrain of simulation, the over-production of meaning, inadvertently opens onto other features of post-modern painting.

In the information society, with its global saturation of communication, meaning, with nowhere to go but itself, implodes; reality has disappeared in the multiplication of models, of simulacra. However, perhaps reality is replaced not by a single hyperreality as Baudrillard proposes, but rather by hyperrealities: absolute fragmentation. And fragmentation has been a constant referent of modern painting itself – the search for meaning, for being, in the face of meaning's lack, succeeded by the post-modern undoing of meaning in the face of meaning's excess. In recuperating modernity's life as the thrust to deconstruct, post-modern practice sites itself in relation to the hyperrealities of 'post-culture' (the term is used by Steiner, 1971). Knowing that art alone, that painting alone, has always been absolutely powerless to change anything, that painting is precisely the other of power, it offers itself as the absolutely passive subversive and puts itself to one side of the positivities of information, of the semiotic sign – not as its simple negative, but beyond its region. Stubbornly signing Nothing in a culture where everything is a sign of something, it resists meaning passively, silently. Perhaps this is the return of the symbol hinted at by Baudrillard.

Working in the gaps between the multiplying hyperrealities, picking its way between the shards of the self-fragmenting information culture, post-modern practice inscribes the Nothing that is the other to the over-drive production of meaning. If we try to hold it within the terms of the semiotic sign we find that all its primary signifieds (Being, Nothing, Writing, Desire, Tradition, this particular painting) turn out to be on a plane which the semiotic sign cannot contain, for as its very possibility they mark the limit of the semiotic sign itself. In a world marked by the penetration of everything by simulation and re-presentation (we are reminded of Benjamin's earlier thesis about the revolutionary power of the camera to insinuate itself into the body of the world, to re-present everything, Benjamin, 1969), where we are confronted by the 'absolute proximity' (Baudrillard, 1983b, p.132) and instantaneity of everything (not-in-itself but as simulacrum), painting serves to remind us of lost things, of the absence of the 'nearness of things' to which Heidegger has also pointed us. The greater the power of simulation the further do Writing-in-general, Being and Desire recede from us. Simulation seeks interminably to defer, absolutely to seal off, passion as the eruption of Desire, as the life in-between, as being-in the gap, through the inertness of fascination. And the project of post-modern painting becomes the preservation of the possibility of passion, its rememoration, the plunge into the gap on behalf of Nothing.

If there is no longer a 'whole', a real or a symbolic whole, but only the deadly play of simulations, art can only work to mark, to re-present, that lack, that concrete nothing. Paintings can only stand as singular re-presentations of the lack of a whole, the relation of the fragment to dispersal, to Fragmentation itself. But this is always within Language, is always in relation to Tradition, and this has always already provided for the possibility of sharing the singular. Insofar as any work gathers itself in relation to the Tradition of art it stands as a metaphor for the whole, the one, albeit the unfinishable whole, of Tradition. Retrospectively 'It' gives the illusion of a complete unity, of closure, a display of the commitment to make art in ways that, within Writing-in-general, metonymically preserve an absolute continuity – the languages of art under the aegis of Art-as-Language – Identity. But prospectively, for the practising artist, the Tradition is always an incomplete whole, a necessarily fractured unity, always providing a space for its own supplementation and transformation by new work. And in secreting this Desire to remember Tradition, origin and beginnings, painting, even in its move into post-modernity, remains fundamentally archaic. The practice 'knows' from the beginning that it can only be the continuous invention of metaphors for that which is only a fragment amongst fragments; lacking a whole, a final system within which each fragment has its place, the re-presented fragments nevertheless are inserted into and take place within Tradition, but a Tradition which they themselves are continually reinventing as difference.

Tradition is the context in which all work is pulled back into meaning. But, at the level of making, creative practice cannot be, if indeed it ever was, either the 're-doubling of the world in space' or the artist copying his or her own difference (Baudrillard, 1981, p.106), for it has to invent its own singular fragments, abandoning style, and knowing that there is no 'right' way to relate bits and pieces. It knows that these shards (everyday life) have meaning only as members of the interminable series which is precisely the passing of the quotidian. The absolute end of modernity (which would entail the death of post-modernity too), the end of this recognition of art practice as the play between the Good of Tradition – a memory trace of wholeness – and the realities of fragmentation could only take place if either Tradition were erased (the holocaust – itself a possibility of modernity) or the fragments were restructured in a way which not merely simulated but enforced an absolutely encompassing system, without possibility of haemorrhage or fissure.

In different ways each of the preceding examples of sign analysis displayed the Desire for mastery of their object of knowledge however this was semiotically defined. And yet painting, approached on its own terms, from the site of its practice (of painting-as-writing and responding-as-reading) displays what, for theory, must be a disconcerting habit of continually escaping, of slipping through the net of method. And perhaps this is because theory, exemplified here by semiotics, can only handle, can only know, re-present, simulate, on its own terms, 'things that have happened', things that have passed, have come to pass: theory marks the death of things. Whereas in painting (and art too) it is precisely Nothing that happens. Or at least nothing but inscription, nothing but painting-as-writing. Writing of the narrative in literature Barthes carries us and himself beyond the semiotic when he proposes that ' "What takes place" in a narrative is from the referential point of view literally *nothing*; "What happens" is language alone, the adventure of language, the unceasing celebration of its coming' (Barthes, 1977, p.124). And if we shift from narrative to writing, and from writing to painting-as-writing, and if we can admit this Nothing to ourselves we may be brought, may allow ourselves to be brought, to the beginning of writing, of painting:

> Writing begins only when it is the approach to that point where nothing reveals itself . . . the force of the writing impulse makes the world disappear. Then time loses its power of decision; nothing can really begin (Blanchot, 1982, p.52).

9
Painting: Criticising

Beware, my friend, of the signifier that would take you back to the authority of a signified (Hélène Cixous, *The Laugh of the Medusa*).

Esthetics is for artists as ornithology is for the birds. . . (Barnett Newman).

Modernity inscribes criticism into the heart of the practice of painting. But painting in its very openness to response invites the other to become critic. Its helplessness and muteness in the face of criticism encourage critique from the beginning, and this is particularly so in a culture where traditional symbols of authority, under whose auspices painting used to live, have been displaced. Painting is the other to the overwhelming need in an instrumental culture to place everything, to make everything reasonable; yet of course there is relative agreement only about the need for such reason and none at all about the grounds which would secure and provide for it. It is thus a defining constituent of the life of modern painting to live amongst warring critical discourses, and it cannot be considered apart from this context: critique as the violent play of difference. But while painting's response to this critical context is always embedded in the works of art themselves in and as the practical aesthetic judgments of artists, criticism, in its need to make criticism and not painting, necessarily separates from painting. And if post-structuralist practice has confused the boundaries between art and criticism by showing that nothing closes off writing, texts or paintings, nevertheless most art critical writing is firmly rooted in alternative models of writing. Notwithstanding the inter-twining of painting and writing, inter-textuality, criticism has needed constantly to display and reaffirm its difference, to show the difference it makes to painting. And if responding to painting begins as reading, the difference reading makes is 'most generally, writing'

(Hartman, 1980, p.19). But reading is a radically creative practice, a re-writing of the painting as text, so the writing that follows reading begins with the necessity to display its own creativity, as a creative adding to the work of art.

If it is a feature of modernity's self-consciousness to know that its works, paintings, are essentially fragments, unfinished and un-finishable (what they begin is continued by the respondent), the writing that reading adds to painting is already part of it from its beginning. Criticism seems to begin with the hope of being true to painting, by meeting its need – by being its necessary supplement; knowing itself to be part of the work of art, its Desire is to begin the interminable work of fulfilling painting by supplementing it with writing. But what draws the need to supplement into the region of the work to begin with? Perhaps art's lack is complemented by a sense of lack within the respondent – a lack which art alone may partially overcome. If anything else would do just as well, and the selection of art to meet the lack was arbitrary, contingent, then art would raise no passions, no commitments. Yet art is precisely the possibility of maintaining, of re-membering the scandal of Desire in our culture. And criticism begins in the midst of this Desire, this need to preserve, this need to write for the scandal of painting, of art, in a calculative culture.

If criticism begins as a drawing-out, an extending, of painting's life, in the face of a plurality of threats, it seems to start from within a care, and a concern, for painting: this proposes an ethics, a politics of criticism in which the latter seeks to show, to write on behalf of the Good of painting, to display itself as a caring-for-painting. Now in order to hold to this, criticism has to seek to know itself as writing, as words; as well as turning away from the quotidian towards art, it has to turn away from art towards itself as discourse. Without grasping its own insinuation into the General Text, its sole commit-ment to write on behalf of painting will be diluted by a multiplicity of powerful extraneous interests and values. The problem for criticism-as-writing in a culture which reduces re-presentation to means is how to care for painting (art) as the in-itself-for-itself, to show its absolute commitment to this concern.

But does this seem to comprehend the project of contemporary art critical practice? What we are faced with in the discourse of critical difference, what assembles the region of critical practice, is, rather, writing as the will-to-power, writing as the violence of negation (frequently of both painting and other writing), writing as self-subservience to extraneous interests (science, politics, theory, self, style, the market, religion, and so on). In this negational context, even though art may not appear to be the prime target of the negation, it is always the death of painting (and art) which is announced.

The death of modernism and the transformation of modernity into its after-text – post-modernity – make the violence of critical practice particularly explicit, for what is in part in question in this transformation is the future of an avant-garde, and this has always been implicated by criticism with politics. Indeed artists' own rhetoric (their discursive justifications, if not the works of art themselves) frequently supported this implication. Competing senses of the avant-garde are to be found in the modern tradition and these differences are still in play and partially seek to define the critical contours of emerging post-modern practice. They provide nodal points of reference around which criticism gathers itself. Modernity itself, from the beginning, was practised within an overarching sense of its own avant-garde status with respect to its surrounding culture, a sense of its being ahead of, somewhere other than that culture. The various metaphysics of the early moderns displayed their rejection of the conventions of cultural re-presentation: rejection and innovation on behalf of art itself as the mark of otherness in bourgeois culture. Artistic vision, committed to a questioning celebration, was, in the broadest sense, in the 'vanguard', through its practical critique of the legacies of re-presentation of European culture.

As a collective phenomenon this radical doubt about the relation between art and cultural convention perhaps peaked with Dada towards the end of the first world war, and at the level of individual practice it continued as one support and motivation for European modernity, as the work of more recent artists, such as Klein, Manzoni and Dubuffet displays. The over-riding threat to the power and sway of this metaphysical doubt within modernity has been the institutionalising of modernity itself through the market, museum and academy. Under these pressures vision (the permanence of doubt) frequently collapses into style. And the same threat hangs over post-modern practice in spite of style being its explicit target. The pressures to repeat, to become mannered, to reproduce identity, are overwhelming. But this general presence of metaphysical doubt provides an opening for criticism to gather painting to politics. It is relatively easy to read painting's metaphysical doubts about both culture and painting itself very concretely and to enclose them within vaguely defined politics. Painting becomes an occasion to develop political criticism (criticism grounded in a politics based on phenomena external to art) with a concomitant loss of any sense of painting's celebration of painting, of Tradition. The Desire for painting is transformed into a Desire for politics, for the social (see e.g. Cork, 1978).

The Russian constructivist and productivist movements, where many of the artists were practically engaged in the alternative political practices that emerged following the Russian revolution, have provided a continuing model for a more directly political sense of avant-garde practice. Criticism which grounds itself on this model re-presents painting(art) as *first of all* a criticism of ideology. Art is only effective (Good) when it dedicates itself to a practical critique of the culture, and especially the culture's dominant modes of producing re-presentations. Because re-presentation in contemporary culture is dominated by the electronic media, by simulation, painting's problem is precisely how to display its otherness to the ubiquity of simulation. This leads the 'critique of ideology' criticism to argue against painting's continued relevance to avant-garde practice, for the practical problem (as formulated by criticism) is to confront the media on their own territory; this requires a switch by the artist into other media such as photography, film, video, or performance. The work of artists such as Cindy Sherman, Sherri Levine, Martha Rossler and Barbara Kruger provides one focus for this criticism (see e.g. Buchloh, 1982b, Krauss, 1981b and Owens, 1983). It is difficult for this criticism to understand painting as anything other than a regressive practice and post-modern painting in particular (with its radical return to imagery) as a decadent appropriation of past styles and gestures. The passion of the artist, the Desire to concretely show in each painting the Good of painting as the in-itself-for-itself in the face of the dominance of simulation, has to be repressed, transformed and brought under the rule of a puritan and violent politics: puritan because of the extremely narrow limits it sets for art practice, and violent because it writes for the subordination of art practice to theory.

Because of its interest in the death of painting this criticism also leans either implicitly or explicitly on the formalist sense of the avant-garde in which modernity became modernism: the linear trajectory towards the reduced material essence of painting. This materialist but non-Marxist reading of modernity, resting heavily on its empiricist conception of seeing as a separable faculty of experience, virtually expunges all traces of the wider metaphysical doubt of European modernity, the doubt, that is, about painting's relationship to its surrounding culture. It narrows modernity down to its search for its own essence (a plainly non-phenomenological essence). Such formalist criticism, with its plainly universalist bent, was well matched to the emergent internationalism of abstract painting fostered by American cultural imperialism in the fifties and sixties and finds its clearest exposition, although not necessarily its worst excesses, in the writings of Greenberg and Fried (see e.g. Greenberg, 1961 and Fried, 1967).

Once the supposed formal material conditions of painting have been established through the cooperation of criticism and practice, painting is left with nothing to do but repeat endless variations of this restricted essence. Again the puritanism of this formulation puts out of play, outside its version of modernity, all contemporary painting that cannot be read as making this reduction its primary concern. The terms and foci of passion, of Desire, are subordinated to the abstraction of form; some of the consequences of this were noted in the discussion of Burnham's semiotic thesis. The re-emergence of imagery and figuration that defines the post-modern response to the self-erasure of modernism centred on European, and specifically Italian and German, painting, and it has called forth a European critical response that differs itself from American formalism (see e.g. Oliva, 1980, Brock, 1981, Parmesani, 1984, Faust, 1981, Lischka, 1984, Wildermuth, 1984). The painting and the critical writing display a return to the earlier metaphysical issues of art's relation to culture (but not from within a narrow political diagnosis) and, against the universalism of formalism, a regionalist concern for the particular local socio-historical experience to which this painting is partially responsive. The point is often made, for example, that several of the German painters who have come to prominence (e.g. Baselitz, Immendorf and Penck) are émigrés from East Germany (for a discussion of regionalism in post-modernity generally see Frampton in Foster, 1983). This work scatters the concept of a unified avant-garde practice which somehow 'leads the way forward', and explicitly raises the problem of likening art to a knowledge which progresses, which goes beyond, which is ahead of other knowledges, within which the other senses of avant-garde practice have placed themselves. In particular it undoes and disseminates the theory of the avant-garde as a privileged reference point for the entire history and field of painting around which much criticism has distributed itself.

Had the concept of the avant-garde not been subjected to such critical constrictions it might still have been possible to gather post-modern practice within it. However as it has been applied in so many instances to practice which has fallen into style, and as style (as generated by modernism) is a key critical issue for post-modernity, its conceptual value evaporates. And if post-modern painting, through its fragmenting of the privileged critical reference points, calls upon critical practice to re-think itself, to re-think its relation to art, writing, culture, and Language, then criticism fails to listen at its own peril.

Painting's mute invitation to its respondents is, as suggested, always to become a supplement, to explore the specific qualities of its lack, its falling short; but this can only be accomplished by the respondent's reflexive turn to his or her own lack that brought them to the work of art in the first place. And it is in this space (the in-between, the dead time, the space of relating itself) that the painting provides for this very confrontation with one's own lack. It is here, if anywhere at all, that art's transformative potential may be at work. Criticism is the writing that has to learn how to find itself in this space and to textualise this learning for others. This is precisely what criticism can learn from painting.

But how can this space that is no-where be found, be real-ised, given that the entire telos of painting is to make itself, to display itself as, utterly powerless in the matter? As the region where power enters a vacuum, the region of absolute impotence, the undoing of subjugation, painting re-presents an absolutely concrete need for a particular other, but can do nothing, and from its inception was totally committed to doing nothing, in the event of this other failing to appear. Painting is a waiting game.

How might the respondent (criticism) be responsive to, learn from, this absolute impotence, given, as is the case with criticism, the Desire to theorise art's practical life? Only through an abrogation of all those forms of control, of power, to which the respondent is subject, which bear upon the possibilities of engagement. It is not so much, as Bachelard puts it, a matter of seizing the specific reality of the work (Bachelard, 1970, p.xv), where the metaphor of seizure retains an immanent violence, but rather of losing one's self to, of trusting one's self to, of placing one's self in the care of the work: allowing one's self to be played with – over-taken by inscription – the pleasure of the text (see Barthes, 1975, for a poetic expansion of the possibilities of this pleasure in relation to the literary text). To provide for the possibility of this self-inscription by the painting the respondent has to let reading be; the supplement of criticism is not the reading itself but only what comes after the reading. Blanchot makes the point in relation to the literary text and it holds for the painting:

> to read is not to write the book again, but allow the book to be:
> written – this time all by itself, without the intermediary of the

writer, without anyone's writing it. The reader does not add himself to the book, but tends primarily to relieve it of an author . . . Reading does not produce anything, does not add anything, it lets be what is (Blanchot, 1982, p.193, 194).

The addition of criticism is the difference that writing makes to the freedom that reading is, the letting be of the text, the painting.

What else could the work of art possibly need other than this letting be, the possibility of its own freedom? But can the iron rule of method, of politics, ever allow one of its subjects into the freedom of such a letting be? Must it not seek to infiltrate and commandeer the very work of reading to prevent it from ever letting anything be? Must it not always work to condition reading in advance to its own ends and endlessly to defer the possibility of such a reading? If criticism follows and grounds itself in a method (a set of unquestioned premises which guide the practice of reading), critical writing, the response to a reading infiltrated by method, will only ever be speaking for and seeking to display method's power. Art becomes a limit or test case through which method can finally display its power to contain anything, even that which stands as its absolute other. Over and against this, painting invites a poetics that is responsible to its need and which will write for the Good of its impotence. And it is modernity itself which, as the tradition of multiplicity and fragmentation, recalls us to difference. The difference modernity (and post-modernity real-ises this) makes to culture is its impotence, its continual rehearsal and reiteration of its absolute inappropriateness to any use whatsoever, and this impotence is accomplished purely through the letting be of differences. Ironically it is in this very vacuumising of power that modern painting finds its greatest strength, has the last laugh: it displays, it enacts, an abandonment of the will to power – but it can only 'do' this through the respondent's letting it be.

Before becoming a critic, the respondent has to 'have' the founding lack doubled through the loss of 'self' necessary to let the reading be. Critique somehow has to provide for, to show, the importance of this doubled lack to any subsequent critical work. And the practice of living-through these lacks is not some 'thing' which can be gathered by method. Critical writing has to show, to preserve in its writing, a memorial to, a trace of, this lack. The obligation of such a writing is to painting's utter excess, its otherness to theory and method – it cannot and will not be had. Only by beginning here (or in some similar region) can criticism (and by extension all the disciplines committed to knowledge and method) begin to understand and find ways of showing what it can learn from painting, of recognising the risk to itself that it takes in engaging painting in the first place, of acknowledging that painting may entail its own death as will, as method. Now this acknowledgment of art's difference opens also onto issues raised within feminism about the construction of sexual difference within Language. For a particular concern in those areas of feminist practice which treat Language as central to their exploration of and intervention in the re-presentation of the feminine, is the deconstruction of textual practices which privilege potency as the power of the phallus (for a discussion of deconstruction and feminist practice see Culler, 1983). And certainly within modernity the common discursive conventions for pointing to painting's involvement with the erotic are, as we saw with Matisse, typically phallocentric (see Kozloff, 1974 and also Pollock, 1979). Equally certainly it is no accident that most of the work by women artists which begins from this concern and which critics have gathered within post-modernity (such as those mentioned in the preceding discussion of the 'critique of ideology' criticism) is carried through in media other than painting.

Post-modernity's displacement of modernism and its re-opening of the question of the significance of modernity recover the play of signifiers, of difference, as its site for practice, and through intertextuality scatter and depotentiate any sense of a primary region of transcendental signifieds for painting. And a prime aim and consequence of both post-modernity and post-structuralism is the displacement of those privileged master texts which traditionally were used to unify the fragments; these were the texts of philosophy and social thought used to ground totalising conceptions of being and reality. Deconstruction and post-modernity say 'no' to all totalising practices by working in the in-between: no privileged metaphors, no more master texts, no more master pieces, only the play of writing, of painting. Mary Kelly speaks for this standing aside in commenting on her *Post-Partum Document*, which is itself a work that displays the post-modern interest of exploring the interface of art and theory (see Kelly, 1983, Pollock, 1979, p.52, Smith, 1982):

> Hopefully, the work is a continual displacement rather than a hierarchisation of certain forms of language. . . . I think that what's discovered in working through the Post-Partum Document is that there is no pre-existing sexuality, no essential femininity; and that to look at the processes of their construction is also to see the possibility of deconstructing the dominant

forms of representing difference and justifying subordination in our social order (Kelly, 1982, pp.34 and 35).

This metaphorises the more general post-modern argument that 'there's no single theoretical discourse which is going to offer us an explanation for all forms of social relations, or for every mode of political practice' (op.cit., p.33).

Even Tradition cannot be gathered as identity but only as texts metonymically linked by their concrete displays of the desire to paint, the Desire for difference. And painting, concretely dominated by men, as a tradition where mastery has been continually in play has become a suspect terrain constantly threatening to pull the feminine search for its difference(s) back under the sway of phallocentrism. If it is mastery itself which is undergoing deconstruction and if the modern tradition of painting is conventionally recuperated as tradition of masters, then feminist practice has not surprisingly tended towards the exploration and celebration of its difference(s) at the margins of painting. In undoing the suspect and logocentric unities of theoretical mastery feminism in both theory and art practice works in-between discourses and media on behalf of another space within writing, which cannot be said, cannot be inscribed, through the terms that theory and modernism have prescribed (see Eisenstein and Jardine, 1979, for further papers on the issue of difference). And yet in this very deconstructive exploration, this celebration of difference, feminist practice re-inscribes itself within Tradition and as fundamental to post-modernity.

Through this deconstructive turn, shared with post-modernity, feminist art practice may yet re-gather itself, its selves, within painting and so re-gather painting for us. Perhaps painting has to be pulled out from under the discursive domination of the rhetoric of power, to be recalled to its own powerlessness. This release of painting to itself, painting as that which hyphenates, that which lies between, may draw us towards a necessary con-fusing of its difference within the play of sexual difference: the inscription not of neutrality, but of the very coming-and-going of difference – the realm of an emergent sexuality which displaces the logocentric, the phonocentric, the phallocentric:

Bisexuality: that is, each one's location in self of the presence – variously manifest and insistent according to each person, male or female – of both sexes, nonexclusion either of the difference or of one sex, and, from this 'self-permission', multiplication of the effects of the inscription of desire, over all parts of my body and the other body (Cixous, 1976, p.884).

Ironising the impotence feared by mastery, painting's other impotence, may be real-ised, as post-modernity's telos and celebration – an opening into hyphenation itself, the swirl of difference.

Painting's very regressive (think of the way 'progressive' may resonate with phallocratic thought) character, so disparaged by the 'critique of ideology' critics, may then turn out to be a virtue, for, in the face of the alternative media engaged by a variety of feminist art practices, painting reminds us that the essence of mastery, the will to power, is actually to be found in the very instrumentalising calculative thought which grounds these media. And, in addition, the mechanical, electronic and information media systems have the nasty habit of recuperating for themselves all attempts to either subvert them from within or to use them for other ends (such as the critique of the re-presentation of the feminine). Perhaps the work of those women painters associated with post-modernity already begins to recognise this (see Pohlen, 1984).

Criticism, committed to its own difference, has somehow to find itself within this play of differences. Insinuating itself into this play, its responsibility is to the painting-as-text, to the respondent and to itself. As Kristeva puts it in her discussion of Barthes, the critic should not seek a transcendence or a repudiation of the reading (responding) subject (Kristeva, 1980). The reader is not someone to be overcome, subdued or put down, but rather must be constituted in the practice of writing itself, as a potential enhancer of painting's freedom in impotence. The question for criticism now is not 'how can the work of art and artistic practice be given their place within existing theoretical schema?', but rather, 'how can our theoretical schema find ways of giving themselves up to the work, of admitting both their own inadequacy and the possibility of their own transformation through this giving up – criticism becoming an opening into, and perhaps an exemplification of, the letting be of hyphenation?'

10

A More Contemporary Pluralogue
Re-gained (and Lost)

Scene: The same
Time: Even later, even darker

(tape (scrap) runs)

(An Unidentified Artist): . . . can hardly be expected to lead back
to the old search for a personal style. The idea of style itself
has become suspe . . .

Wolfgang Max Faust: . . . If you want to be somewhere else . . .

Franz Kafka: (very faintly) . . . 'Away-From-Here' . . .[63]

Wolfgang Max Faust: . . . you have no use for a static point of
view. You have to change continually, to keep moving you have
to be 'here' and yet keep your lines of escape open.[64]

Francesco Clemente: . . . to see how far away from oneself and
from one's own tastes one can lead the work.[65]

An Interpreter: It sounds, Francesco, as if you have . . .

Rainer Crone: (interrupting) . . . an aversion toward a normative
stylistic integration, displaying instead an outright rejection,
which leads even to a negation of 'personal style', and to the
elimination of such supposedly conflicting terms as 'abstract'
and 'figurative'.[66]

Jiri Georg Dokoupil: I am interested in working with disruptions,
contradictions . . . we do not want a new style or a new
direction.[67]

An Interpreter: If you are saying that post-modern painting is
committed to the subversion of style then this seems to pose a
crucial problem for criticism and for respondents because the
very lexicon of modern criticism has grown from within the need
to recognise and conceptualise difference as style. The history of
modernity is understood as the play of stylistic differences –
stylistic difference as a display, a re-presentation, of the artist's
subjectivity. But how can the post-modern painter prevent self-
thematisation lapsing into style?

Armin Wildermuth: . . . self-thematising painting . . .

AN INTERPRETER: . . . which modern painting has in any case been
from the beginning . . .

ARMIN WILDERMUTH: . . . demands a self-thematising
interpretation, because the whole framework of interpretation
used by regular criticism and so-called art history has been
anticipated by the painters . . . They know the styles and
qualitative standards by which paintings have been judged so far
– and they retreat with them behind the images into the depth of
the creative process. This interpretive self-thematisation is also
an act of disconnection . . . liberating itself from all constraints of
style and content, but also gaining the capacity to use all possible
imagery . . . The current 'disconnection' from styles and trends
is expressed in an ecstatic affirmation of life . . . an unobstructed
play of continually outwitting rational thought . . .

AN INTERPRETER: . . . and specifically the categories and methods
of schools of criticism. But how can criticism, committed to
rational thought, touch this practice? What does it need to do?

ARMIN WILDERMUTH: In order to explore this, we would need an
ethnomethodology . . .

AN INTERPRETER: . . . I'm glad you said that mouthful and not
me . . .

ARMIN WILDERMUTH: . . . of art, a form of *phenomethodology* which
shows that we must free ourselves from the confusion between
reality and method.

AN INTERPRETER: Well, just as long as your method can allow itself
to be subverted by a painting practice which is already in its very
being the scattering of all methods . . .

ARMIN WILDERMUTH: . . . *Yes* . . . it becomes evident that the
painters are so familiar with current interpretations and
reactions that they can play with them ironically . . .[68]

AN INTERPRETER: . . . and lovingly too, perhaps, once again
leaving criticism floundering elsewhere, caught within its own
simulations. But let's get back to this affirmation of life, because
painting is, first of all, given what you said about self-
thematisation, affirmation of painting, and paintings are the
other of life – they hyphenate life and death.

LOREDANA PARMESANI: Here at the conclusion of the modern era
art is rediscovering the themes that characterised the beginning
of modernity, and, above all, the theme of death . . . From this
point of view, apparent recuperation of the past . . .

AN INTERPRETER: . . . what some critics see as a straight
appropriation of past styles and themes . . .

LOREDANA PARMESANI: . . . is an indication of the death of the past:

its reduction into media, and the overwhelming of humanism at the hands of technology . . .

AN INTERPRETER: . . . the erasure of Being . . .

LOREDANA PARMESANI: If the modern period opened with a search for death – being-for-the-sake-of death – the so-called post-modern era finds its origins in death itself – being-from-out-of-death . . . No longer sustained by an aesthetic . . . and entirely abandoned to itself . . . the duty of art as a moral and categorical imperative of the modern era . . . is replaced in the post-modern era with the will to art, with art as the will to life . . .

AN INTERPRETER: . . . yes, but we have to ensure that this will to art does not lose itself to the will to power; the will to art is the will to the undoing of power as we know it . . .

LOREDANA PARMESANI: . . . *O.K. But* . . . Faced with a world controlled by industry and in which science is the ally of industry, the craftsmanly techniques of art can no longer retain their status as something scientific and cognitive.

AN INTERPRETER: So while it might just about have been possible to gather art with knowledge and progress within modernity, as the avant-garde sought to do, the post-modern consciousness, realising the awe-ful error of this association and its disastrous consequences for modernity within art, seeks to retrieve another site for creative practice – an elsewhere to modernism. In this very separation of itself art becomes a judgment of the totalising annihilative will to power which encompasses it.

JO BAER: From this point on to act as if innocent showdowns could be staged against the ideological weight of the market was tantamount to the belief that a fish can ride a bicycle.[69]

LOREDANA PARMESANI: The cadaver of art . . . still finds itself with two possibilities: it can surrender to high performance know-how . . .

AN INTERPRETER: . . . accepting and trying to turn the deadly technology of simulation to its own ends . . .

LOREDANA PARMESANI: . . . or it can recognise the annihilation of humanism and turn itself into its ghost . . . Starting out from its own death, and from death in general, it can seek out the experience, turning Heidegger inside out . . .

AN INTERPRETER: . . . poor old Martin . . .

LOREDANA PARMESANI: . . . of what I would call an 'Angst' for life, an emotional anticipation of life . . .[70]

AN INTERPRETER: . . . the not-yet of life, the ghost of a life yet to be, appearing in the society where life has been caught by the continuous reproduction of its own copy. In its resolution of this choice art displays its freedom . . .

WILLEM DE KOONING: It is exactly in its uselessness that it is free . . . freedom of indifference.[71]

AN INTERPRETER: And freed by indifference to function without intervention (more or less), art has no end, no reasons, no point, and yet is still, as a breath of life . . .

FRANCESCO CLEMENTE: (interrupting) . . . You know the story about who is the first painter, what he did?

AN INTERPRETER: No. Tell us!

FRANCESCO CLEMENTE: He had the colour in his mouth, and then he put his hands on the wall, and spit the colour. Then he takes his hands off the wall and there is . . .

AN INTERPRETER: . . . the outline of his hands . . .

FRANCESCO CLEMENTE: Yes. So that is the first painter. That was the first posture of a painter.[72]

ART-LANGUAGE: Painting By Mouth![73]

AN INTERPRETER: Painting by breath! But this inscription of the body in its very uselessness is absolutely necessary.

AD REINHARDT: Art necessary, but necessary for nothing.[74]

AN INTERPRETER: Ah! I'm glad you came back, Ad, I've missed your pithiness. You say art is necessary for nothing and Willem says it's useless. These slogans certainly throw art out of joint with the world of everyday life! But maybe if we consider some of the resonances of 'use' and the 'useful' in our culture we might just catch a glimpse of the absolute value, the indispensability of this uselessness. Perhaps the instrumentalism of our culture, constantly transforming beings into things-to-be-used-and-consumed, works continuously to violently subdue beings, phenomena, into means. The culture is committed at its very non-heart to the endless production of means, and in so doing obliterates, erases, the question of ends, of an end to its own endless rule. To face these questions would require the culture to recognise end as its absolute other, that which it lacks, so it has constantly to work to repress the surfacing of this recognition. The culture of means is a mean culture that has to close off the possibility of its own end by ensuring that beings are constantly transformed into things-to-be-used. To erase this inscription within us of the necessity of relating to beings, and specifically to art, in terms of their use, is an awe-ful task: and yet this is what art asks of us. The marginalising of art – Willem's indifference – in a culture grounded on the reduction of all things to instruments of use is then understandable, for art is one of the very few practices which ceaselessly strive to re-present to the culture and to keep open that other possibility, the Good of ends. And art is perhaps the only practice which has as its principal ground and end the celebration of its own uselessness. It opens itself as the absolute other to the culture of means (market and museum notwithstanding) and stands as a constant needling reminder of this. Cézanne told us that art was the horror of the bourgeoisie and we can see the force of this when we recognise that art makes an absolute virtue out of its uselessness. This is the Good in Ad's negative. That most artists for most of the time are absolutely committed to working very hard for Nothing (and for nothing very often) is itself the guarantee of art's strength in the face of the endless rule of means. Its very marginality is paradoxically a sign of its central importance for the struggle to keep open a space in that culture for the inscription of otherness. If it were to lose its marginality in a mean culture it would cease to be art through its transformation into means – Loredana's first alternative.

ACHILLE BONITO OLIVA: Tight rope walking . . .

AN INTERPRETER: . . . yes, art currently walks the tight rope between on the one hand preservation of itself as its own end and hence the icon of otherness, and on the other hand its absorption into the culture and structure of means in which it is seen as a means to simulation. Breaking with the world, it re-presents itself as . . .

ACHILLE BONITO OLIVA: . . . an operation which doesn't measure itself with the world but rather with the history of its own language.[75]

AN INTERPRETER: Indeed, no longer finding a world reality, but only totalising systems of simulation and information, only fragmented worlds, art works in the cracks, gaining its sustenance not from the world but from the void, . . .

ALICE: . . . arctic rations . . .[76]

AN INTERPRETER: . . . from itself . . .

JEAN DUBUFFET: . . . the voice of the dust, the soul of the dust. . .[77]

MARCEL DUCHAMP: . . . dust breeding . . .[78]

AN INTERPRETER: . . . painting in the dark, but . . .

HÉLÈNE CIXOUS: . . . The Dark Continent is neither dark nor unexplorable . . .[79]

PHILIPPE SOLLERS: We live in the false light of a dead language with narrow significations; we lack daylight to the extent that we lack the night that we are . . .

AN INTERPRETER: . . . painting blind . . .

PHILIPPE SOLLERS: But we are nothing other than this nocturnal and

diurnal movement of the legible and illegible, in us, outside us –
and this is precisely what we would rather not know.[80]

JAMES JOYCE: When morning comes of course everything will be
clear again.[81]

MAN RAY AND MARCEL DUCHAMP: (together, in a low sing-song)
Behold the domain of Rrose Selavy
How arid it is – How fertile – How joyous – How sad![82]

AN INTERPRETER: . . . painting as the opening of the body to its
own erotic writing; the body's self-inscription, self- . . .

JACQUES LACAN: . . . the insistence of the letter in[83]

AN INTERPRETER: . . . lettering.

ECHO: (distantly) . . . lettering
                           let tearing
                           let erring
(getting fainter)   let tear in
                           letter in
                           let ur in
                           let 'er in
(inaudible)   let her in

MARCEL DUCHAMP: (cutting in across a groundswell of muttering)
. . . the arrhe of painting is feminine in gender.[84]

AN INTERPRETER: . . . but surely Marcel, you and Man have just
shown us that the domain of Rrose Selavy is the in-between,
within the caesura . . .

HELENE CIXOUS: . . . the other bisexuality . . .[85]

MICHAEL BALDWIN: . . . *and* another thing about painting a
picture by mouth is that you take away a certain amount of
masculine aggression associated with expression or expressive
types of works by tradition. It is difficult to be masculinely
aggressive with your arse stuck in the air and a brush in your
mouth.[86]

AN INTERPRETER: . . . and it radically confronts respondents with
the question of their responsibility for all the judgments made in
constituting a work of art, particularly questions about the brush
mark as a vehicle for expressiveness.

MEL RAMSDEN: Is it a competent (expressionistic) painting (by
mouth) or an expressive (incompetent) painting by mouth or
. . . ? The work has to live within a sort of disquieting
undecidability; that's where the work lives. Its value is in terms
of these sorts of details.[87]

AN INTERPRETER: Ah! Ha! We're thrown back into the in-between
again! But, whether painter or respondent, you have to Desire
that thrownness, you have to want to lose yourself in the play of

this useless questioning, and you have to know that is what you want . . .

MICHAEL BALDWIN: What have you got to know? How are you going to puzzle out and deal with a modern work of art without that sense of glory in the puzzle, the horror and insignificance of the game, the combination of life and death in ruined playfulness? It would seem to me that is all we have left in a modern work of art.[88]

AN INTERPRETER: Of course if you were to continue Painting By Mouth you might be able to get Art-Language registered as a charity, but that would inevitably entail a lapse into style . . .

ENID TOMORROW: (insistently cutting in) NO MORE INTERPRETATION!

PETER DE FRANCIA: (sotto voce) . . . Yet is it not peculiar that someone so rudimentarily equipped, manipulating a bit of wood with some bristles tied to it, using a surface and some pigment – the prototype of archaism – can hold their own so successively against the bellowing of the so-called competition of other media? And might it well be that the latter are the dinosaurs? And is it not conceivable in this context that certain people have misread their Darwin and their Ma . . .[89]

(tape snaps)

References to the Pluralogues

1 Ashton, 1972, p.140.
2 Merleau-Ponty, 1968, pp.181–7.
3 Merleau-Ponty, 1968, p.188.
4 Ibid.
5 Ashton, 1972, p.34.
6 Heron, 1958, p.2.
7 Hitchens, 1979, p.10.
8 O'Hara, 1965, p.70.
9 Rosenberg, 1973, p.205.
10 Law, 1978, unnumbered.
11 Blamires, 1978, p.27.
12 Blamires, 1978, p.30.
13 Merleau-Ponty, 1968, p.166.
14 Heidegger, 1971b, p.59.
15 Heidegger, 1971b, pp. 74–5.
16 Heidegger, 1971b, p.84.
17 Heidegger, 1971a, p.135.
18 Heidegger, 1971a, p.166.
19 Heidegger, 1971a, p.170.
20 Merleau-Ponty, 1968, p.180.
21 Arikha, 1978, pp.3–6.
22 Russell, 1979, p.112.
23 Rosenberg, 1972, p.105.
24 Rose, 1975, p.111.
25 Rose, 1975, p.142.
26 Rose, 1975, pp.191–3.
27 Merleau-Ponty, 1964, p.57.
28 Merleau-Ponty, 1968, p.188.
29 Johnson, 1976, p.110.
30 Bachelard, 1970, p.xxii.
31 Penrose, 1978, pp.173–3.
32 Penrose, 1978, p.173.
33 Hess, 1972, pp.22–4.
34 Herbert, 1964, p.132.
35 Macke, 1969, front text.
36 Marcuse, 1972, pp.88–9.
37 Rose, 1975, p.59.
38 Klee, 1961, p.17.
39 Rimbaud, 1974, p.8, p.77.
40 Francis, 1972, p.134.
41 Rose, 1975, p.18.
42 Paz, 1974, p.192.
43 Rosenberg, 1962, Title.
44 Bachelard, 1968, p.117.
45 Bachelard, 1968, p.122.
46 Bachelard, 1968, pp.122–3.
47 Crichton, 1977, p.75.
48 Crichton, 1977, p.76.
49 Crichton, 1977, p.77.
50 Baudrillard, 1983a, p.2.
51 Bachelard, 1970, p.xv.
52 Bachelard, 1970, p.xix.
53 Bachelard, 1970, pp.xv-xix.
54 O'Hara, 1965, p.70.
55 Rosenberg, 1977, p.43.
56 Ashton, 1972, pp.101–4.
57 Heidegger, 1971b, p.80.
58 Heidegger, 1971a, p.137.
59 Rose, 1975, p.111.
60 Lambertini, 1980, p.26.
61 Auerbach, 1978, p.17.
62 Buchloh, 1980, p.58.
63 Kafka, 1971, p.189.

64 Faust, 1981, p.33, p.36.
65 Clemente, 1984, p.13.
66 Crone, 1983, p.51.
67 Crone, 1983, p.53.
68 Wildermuth, 1984, pp.9–10, 13, 15.
69 Baer, 1983, p.137.
70 Parmesani, 1984, pp.56–60.
71 Rosenberg, 1973, p.144.
72 Clemente, 1981, pp.19–20.
73 Art-Language, 1982, p.45.
74 Rose, 1975, p.111.
75 Oliva, 1981, p.28.
76 Art-Language, 1982, p.65.
77 Ashton, 1962, p.178.
78 Sanouillet and Peterson, 1975, p.53.
79 Cixous, 1976, p.884.
80 Sollers, 1983, p.197.
81 Ellmann, 1982, p.546.
82 Sanouillet and Peterson, 1975, p.52.
83 Ehrmann, 1970, p.vi.
84 Sanouillet and Peterson, 1975, p.24.
85 Cixous, 1976, p.884.
86 Miller, 1984, p.13.
87 Ibid.
88 Ibid.
89 de Francia, 1978, p.94.

Bibliography

Arikha, A. (1978), *Avigdor Arikha*, London, Marlborough Gallery.

Art-Language (1982), *Art-Language*, vol.5, no.1.

Ashton, D. (1962), *The Unknown Shore*, London , Studio Vista.

Ashton, D, (1972), *Picasso on Art*, London, Thames & Hudson.

Ashton, D. (1976), *Yes, But . . .*, New York, Viking Press.

Auerbach, F. (1978), *Frank Auerbach*, London, Arts Council of Great Britain.

Bachelard, G. (1968a), *The Philosophy of No*, New York, The Orion Press.

Bachelard, G. (1968b), *The Poetics of Space*, Boston, Beacon Press.

Baer, J. (1983), 'On Minimalism and Painting', *Art in America*, October, p.136.

Bann, S. (1970), *Experimental Art*, London, Studio Vista.

Barthes, R. (1967), *Writing Degree Zero*, New York, Hill & Wang.

Barthes, R. (1969), *Elements of Semiology*, London, Jonathan Cape.

Barthes, R. (1975), *The Pleasure of the Text*, New York, Hill & Wang.

Barthes, R. (1977), *Image-Music-Text*, Glasgow, Fontana.

Barthes, R. (1982a), *Camera Lucida*, New York, Hill & Wang.

Barthes, R. (1982b), *Barthes by Barthes*, New York, Hill & Wang.

Baudrillard, J. (1975), *The Mirror of Production*, St Louis, Telos Press.

Baudrillard, J. (1981), *For a Critique of the Political Economy of the Sign*, St Louis, Telos Press.

Baudrillard, J. (1983a) *Simulations*, New York, Semiotext(e) Inc.

Baudrillard, J. (1983b), *In the Shadow of the Silent Majorities*, New York, Semiotext(e) Inc.

Baudrillard, J. (1983c), 'The Ecstasy of Communication', in Foster (ed.) (1983)

Benjamin, W. (1969), *Illuminations*, New York, Schocken.

Blamires, D. (1978), *David Jones*, Manchester University Press.

Blanchot, M. (1982), *The Space of Literature*, Lincoln, University of Nebraska Press.

Brock, B. (1981), The End of the Avant-Garde?, *Artforum*, summer, p.62.

Bryson, N. (1981), *Word and Image*, Cambridge University Press.

Bryson, N. (1983), *Vision and Painting*, London, Macmillan.

Buchloh, B. (1980), 'Marcel Broodthaers: Allegories of the Avant-Garde', *Artforum*, May, p.52.

Buchloh, B. (1981), 'Figures of Authority, Ciphers of Regression', *October*, 16, spring, p.39.

Buchloh, B. (1982a), 'Parody and Appropriation in Francis Picabia, Pop, and Sigma Polke', *Artforum*, March, p.28.

Buchloh, B. (1982b), 'Allegorical Procedures: Appropriation and Montage in Contemporary Art', *Artforum*, September, p.43.

Buchloh, B. (1982c), 'Documenta 7: A Dictionary of Received Ideas', *October*, 22, fall, p.105.

Buchloh, B., Krauss, R., and Michelson, A. (1980), 'Joseph Beuys at the Guggenheim', *October*, 12, spring, p.3.

Buren, D. (1981), 'Why Write? or: Once doesn't Constitute a Habit', in B. Buchloh (ed.), *'Les Couleurs: Sculptures, Les Formes: peintures'*, Nova Scotia, Press of the Nova Scotia College of Art and Design.

Burnham, J. (1973), *The Structure of Art*, New York, George Braziller.

Cabanne, P. (1971), *Dialogues with Marcel Duchamp*, London, Thames & Hudson.

Cixous, H. (1976), 'The Laugh of the Medusa', in *Signs*, I, p.875.

Clemente, F. (1981), 'Interview with Francesco Clemente by Robin White', *View*, Oakland, Crown Point Press.

Clemente, F. (1984), 'Francesco Clemente, Interview by Giancarlo Politi', *Flash Art*, no.117, April–May, p.12.

Cork, R. (1978), 'Art for Society's Sake', in *Art for Society*, London, Whitechapel Art Gallery, p.47.

Crichton, M. (1977), *Jasper Johns*, New York, Harry N. Abrams.

Crimp, D. (1981), 'The End of Painting', *October*, 16, spring, p.69.

Crone, R. (1983), 'Dokoupil', *Artforum*, March, p.51.

Culler, J. (1983), *On Deconstruction*, London, Routledge & Kegan Paul.

Damisch, H. (1979), 'Eight theses for (or against?) a Semiology of Painting', *Enclitic*, vol.III, no.1, spring.

de Duve, T. (1983), 'Who's Afraid of Red, Yellow, and Blue?', *Artforum*, September, p.30.

de Francia, P. (1978), excerpted from a discussion in *Studio International*, 2/78, vol. 193, no.987, p.94.

Deleuze, G. and Guattari, F. (1983), *On the Line*, New York, Semiotext(e) Inc.

de Man, P. (1980), *Allegories of Reading*, London, Yale University Press.

Derrida, J. (1968), 'Semiology and Grammatology', in *Social Science Information*, vol.III, no.3, p.135.

Derrida, J. (1973), *Speech and Phenomena*, Evanston, Northwestern University Press.

Derrida, J. (1974), 'White Mythology', in *New Literary History*, vol.VI, no.1, p.5.

Derrida, J. (1976), *Of Grammatology*, London, Johns Hopkins University Press.

Derrida, J. (1978a), *La Verité en Peinture*, Paris, Flammarion.

Derrida, J. (1978b), *Writing and Difference*, London, Routledge & Kegan Paul.

Derrida, J. (1978c), 'The Retrait of Metaphor', *Enclitic*, vol.2, no.2, p.5.

Derrida, J. (1979), 'Living On', in H. Bloom *et al.*, *Deconstruction and Criticism*, New York, Seabury.

Derrida, J. (1981), *Positions*, London, Athlone Press.

Derrida, J. (1982), *Dissemination*, University of Chicago Press.

de Saussure, F. (1959), *Course in General Linguistics*, New York, McGraw-Hill.

Descombes, V. (1980), *Modern French Philosophy*, Cambridge University Press.

d'Harnoncourt, A. and McShine, K. (eds) (1974), *Marcel Duchamp*, London, Thames & Hudson.

Eco, U. (1976), *A Theory of Semiotics*, Bloomington, Indiana University Press.

Ehrmann, J. Ed., (1970), *Structuralism*, New York, Anchor Books.

Eisenstein, H. and Jardine, A. (eds) (1979), *The Future of Difference*, Boston, G.K. Hall.

Ellmann, R. (1982), *James Joyce*, New York, Oxford University Press.

Faust, W.M. (1981), ' "Du hast keine Chance. Nutze Sie!" With it and Against it', *Artforum*, September, p.33.

Fincman, J. (1980), 'The Structure of Allegorical Desire', *October*, 12, spring, p.47.

Flam, J.D. (ed.) (1978), *Matisse on Art*, London, Phaidon.

Foster, H. (1982), 'Re: Post', *Parachute*, spring, 26, p.11.

Foster, H. (ed.) (1983), *The Anti-Aesthetic, Essays on Postmodern Culture*, Washington, Bay Press.

Foster, H. (1984), 'For a Concept of the Political in Art', *Art in America*, April, p.17.

Foucault, M. (1982), *This is not a Pipe*, London, University of California Press.

Francis, S. (1972), *Sam Francis*, Buffalo Fine Arts Academy.

Fried, M. (1967), 'Art and Objecthood', *Artforum*, summer, p.21.

Gohr, S. (1982), 'In the Absence of Heroes. The Early Work of George Baselitz', *Artforum*, summer, p.67.

Greenberg, C. (1961), *Art and Culture*, Boston, Beacon Press.

Hartman, G. (1980), *Criticism in the Wilderness*, London, Yale University Press.

Heidegger, M. (1967), *Being and Time*, Oxford, Basil Blackwell.

Heidegger, M. (1971a), *Poetry, Language, Thought*, New York, Harper & Row.

Heidegger, M. (1971b), *On the Way to Language*, New York, Harper & Row.

Heppenstall, R. (1966), *Raymond Roussel*, London, Calder & Boyars.

Herbert, R. (ed.) (1964), *Modern Artists on Art*, New Jersey, Prentice-Hall.

Heron, P. (1958), *Braque*, London, Faber & Faber.

Heron, P. (1978), *Paintings by Partrick Heron*, University of Texas Press.

Hess, T. (1972), *Barnett Newman*, London, Tate Gallery.

Hitchens, I. (1979), *Ivon Hitchens*, London, Royal Academy of Arts.

Jakobson, R. and Halle, M. (1971), *Fundamentals of Language*, Atlantic Highlands, New Jersey, Humanities Press.

Johnson, E. (1976), *Modern Art and the Object*, London, Thames & Hudson.

Joyce, J. (1958), *Ulysses*, London, Bodley Head.

Kafka, F. (1958), *Parables and Paradoxes*, New York, Schocken.

Kandinsky, W. (1964), *Concerning the Spiritual in Art*, New York, George Wittenborn.

Kandinsky, W. and Marc, F. (eds) (1977), *The Blaue Reiter Almanac*, London, Thames & Hudson.

Kelly, M. (1982), 'No Essential Femininity: a conversation between Mary Kelly and Paul Smith', *Parachute*, no.26, spring, p.31.

Kelly, M. (1983), *Post-Partum Document*, London, Routledge & Kegan Paul.

Klee, P. (1954), *On Modern Art*, London, Faber & Faber.

Klee, P. (1961), *The Thinking Eye*, London, Lund Humphries.

Klee, P. (1973), *The Nature of Nature*, London, Lund Humphries.

Kozloff, M. (1970), *Renderings*, London, Studio Vista.

Kozloff, M. (1974), 'The Authoritarian Personality in Modern Art', *Artforum*, May, p.40.

Kramer, H. (1983), 'Signs of Passion', in *Zeitgeist*, London, Weidenfeld & Nicolson.

Krauss, R. (1981a), 'In the Name of Picasso', *October*, 16, spring, p.5.

Krauss, R. (1981b), 'The Originality of the Avant-Garde: A Postmodernist Repetition', *October*, 18, fall, p.47.

Kristeva, J. (1980), *Desire in Language*, Oxford, Basil Blackwell.

Kuspit, D. (1981), 'The New(?) Expressionism: Art as Damaged Goods', *Artforum*, December, p.47.

Kuspit, D. (1983), 'Flak from the Radicals', in J. Cowart, *Expressions: New Art from Germany*, St Louis Museum.

Lambertini, L, (1980), *Victor Pasmore*, London, Thames & Hudson.

Law, R. (1978), *Bob Law*, London, Whitechapel Gallery.

Lischka, G. (1984), 'The Postmodern: A Multilateral Approach', *Flash Art*, 115, January, p.22.

Lodge, D. (1977), *Modes of Modern Writing*, London, Routledge & Kegan Paul.

Lyotard, J.-F. (1981), 'The Works and Writings of Daniel Buren', *Artforum*, February, p.57.

Lyotard, J.-F. (1982), 'Presenting the Unpresentable: The Sublime', *Artforum*, April, p.64.

Macke, A. (1969), *Tunisian Watercolours and Drawings*, New York, Harry N. Abrams.

Marcuse, H. (1972), *Counter-revolution and revolt*, Boston, Beacon Press.

Marin, L. (1979), 'To Destroy Painting', *Enclitic*, vol.III, no.2, fall.

Martin, K. (1975), *Kenneth Martin*, London, Tate Gallery.

Matejka, L. and Titunik, I. (eds) (1976), *Semiotics of Art*, Cambridge (Mass.), MIT Press.

Melville, S. (1981), 'Notes on the Reemergence of Allegory . . .', *October*, 19, winter, p.55.

Merleau-Ponty, M. (1964), *Signs*, Chicago, Northwestern University Press.

Merleau-Ponty, M. (1968), *The Primacy of Perception*, Chicago, Northwestern University Press.

Miller, S. (1984), 'Art and Language: Mike Baldwin and Mel Ramsden. A Discussion', in *Artscribe*, no.47, July–August, p.13.

Motherwell, R. (1978), *Robert Motherwell*, London, Royal Academy of Arts.

O'Hara, F. (1965), *Robert Motherwell*, New York, Museum of Modern Art.

Oliva, A.B. (1981), *The Italian Trans-avantgarde*, Milan, Giancarlo Politi.

Owens, C. (1980a), 'The Allegorical Impulse: Toward a Theory of Postmodernism, I', *October*, 12, spring, p.67.

Owens, C. (1980b), 'Towards a Theory of Postmodernism, II', *October*, summer, p.61.

Owens, C. (1983), 'The Discourse of Others: Feminists and postmodernism', in Foster (ed.) (1983)

Owens, C. (1984), 'The Medusa Effect, or, The Specular Ruse', *Art in America*, January, p.97.

Parmesani, L. (1984), 'From Life to Death: From Death to Life', *Flash Art*, 117, April–May, p.56.

Paz, O. (1974), *Children of the Mire*, Cambridge (Mass.), Harvard University Press.

Penrose, R. (1978), *Tàpies*, Paris, Editions Galilée, Dutron.

Perkins, D. and Leondar, B. (eds) (1977), *The Arts and Cognition*, Baltimore, Johns Hopkins University Press.

Picon, G. (1978), *The Birth of Modern Painting*, New York, Rizzoli.

Pohlen, A. (1984), 'Obsessive Pictures or Opposition to the Norm', *Artforum*, May, p.44.

Pollock, G. (1979), 'Feminism, Femininity and the Hayward Annual Exhibition, 1978', *Feminist Review*, no.2, p.33.

Raphael, M. (1968), *The Demands of Art*, London, Routledge & Kegan Paul.

Rewald, J. (1976), *Cézanne's Letters*, Oxford, Bruno Cassirer.

Ricard, R. (1981), 'About Julian Schnabel', *Artforum*, summer, p.74.

Richter, H. (1965), *Dada*, London, Thames & Hudson.

Ricoeur, P. (1978), *On Metaphor*, London, Routledge & Kegan Paul.

Rimbaud, A. (1974), *A Season in Hell, The Illuminations*, Oxford University Press.

Rose, B. (1975), *Art-as-Art . . .*, New York, Viking Press.

Rosenberg, H. (1962), *The Tradition of the New*, London, Thames & Hudson.

Rosenberg, H. (1969), *Art-Works and Packages*, London, Thames & Hudson.

Rosenberg, H. (1972), *The De-definition of Art*, London, Secker & Warburg.

Rosenberg, H. (1973), *De Kooning*, New York, Harry N. Abrams.

Rosenberg, H. (1977), *Barnett Newman*, New York, Harry N. Abrams.

Roussel, R. (1970), *Locus Solus*, London, Calder & Boyars.

Rubin, W. (1977), *Cézanne: The Late Work*, London, Thames & Hudson.

Russell, J. (1979), *Francis Bacon*, London, Thames & Hudson.

Sanouillet, M. and Peterson, E. (eds) (1975), *The Essential Writings of Marcel Duchamp*, London, Thames & Hudson.

Schapiro, M. (1969), 'On Some Problems in the Semiotics of Visual Art', *Semiotica*, 1, p.223.

Smith, P. (1982), 'Mother as Site of Her Proceedings', *Parachute*, no.26, spring, p.29.

Sollers, P. (1983), *Writing and the Experience of Limits*, New York, Columbia University Press.

Steinberg, L. (1972), *Other Criteria*, New York, Oxford University Press.

Steiner, G. (1971), *In Bluebeard's Castle*, London, Faber & Faber.

Stokes, A. (1978), *The Writings of Adrian Stokes, Vol.II*, London, Thames & Hudson.

Wildermuth, A. (1984), 'The Crisis of Interpretation', *Flash Art*, 116, March, p.8.

Index

Index